THE GREE

THE GREEKS IN HISTORY

Alan E. Samuel

Edgar Kent, *Publishers Inc*
TORONTO 1992

Copyright ©1992 by Edgar Kent, Inc., Publishers

All Rights Reserved

Edgar Kent, Inc., Publishers
University of Toronto Press
340 Nagel Drive, Buffalo, New York 14225 U.S.A
5201 Dufferin Street, Downsview, Ontario Canada M3H 5T6

Canadian Cataloguing in Publication Data

Samuel, Alan Edouard
    The Greeks in History

Includes bibliographical references and index.
ISBN 0-88866-639-X

1. Greece - Civilization - To 146 B.C.
2. Greece - History - To 146 B.C.   I. Title.

DF77S26 1992   938   C92-094709-3

Design: Peter Maher

Printed in the United States of America

To Valerie

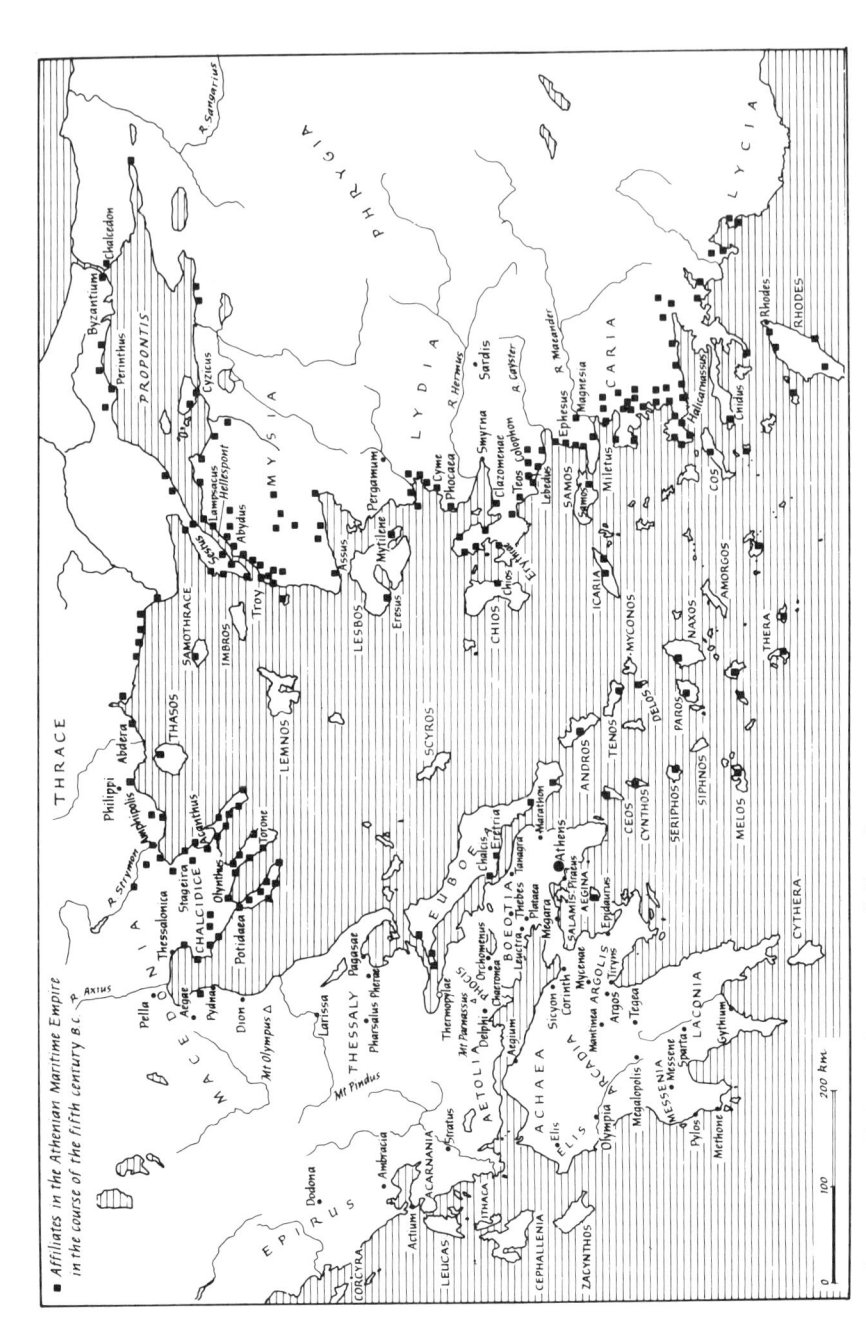

1 The Aegean world, showing the cities controlled by Athens

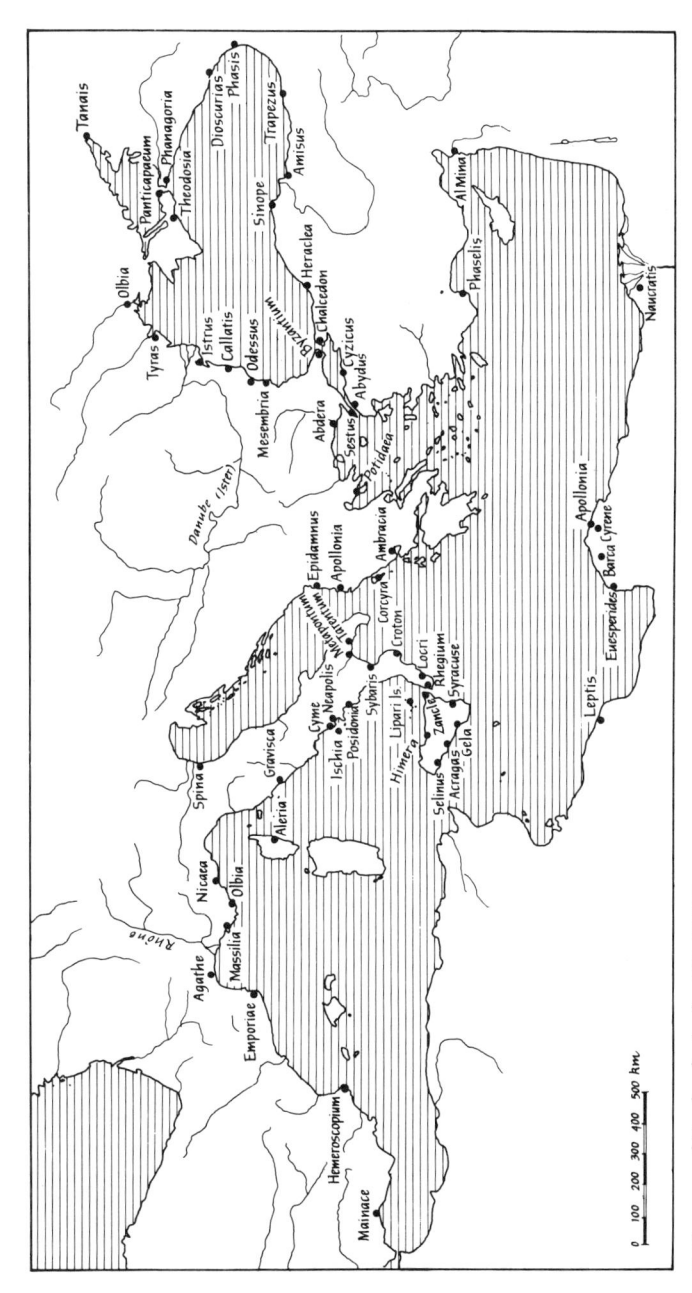

2 The scope of Greek colonization 750–550 BC

Contents

Maps vi

Preface xi

1. Why Greek History? 1

2. City and Citizen 11

3. "We Know How to be Greek" 39

4. Greek Imperialism 74

5. Civic Values 121

6. The Oppressive Society 138

7. One-Man Rule 154

8. Hellenism and Culture 171

9. Forward from the Greeks 190

Bibliographical Note 195

Chronological Table 199

Index 203

Preface

This book is intended for people with no prior knowledge of Greek history, but I hope that some of the ideas and interpretations will be of interest and value to those who already have much of the specific information contained in some of the chapters. The study of Greek history has always been rewarding for those whose horizons have opened with knowledge of human experience in the past, and I have tried to make that the major goal of the book, while not neglecting the facts and events which make up part of that knowledge. Some chapters, therefore, have more specific information, while others concentrate on interpretation and evaluation. I hope that readers will find the balance satisfactory, and I hope even more that in avoiding a strictly chronological account, I have remembered in each chapter to present the information essential to the interpretation and comment.

There are also characteristics of the account which may seem strange to some academic readers: no footnotes, no specific citations of quotations from ancient authors, and no quotations of modern historians. There are fewer dates than one might expect in a "history" book, and little discussion of battles beyond the statement of how they came out. Part of the reason for writing this way relates to my own interests, and part is deliberate. I am not expecting to emulate ancient historical writers by omitting page references, but I hope my text will flow a little more amiably if I do so. I cannot imagine most people needing to know precisely where in Thucydides' or Herodotus' or other texts my quotes can be found, and they are all such well-known items that professional historians will have no difficulty in recognizing them as genuine. I have avoided footnotes because most of what I have written is, in terms of fact, basic, and need not be argued or supported. Where I interpret, I see no point in burdening the reader with the names of those with whom I agree or disagree.

Dates, unless specifically noted, are all B.C., and I have used that designation at the beginning of the book to establish it in the reader's mind. Greek names have usually been given in accepted English style, rather than in transliteration. In most instances, I have avoided Greek terms when English will do, preferring heavy-armed infantryman, for example, to hoplite. Where I do use Greek words as part of the text, as I do with "metic," I use the word in its English form or italicize a transliteration. All this aims at a little reduction in the bewilderment so often produced by the barrage of unfamiliar names and terms in books about the Greek world.

In readying this for the press, I have had the kind and invaluable help of Professors Catherine Rubincam and Gary Reger, and of Richard Hazzard, all of whom were kind enough to read the work in proof just before it went to press. They alerted me to many points at which the text could be improved, and I am very grateful for their advice and suggestions. The weaknesses that remain are, of course, my faults of haste and perversity, and I hope that they will not mislead too many and will amuse some. The present volume is, in a way, a preliminary edition, which I hope to follow in a second edition in the not too distant future. I will be very grateful for comments, advice and corrections for that edition.

Toronto, July, 1992

THE GREEKS IN HISTORY

1 Why Greek History?

One of the most famous episodes in Greek history is the story of Croesus, king of Lydia. When he asked the oracle at Delphi what would happen if he attacked Persia, it told him that if he did that, "he would destroy a great kingdom." The oracle was right, but the kingdom destroyed as a result was Croesus' own. There is another oracular story: Hippias, the son of the tyrant of Athens, and who had been tyrant in his own right, was told that he would be buried in Athenian soil. When he was very old, and after he had been expelled from Athens, he was part of a Persian force invading Attica, confident of success because of the prediction of Hippias' eventual location. As the troops landed, Hippias sneezed, and one of the old man's teeth fell out. It was the only part of Hippias to be buried in Athenian soil, and the invasion failed.

So oracles worked, and the gods knew the future of Greece. People did not, however, and they repeatedly sought prophetic revelations. There is a bit of logical inconsistency here, however: if prophecy can work, what good does it do? If the universe is to unfold, what is the advantage of knowing in advance what cannot change? The Oedipus story is a case in point. Oedipus' parents, king and queen of Thebes, received a prophecy that their son would kill his father and sleep with his mother. Trying to evade that doom, they ordered a shepherd to take the infant and leave him to die in the wilderness. Pity for the child led to his being let live, and eventually he found his way into the family of the king and queen of Corinth, where he was raised as that couple's child. He then heard of the prediction of his terrible future, but thinking he was actually the son of the parents he knew, he left the palace to avoid fulfilling the prophecy. In his travels, he met his (birth) father on the road and killed him, and later found his way to the city where he had been born, and married his mother, the widowed queen.

So prophecy was fulfilled, and human attempts to evade it futile. But they are more than futile—they are logically inconsistent. If you believe in prophecy enough to have an infant killed, why do you not believe in it enough to abandon the attempt to evade it? Greeks, I suggest, did not worry so much about this logical inconsistency, or even the logical problems created by a belief in fate. These are issues of real importance only when the issues of divine goodness and free will emerge as critical Christian problems, and I do not intend to deal with them here. Rather, I want introduce these oracular stories as a reminder that the Greeks had very different mental constructs to deal with issues they had in common with us. Dealing with oracles is another way of treating questions of choice and chance, and these are matters at the heart of history.

To ask the question "Why study History?" is to make so general a query as to call for too vague an answer. Why study Greek History? works as well, because it allows for some specific answers to fill out the response to the wider question. But even the more specific question requires some clarification about the subjects of study. Do we mean events, all events, social, cultural, personal and economic, or just political events, or some but not all of these? And do we mean to study only those events which come to public notice, or seem to relate to public events, so that a politician's sexual habits are of interest, even though private matters, while those of his brother-in-law's second cousin once removed are of no interest to history? Or is it not events we study, but causation, in order to understand why things happen, perhaps to help us in decisions in the future, as some ancient Greek historians thought as they sat down to write.

Actually, worrying about all these matters is a little silly; they are questions historians tend to ask as they work up to speed on their keyboards or as a kind of running in place before lectures start in earnest. Important questions about Greek history, or history in general, however, are those implied by the stories of prophecy and oracles like those of Croesus, Hippias and Oedipus. Take the story about Hippias, for example. The fulfilment of the oracle of his burial in Athenian soil was achieved when his tooth fell to earth. So the prophecy was true, but had been misunderstood, and the invasion, which had been thought to be supported by Hippias' future. failed. But what would have happened if Hippias had not sneezed? Was the sneeze itself a matter of chance, or was it in fact part of the unfolding future only partly revealed by the oracle? Was Hippias himself a matter of chance—the outcome of the nearly 50-50 lottery which at conception produces male or female offspring? These questions can be, and have been, phrased in different ways about different periods of history, and there are, essentially only two ways of answering them. To a question, "Would the world have been a fundamentally different place in the nineteenth century if Napoleon had not been born? we can answer yes or no. If we answer "yes" we are lining ourselves up with a view of history that sees it as influenced at least in part by chance, undeterministic, allowing for the effects of human will and choice at least in part. This view asserts that at any given point in the flow of history, there are different possibilities for the future. Some may be more probable than others, and some may be almost impossible in view of the status quo at time of thinking. But of the "probable futures," the one that is actually realized will be due to some combination with chance and volition.

The other answer, "no," asserting that the world would have followed the same course regardless of the presence or absence of Napoleon, is predicated on a completely different concept of the relationship between past, present and future and the impetus events give to their successors. It is a concept endorsed by belief in the truth of oracles, and it is a deterministic concept, although it may present itself in more attractive terms and verbal descriptions. In the form fashionable today, the deterministic view would say of Napoleon and his impact something like, "If Napoleon himself had not existed, someone would have occupied his place and the flow of history in the nineteenth century would have been essentially the same." This view asserts that the sum total of social, economic and political conditions will constrain future social, economic and political developments within very narrow limits. It can be asserted in another way: the material condition of the world at any time determines the possibilities and ideas which can exist at that time. That means that the material condition of the world, in determining possibilities and ideas, also eliminates chance and choice as influences. In the context of Napoleonic times, the material condition of the world established the ideas which allowed for and led to the conflict between European powers, and excluded ideas and possibilities of cooperation and idealization of peace. The European wars of the early nineteenth century were the necessary outcome of the conditions obtaining in 1800, and an alternative arrangement, let us say a half-century of peace, while conceptually possible, was in fact historically impossible given the state of the world at the time. Note that this view asserts not that the outcome was unlikely or improbable, but claims that conditions made it impossible.

While I personally believe in the first of these two alternatives, accepting chance and choice in affecting the future, a conception of the influence of the past in no way depends on that choice. In the first alternative, knowledge of the past—or lack of knowledge—influences the choices made in the present to create the future. At the very least, a knowledge of the past affects attitudes about the nature of the human being and what it is to be human, and those attitudes affect decisions. If we read Thucydides and conclude with him that the holders of power grip that power with a tenacity that obliterates feelings of pity and mercy or kindness for fellow human beings, then our opinions about dealing with those in power will rest on that assumption. If, on the other hand, we are Socratic in our confidence that no one does evil knowingly or willingly, we are rather more likely to try reason for a very long time before reaching for the sword. And those opinions, attitudes and decisions will influence the state of the world in its next stage.

On the other hand, if we believe that the state of the world at any instant leads relentlessly to its next state, determined by the sum effect of all its conditions (presumably we could, like an oracle, know it, if we knew all the existing conditions), history still has a force. For, under those circumstances, the knowledge of the past becomes one of the conditions of the present and one of the phenomena that lead inexorably to the next state of the world, so that knowledge of history, or at least, conceptions of what took place in the past, are a factor in the creation of the future.

There is nothing difficult about any of this, and, once stated it all becomes obvious. But it is just as well to state it, so that no one will think any of it is left out of consideration in approaching the study of Greek history. It is also well to have these considerations in mind as we turn to actual decisions about what we do in the study of history, whether we are studying as scholars and historians or are contemplating a period about which we intend to acquire basic information.

I have in mind an episode from the beginning of my own historical activity. I was writing about the organization of the Macedonian calendar in Egypt in the period after 300 B.C., and I had occasion to refer to the death of Alexander the Great. At that time, Alexander's death was generally given as June 13, 323 B.C., a calculation made with some accuracy from the information available to us in ancient sources. Discussing the implications of the allusions to the event in the sources with Otto Neugebauer, a distinguished historian of mathematics at Brown University, I was told "No, no, no. Not June 13, but June 10." Neugebauer showed me a transcription and translation of a contemporary Babylonian clay tablet giving the day of the (ancient) month as 29, equivalent to June 10. It was a fortunate find for me, because "day 29" confirmed my theory about the way the calendar worked, but it also meant that, as a contemporary source, we had a new date—three days earlier—for Alexander's death. Historians of Alexander, who hitherto had been unaware of the Babylonian text, from then on began to give June 10 as the date of the king's death.

The point of this story is to raise the question, "did it matter, and does it matter?" The information was useful to me for my calendar work, but the change in date for Alexander's death seems to me a completely inconsequential fact, unless someone can show how the difference affected later events. By inconsequential, I mean that the events after Alexander's death would have been the same whether he had died on June 13, as we used to think he he did, or on June 10, as we now think, and that our assessment of Alexander and his effects remains the same regardless of the date. If my view of this matter is right, it is not an urgent matter to spend time on such details *for historical purposes*; that is, in Aristotle's mode, we should decide that some forms of precision are less necessary than others for historical research. This is not to say we should not use precise dates or facts in history, or use them as a matter of course if doing that does not entail an unnecessary effort, but rather to say that there is no requirement to be more precise than needed to make a statement of consequence. In example, the two following statements are equally acceptable: (1) The Persian Wars at the beginning of the fifth century B.C. laid the groundwork for the growth of Athenian power; and (2) The Persian Wars between 490 and 479 B.C. laid the groundwork for the growth of Athenian power.

This is to say that the investigation of facts and details for their own sake and for the sake of an abstract accuracy plays the same role in "History" as the imposition of the rules for rhyme in sonnets plays in "Poetry." If you want to write a certain kind of poetry, a Petrarchian sonnet, say, then you must use rhyme in the patterns established by Petrarch. If you do not, then you have not written a Petrarchian sonnet, even if what you have written is still poetry. Thus historical writing with the aim of improving or teaching precise data about the past can be a form of "History," but it is not the only kind of historical writing with legitimacy. And as practiced today, it is something of an extension from the days of St. Jerome, who was concerned in the first place to establish dates not so much for their own sakes as to make possible an understanding of sequence for the centuries before the Christian era in order to erect a consistent and broadly applicable chronological framework.

Greek historical writing has been particularly occupied with establishing data, with "the importance of getting things right" as a colleague described the effort to me years ago. The reason for this is, of course, the number of items of data about which we have lost precision over time. The problem is not new. Plutarch, writing at the end of the first century or beginning of the second, noted, for example, serious chronological difficulties involved in dating Solon's activity, and here, in fact, the decisions on dating, ranging today over a twenty-year period from about 590 to 570 B.C. influence one's interpretation of events. With regard to the early lawgiver of Sparta, Lycurgus, Plutarch's assessment of the dating problem makes it so severe that he proposes the hypothesis of "two Lycurguses." Now, almost two thousand years after Plutarch, it is small wonder that we still notice the chronological anomalies, or argue about the existence of a fifth-century B.C. "Peace of Callias" mentioned by one source and not another.

It is also the case that in the last 150 years we have obtained more new information about Greek history than in the preceding 1500 years. Whole cities have been unearthed. Greek history has been pushed back a millenium, into the Bronze Age, and tons, literally, of stone inscriptions now give us many details about public and private life. Even books have come to light, as papyrus texts from the sands of Egypt give us works such as Aristotle's history of the constitution of Athens, plays of the fourth-century B.C. dramatist Menander, and fragments of lyric poetry from before the fifth century. The excitement of discovery inspired more searches which in turn brought more discoveries, and all the discoveries molded a form of history which could use them. A type of history which its practitioners like to think of as scientific and which can now best be called "technical" history evolved to fit the new data into, and in turn create, a picture of antiquity.

There is nothing wrong with this technical history. It is intellectually stimulating and provides the possibility of a more objective basis for reputations to take aspiring middle-class academics all the way to the professoriate. The skills to pursue it are teachable, and within reasonable limits, learnable by anyone. Best of all, it can be seen to inspire the use of, and teaching of, critical thinking, as historical understanding becomes a matter of comprehending and manipulating the evidence. Even its weaknesses, often related to the proliferation of evidence more and more difficult to master, can be thought to have the merit of refining conclusions as data accumulates.

However, the value and interest of technical history ought not to invalidate the practice of other kinds of historical writing. I do not refer here to the kind of history referred to, often derogatorily, as "popular," or "textbook" history, written for non-specialist, i.e., non-academic, readers, or for students—"students," that is, defined as people taking courses for credit. There is also nothing wrong with this kind of history writing, taking the findings and publications of technical history and turning them into writing of a more general, and perhaps more palatable, nature. However, there is still another kind of history, rarely written today except by journalists like William Shirer. We are familiar with this kind of history, and in fact, we read it as a part of our study of antiquity. Thucydides wrote it; so did Herodotus, and Tacitus. Later on, Orosius wrote it, and in more modern times, Gibbon and George Grote. It is opinionated history, permeated by its authors' views about the nature of the world and the people in it, written to express moral and cosmological opinions and even to mold the attitudes of readers. Hardly technical in itself, it still influenced the attitudes of the great founders of technical history like Theodor Mommsen, and it was the kind of historical writing and thinking which provided the basis from which writers like Marx, Freud and Nietsche levered thought into the modern world.

The ancient Greek experience is particularly suitable to the writing of this kind of history. In the first place, as I have written in another context, the attitudes and writings of Hellenism have been so influential in the development of western culture that they have molded some of our most basic attitudes, and in so doing, they have insured that Greek works remain understandable and accessible to us. We do not understand the *Oresteia*, Homer, Plato and Herodotus intuitively; we understand them because they provide some of the bases of our own attitudes. We do not have to study for years, or learn Greek, to do this. Sophocles is as close to us, perhaps even closer, than Shakespeare, and we have only to compare our cultural familiarity with Hellenism against the mystique of Egyptian antiquity, or even the Semitic experience, to make the point. In this respect Moses Finley's insistence on the "desperately foreign" quality of the ancient world is the insight of a technical historian. A second reason for the Greek experience suiting this kind of history is its relative simplicity. There were not many players, or we do not know many players, on the stage of Greek history, and their lines are relatively clear. The stories of the Persian Wars and of the Athenian Empire are short and sweet, and both had the advantage of superb narration, the Persian Wars by a historian with a magnificently broad and deep cosmological view, and the Athenian Empire by a great moral historian.

The Greek experience also provides wonderful evidence for this kind of history. From the shelves of the studies of classics professors come a large number of works involving an interpretation of human behavior and activity and of the relationship between the human being and the environment, or, as a Greek might say it, between humanity and the cosmos. Yet it is not all abstract, a disembodied mind full of ideas, expressing itself like Ionescu's "Mouth." What Greeks thought and wrote existed in a context about which we know a good deal, certainly enough to understand the ideas and what their authors meant. In one sense, the history of the Greek experience can be an account of an experiment in human living, a closed experience traceable in its broad outlines from an obscure beginning through its evolution into a great culture. Taking another tack, an account of Hellenism can provide us with a number of human enterprises in which we can see events and ideas interacting. Or moving laterally, we can see Greek culture not in political or ideological terms, but in its artistic expression, or religious, or purely literary development. Only in music are we excluded from sharing experience with the occupants of the Greek peninsula from 900 to 300 B.C.

With all this at hand, the Greek experience has the potential of providing us with the material for deeply meaningful history. If history can be an art form for commenting on the present, there is in Hellenism plenty of sources of comment. Approaching the writing of history in this way means, of course, allowing personal interpretations, even personal opinions, into the discussion. More than that, it inevitably has the lack of objectivity created by omission, a lack of objectivity more subtle and thus potentially more dangerous than the open espousal of opinions and value judgements. Still, with all the dangers, I will try out this kind of history in this volume. I will examine a number of aspects of Hellenism as it developed and existed from about 800 to 300 B.C., a half-millenium of time, and I will do this with a focus on the aspects themselves, rather than on the availability or non-availability of evidence. So if I write of "Homer" or Hesiod, I will permit myself the liberty of mere acknowledgement of the paucity of data about their context, and I shall not worry about filling the reader in on obscure events if they do not cast light on a theme I am pursuing. I will also completely ignore chronology, in the sense of trying to tell a story in a sequential way. I do this partly as an experiment, to see if some of the significance of Hellenism is clearer if themes rather than sequence are pursued, and partly as a deliberate device to eliminate the urge of the writer or the reader to present or seek information just to fill out a narrative or provide "completeness."

Furthermore, this book focuses especially on those aspects of the Greek experience which seem to be of interest today because of their relation to modern problems. The Athenians advanced further along the road to citizen-government than have any other people until the end of the eighteenth century of our era; their successes and failures are enlightening when large parts of the world are embarking on the path to "democracy." The concept is imperfectly understood at best, and even in those regions with 200 years of experience with the idea, there is serious questioning of goals and values, and perhaps a reshaping of political myths by which people live. The consideration of the Greek experience, while not likely to solve our problems or answer our questions, will at least have the merit of making many of them clear.

2 City and Citizen

So far as we can tell about the societies of the ancient Mediterranean outside Greece, and in Greece itself before the first millenium B.C., authority was unitary and most people were subjects of government, rather than participants in it. It is hardly surprising that such should be the case, for this has been the prevailing mode of government in human society in most places and times. Apart from the ideology of "democracy" in modern times, notions of citizen-government have appeared rarely: ancient Greece, Berber villages in North Africa, some European communities in late medieval and early renaissance times come to mind.

In Greece itself, government was, apparently, unitary until the first millenium. The patterns of authority in the eastern Mediterranean were essentially the same everywhere, in Egypt, in the river valleys of Syria and Babylonia, in the promised land of Canaan and in the highlands of Anatolia, government was in the control of single individuals who might be thought of primarily as kings or as priests, but who in fact exercised the ultimate authority in what we would call political matters, and often were the chief religious figures as well. In Greece, during the Mycenaean period, as the Bronze Age is called there, palace-focused centres seem to have provided the organizing principle for society. At Mycenae, Tiryns, Argos and Pylos in the Peloponnesus in the south of Greece, at Athens, Thebes and other sites in central Greece, large palaces constructed of huge cut stones have left their foundations, and in some cases, parts of their walls, to the investigations of modern archaeologists. Greeks of the classical period and after, looking at the super-scale of the masonry at Mycenae and elsewhere, attributed the structures to the cyclopes, giants who inhabited the earth in earlier times. Cyclopes or not, the inhabitants of the palaces and the towns around seem to have organized themselves differently from the civic structures of Greek communities in classical times. The architecture itself, with a large room on which the palace focuses, points to some form of monarchic orientation. And, now that we have been able to decipher the pre-alphabetic script of the many clay documents found on the palace sites, we have a little insight into the activities of the society. Bureaucratic, economically somewhat complex, with official titles meaning something like "lord" or "king" in later Greek, the documents suggest a social structure with the centralism of Near Eastern autocracies.

The earliest literature of Greek culture is related to this Mycenaean period. The kings of Homer belonged, in Greek tradition, to the time of the cyclopean palaces; they lived a Bronze Age life, in fact, with bronze the metal of shields, swords, knives, helmets and armour, as the epics *Iliad* and *Odyssey* describe the materials of civilization. The epics have, of course, a complex mixture of holdovers of the past, before 1000 B.C., with intrusions from the centuries after, as the poems were repeated and reformed by oral bards in the generations after the collapse of the Mycenaean centres. Nevertheless, the epics make it clear that the world of which they sang was a world in which authority and decisions were the prerogative of a few kings, princes or lords, and that ordinary people were of little or no consequence, and that they were seen as the myrmidons, or "ants" who made up Achilles' troops.

The influence of this earlier period can be seen in the fact that the concept of kingship never died out in Greece. Even in the most radical of non-autocratic cities, Athens, the tradition was firm that control of the city had in early times been in the hands of a king. At the next stage authority was exercised by a life-time archon [Greek *archon* literally means "governor" or "ruler"], and life-time archons gave way to ten-years archons and eventually to magistrates with one-year terms. At other places we find survivals of this early kingship in a number of forms. At Sparta in historical times among other officials there were two hereditary kings with constitutionally limited power, and at Corinth, Argos and Athens there were elected magistrates with the title of "king." At Corinth, one family, the Bacchiadae, provided kings in a series, and then formed a ruling group to make up a very close oligarchy. There were similar arrangements in Mytilene, Ephesus and other cities, where individual clans held a monopoly on office, or the Cretan cities and others where there was a limitation of eligibility to office, although the privilege was extended to a somewhat wider group than at Corinth.

A genuine kingship survived in the northern parts of Greece. In Macedonia, which dominated the peninsula by the end of the fourth century B.C., we can see something of its workings at a time when we have some real evidence of its nature. Although there is still a great deal of scholarly debate about the "constitutional" quality of the government run by Philip II of Macedon and his son, Alexander (the Great), the most important characteristics are clear, and they cast some light on the development of government generally in Greece. The Macedonian kingship was, in principle, hereditary, although the kingship might move laterally to a brother rather than to a minor son. The king was an autocrat, but had to meet some expectations to hold on to power. He had to be an effective war-leader, and he had a warrior aristocracy to contend with and to satisfy. His was personal leadership, maintained so long as he was bringing results in terms of wealth and power, but always threatened if a king was weak or if he was not meeting the expectations of the lords. Alexander saw himself as an Achilles-figure, and the war-ideology of the *Iliad* remained part of the ideology of Macedonian kingship.

The expectations of the warriors made for practical limitations on the king's exercise of his autocracy. In a general sense, the Macedonian king remained as leader and could constrain the loyalty of his lords to the extent that he provided a political and military environment in which they could fulfil their personal aims. The process of the new king being presented to the army, as in the case of Alexander, fits this concept, and the practical constraints on the monarchy have led some to conceive of Macedonian kingship as strictly and formally limited constitutional monarchy. It was probably not that, but in its relationship to the society as whole, it was closer to other forms of government in Greece than it was to the absolute autocracies of the Near East.

The general theory of the evolution of democratic constitutions, like that of Athens, is still more or less like that underlying Aristotle's historical survey of Athenian government. The theory grows primarily out of common-sense assumptions: at first cities were governed by kings who ruled by their own fiat. Gradually, the more powerful nobles demanded increasing control over policy and actions, and after a period of conflict between kings and their families on the one hand, and the leaders of other powerful or aristocratic families, the latter won out, and power rested in the collective of the leaders of the wealthy aristocratic clans. In the next stage of evolution, a wider group of residents of a city struggled to wrest control from the aristocrats or oligarchs, and the decision-making power was more and more disseminated until, in the most radical of democracies, as fifth-century Athens was seen, the exercise of power was shared by all male adult citizens.

This makes a neat picture, and it fits the metaphysics of Aristotelian thought. But all was not smooth, and the bumps on the way to democracy experienced by many Greek cities call for some modification of the idea. Assuming a general pattern is risky, since the nature of society in the eighth and seventh centuries, during which these aristocracies were prevalent in their domination, is difficult to assess. It is not safe to generalize from the limited evidence, showing one characteristic at one place, another elsewhere, to put together a reliable composite picture. In a few cities the body of aristocrats holding control seems to have come through the turbulent early centuries down into the historical period, while in others their formal power was long gone by the time we have any hard evidence about political life. Some cities met changing conditions by modifying their institutions, and the activity of formal lawgivers, like Charondas and Zeleucus in Greek cities of South Italy in the early seventh century B.C., or Pheidon or Philolaus at Corinth, in its mere existence shows some relaxing of the tightest form of aristocratic control. To promulgate law, however limited its application, is to limit the authority and arbitrariness of clan leaders, who earlier might have exercised their judicial power with no consistency or fairness whatever. We have an indication of some such injustice in Hesiod's *Works and Days*, where the poet complains of the "crooked judgements of the corrupt judges."

In some cities, domination was eventually taken from the aristocracies and grasped by a single man, who was called *tyrannos*, in Greek, to designate a ruler who held monarchical power by force or unconstitutional means, not by the inheritance of royal position. In later times, most of the tyrannies had acquired a bad reputation, but there is really not much detail about most of the individual tyrants. Thucydides, the fifth-century Athenian historian, was one of the few to attempt a general understanding, when he wrote, "With Hellas increasing in power and becoming wealthier than before, tyrannies were established for the most part in the cities." Some of the comments of the early poets also suggest that an increase of wealth was not always the accomplishment of the aristocrats, or even welcome to them. There are remarks like "Money makes the man, and no poor man is noble or good" (Alcaeus) or "Money confounds birth" (Theognis). Thucydides' statement implies that the increase in wealth generated political stresses which opportunists could use for the seizure of power. Aristotle certainly blamed the pursuit of wealth for those animosities which unsettled the stability of ruling oligarchies, but he, like us, may have been extrapolating back to earlier times the strains and troubles of his own days. Herodotus, explaining the genesis of tyrannies, thought that factionalism was endemic to oligarchies, for "out of these come factions, and from these bloodshed, and from bloodshed emerges tyranny." In other words, the very nature of aristocratic rule eventually brings about conflict within the ruling oligarchy, and in its divided state, with civil war at hand, the single, powerful man can seize control. Or, in the view of Solon, from the great men destruction comes to the state, and the people in its ignorance falls into slavery to the tyrant, or of Theognis, "from corrupt judges factions come and civil slaughter and tyrants," this last singling out injustice as a cause of tyranny.

There must have been a number of reasons why tyrants arose in those times in Greece. It is not enough simply to cite "changing times," for the tyrants were as much the cause as the result of the times changing. All the causes identified or hinted at by Greek authors were probably relevant at one place or time or another. Factionalism in an oligarchy arising purely from the orneriness of human nature may have been the sole cause on one occasion; elsewhere, a shifting focus of wealth, skewing economic power into the hands of non-aristocrats who were forced to use uncommon devices to alter the political structure may have provided an opportunity; a patron of the exploited may have used dissatisfaction with the ways of a corrupt and self-serving oligarchy to find a third route to tyranny. Or, to add a completely different possibility, familiarity with the success of the dynasts of Lydia and other West Anatolian societies may have prompted experimentation. Whatever the cause or causes, the phenomenon was common from the seventh century on. In peninsular Greece, at Corinth, Megara, Sicyon, and Epidaurus there were tyrannies in place by the end of the century, and they lasted on into the sixth century, when such places as Athens and Naxos fell under the sway of tyrants, and the institution spread west to Italy and Sicily. But, while widespread, tyranny was not an inevitable stage in the development of government in the Greek cities, and many came through these early centuries without it.

The story of tyranny at Athens provides some insights, not only into the institution and its causes but even more, into the underlying attitudes about government and society which affected political activity and allowed for the establishment of these irregular autocracies. Athens, according to some modern scholars, came late to the realization of the city-state structure, although the Athenians, I am sure, would not have thought so. Their great reformer, Solon, came later than the Spartan Lycurgus or the reformers at Corinth and elsewhere, and this alone may indicate a somewhat slower development. Solon's reforms, apart from some constitutional changes that accord reasonably well enough with political structure elsewhere, point to an attempt to settle domestic disturbances and have been taken to show turmoil at Athens parallel to that in other cities a half-century before Solon's time. Solon's year of government is assigned by the Athenians to the year which works out for us to 594 B.C. (or in some systems, 592), but I have little doubt that the reforms attributed to him stretch over a long period perhaps spanning the first half of the sixth century B.C., and that Solon the man (as against Solon the year) may have been contemporary with Croesus of Lydia and Amasis of Egypt—in the 560's—as Herodotus says Solon was. The problems of dating occupying some historians today may be the best evidence for the prolonged period of reform.

Be this as it may, the reforms and the poetry of Solon suggest a period of serious disturbance, and the effects of the reforms attributed to him may have been, as so many have said they were, to weaken the grip of the old landed aristocracy and increase the power and promote the growth of a new commercial class. Solon's activity may have been part of Athenian development which created a society in which the lowest economic class ultimately had more protection against the rich and powerful minority than it had in any other Greek city—what Aristotle meant by the movement toward democracy, as he evaluated the reforms. It would be nice to think that any politician could be so farseeing, but even if we cannot be sure that the reforms had such purposes, Athens was a changed place after them, and the structure of political government ruled supreme over people's lives. However, the turmoil of which Solon wrote was not ended, and Athenians went on rousting each other about in the streets through the first forty years of the sixth century, so that if we insist on believing, as so many do, that Solon had done his work by 594 or 592 B.C., we will have to admit that it was not very successful. Within a few years of that assigned to Solon, there was, according to Aristotle, *anarchia*—no government—in which archons could not be elected because of civil strife, and in an archon year which works out to 581/80, one Damasias held on to his office longer than the proper period and had to be ejected. Aristotle's account goes on to report that thereafter, a board of ten archons were elected, with the selection providing for representation of diverse interests in society, so that government could resume with the major groups satisfied that their interests had some spokesmen. Five of the ten represented the eupatrids—the well-born, or aristocratic families; these must correspond to the group later called the people of the plain, the aristocrats with the great estates in the good land around Athens and houses in the city, of whom we hear much more, later. Of the remaining five on the board, three came from the country people, the *agroikoi*, and two from artisans, or *demiourgoi*. There is not much difficulty in identifying the *agroikoi* with the inhabitants of the inland farms of Attica, beyond the hills, another of the three groups into which later Athenians reported that the citizen body had been split. The artisans, who probably lived in the city, may—although it is hard to be certain of this—be part of the third group, the people of the shore, along with the landowners who are thought to make up this faction

The board of ten did not solve the problems either, and in 561/60, the Athenians got their first taste of tyranny. The story is again clearest in Aristotle's history of the Athenian constitution. A noble named Pisistratus, who had distinguished himself in a war against Megara, tricked the populace by showing them some self-inflicted wounds he blamed on political opponents, and induced people to vote him a bodyguard. With that, he seized the Acropolis, and maintaining himself with the support of the hill people, as well as those who had been impoverished by Solon's cancellation of debts and those who had recently become citizens under Solonic legislation, he held power briefly. His opponents were the traditional aristocrats of the plains around the city, led by one Lycurgus, and the people of the coastland, who were led, interestingly enough, by another great noble, Megacles, head of the clan of the Alcmaeonids. Together, these were able to command enough support to expel Pisistratus, in the year 554/3 B.C.

Pisistratus is the only tyrant of peninsular Greece for whom we have real information, and that is scanty enough. What we do know we owe to Herodotus, and still more to Aristotle's *Constitution of Athens*. It is Aristotle who writes of the division of the population into three groups, the *paraloi*, or coastal people, with Megacles the Alcmaeonid seeking a compromise government, the *pediakoi*, or plainsmen, seeking an oligarchy under the leadership of Lycurgus, and the *diakrioi*, led by Pisistratus and seeking the fullest democracy. Aristotle continues the story of Pisistratus with his return in 549/8 B.C., escorted by a tall and beautiful woman purporting to be Athena, and supported this time by Megacles. The combination of the two elements assured Pisistratus of power so long as the coalition lasted, and the cooperation between the two was confirmed by Pisistratus marrying Megacles' daughter. Support by Megacles collapsed in 543/2 B.C., when his daughter's naive queries of her mother revealed that the marriage—seven years of it, indeed—had remained unconsummated, so that Megacles could not expect an heir from the alliance. Pisistratus had to flee again, and this time he remained away for ten years, raising money from silver mines and timber on the Thracian coast across from Thasos. With additional support from Lygdamis, the tyrant of the island of Naxos, he eventually returned with an armed force and landed in Attica at Marathon. His forces defeated the Athenians from the city in a battle at Pallene, and Pisistratus was now in secure control of Athens, having occupied the Acropolis, disarmed the citizens, and holding the sons of the major families hostage. He grew old and died in power in 528/7 B.C., basing his power on money, foreign mercenaries and alliances, and, if we are to believe both Aristotle and Herodotus, having maintained a salutory, beneficent and mild rule.

The story of Pisistratus provides a number of valuable guides to understanding the workings of the Greek political community, particularly if we compare modern analyses with ancient views of the tyranny and its dissolution. Pisistratus is the only Greek tyrant who comes through with a good reputation from antiquity. Both Herodotus and Aristotle agree on the benefits he conferred on the Athenians, with loans to the poor to encourage farming, circuit judges sent around the land to administer justice, and an absence of exploitation and oppressive measures. The politics of his success are a little difficult to follow, for his support from the small farmers of the hinterland would not seem to call for further support and alliance with the coastal dwellers led by Megacles, unless we develop the hypothesis that these two groups had political and or economic interests in common as against the traditional aristocracy of the plains. Aristotle does not allege any economic motivations for the alliances, and he was no fool in his understanding of economic causes and motivations. The alliance with Megacles also seems as much based on Megacles' aim of family advancement as on any economic motives.

During the period of Pisistratus' government, Athens was opened up to immigration of Ionian artisans, and the tyrant pursued an aggressive international policy. He developed strong alliances in the Aegean, established his friend Lygdamis as tyrant of Naxos, and Lygdamis in turn made Polycrates tyrant of Samos. Pisistratus appointed his own son at Sigeum in the Troad, and carried out a purification of Apollo's sacred island of Delos called for by an oracle. All these outposts and activities fitted the times, when Athenians, with a fine pottery ware that was even more popular than that of Corinth, were striking out across the Aegean and to the Hellespont and northwards in vigorous trading activity. The prosperity of Pisistratus' reign made it possible for him to attract artists, particularly refugees from the expanding power of Persia, and he is famous for his public works and his increasingly lavish celebration of religious festivals and rites. It was under his patronage that complete versions of the *Iliad* and *Odyssey* were written down. When he died in 528/7 B.C. he left a flourishing, commercially burgeoning and artistically exciting Athens to the administration of his sons, Hippias and Hipparchus.

Pisistratid rule ended with the assassination of Hipparchus and the expulsion of Hippias. Again, there is a striking and significant difference between the explanations of ancient writers and the analyses of modern historians. Writers today look at a worsening international position of the Pisistratids, with their friendly tyrants on Naxos and Samos falling from power, combining with expansion of Persian power and contraction of Athenian trade and prosperity, complicated by the collapse of a friendly relationship with Thebes, Argos and Thessaly on the mainland. Ancient writers—Herodotus, the supremely rational Thucydides, and the polymath philosopher Aristotle— all agree on a personal motivation for the beginning of the end. These sources make it clear that the Pisistratids had created powerful opposition forces by expelling some people from the major clans, including a number of the powerful Alcmaeonid family, who had developed a close friendship with the priests at Delphi. There had been a number of attempts on the part of Alcmaeonid family members to return to Athens, but all had been frustrated. Meanwhile, at Athens, two young nobles, Harmodius and Aristogiton, for private reasons according to the traditioal account, made an attempt on the lives of the tyrants and succeeded in killing one of them, Hipparchus. This happened in 514 B.C., according to standard chronology. As a result of the attack, the surviving tyrant, Hippias, became generally suspicious and ruled much more oppressively. A little later, the Alcmaeonids won a contract to rebuild the temple at Delphi, and by exceeding the contractual requirments so pleased the priests that the oracle began telling Spartans, whenever they came to consult, that they must depose the Pisistratids. The Spartans yielded in 511/10 B.C., attacked Athens, shut the forces of Hippias up on the Acropolis, and by luck captured the young Pisistratid sons. The fight was over; Hippias capitulated and withdrew to Sigeum in western Anatolia and Athens was free from government by tyranny.

It is not naiveté that makes ancient writers explain all these events in personal terms. We have that explanation from three different kinds of thinkers and writers from three different places. Herodotus, a fifth-century writer who saw the march of history in terms of the cyclic rise and fall of powerful states, came from western Asia. Thucydides, a slightly younger contemporary of Herodotus, wrote of Athens' history from the point of view of the moral and practical aspects of the excercise of power, and he came from Athens itself. Aristotle, the fourth-century philosopher who went to Athens at the age of 17 to study with Plato and who investigated the history of the Athenian constitution as part of the study of the development of political institutions, originally came from Macedon. All three made the same basic assumptions about the nature of Athenian society, and these assumptions influenced their understanding of the rise and fall of Pisistratid power. One assumption relates to their view of the relationship between political power and members of the citizen group in a Greek city.

To our three writers, it seemed entirely natural that a body of people, adult males, should be the repository of power and decision-making, and further, that the body might break into divisions along lines of personal or sub-group self-interest. Such were the three groups whose conflict and shifting alliances led to the see-saw accretion of power into the hands of Pisistratus. Such was the family of the Alcmaeonids, making up almost a faction unto itself in the later sixth century B.C. And this comprehension of political action still makes sense in the modern world, even if modern historians do not always adopt it, because politics and social conflict in today's societies are usually set out on a conceptual framework partly derived from the Greek, or at least Athenian, experience. Using this framework, the whole history of the Pisistratids, from the first to the last, can be explained in terms of personal political motives, just as the ancients saw it. Pisistratus' first abortive assault on power seems to have used only his own resources; his second had the aid of Megacles, the Alcmaeonid, whose support can be explained purely in terms of personal family advantage. The tyrant's later expulsion of the leading families would lead inevitably to pressure from them and internal turmoil, if they could arrange it, and the final success of the Alcmaeonids came after a chance attack led the remaining tyrant into misjudged behavior. However much the international scene might have been changing—and we do not really know whether the changes had very much effect on Athens politically or economically—the major political forces at Athens seem to have concentrated on asserting their own control over the city.

Pisistratus' success in holding on to power and passing it on to his sons for an aggregate of over 20 years seems to have come from the tyrants' understanding and playing of the power and goals of the forces in the city. Even as far back as the time of Solon, some elements in the city thought that they were being deprived in some measure of their share of the benefits of being Athenian. Solon's poetic insistence on the balance of his political settlement reflects that. He claims that he did not give more to the populace than they deserved, and neither lowered them nor gave them too much, while for the powerful and rich, he aimed that they not feel aggrieved. Some of the poorer classes must have been dissatisfied, or later renewed that attitude, in order for Pisistratus to have used that group in his grip on power. The later tradition that Pisistratus based himself on the support of the *diakrioi*—the small farmers—shows two things about political assumptions in early Athens. First, it demonstrates that in the power structure of society, small farmers could be, at least in aggregate, a political or social force important enough to provide strength. Second, it underscores what seems to be the assumption in Athenian politics that even the less endowed socially and economically could insist on a share, perhaps an improving share, of political and economic rewards.

In recent years scholarship has focused on this very important characteristic of early Greece, trying to discover whether the attitudes of the classical city represented the culmination of change, and on the conclusion that they did, the reasons that such a change took place. Modern predilections for material explanations propose a sequence beginning with rising populations, and increased population generating need for a greater agricultural base, leading to a kind of warfare aiming at acquiring and holding territory. Earlier wars, this reasoning proceeds, were fought by aristocratic champions, who, like the heroes of the *Iliad*, rode to battle in their chariots and clashed in feats of prowess with opposing nobles. With the need to take and hold land imposing new strategies and massings of troops, the assembled soldiers were no longer the negligible ants of Achilles' force of myrmidons. With the emerging military importance of the heavy-armed infantryman, or hoplite, to use the Greek term, came an increasing dependence on the service of the much larger number of members of society who could provide the arms and armor for this kind of fight—larger in number, that is, than the number of those who could afford chariots, horses and grooms. And so this larger number claimed more and more rights over policy and demanded more and more share in the group's gains.

The theory is reasonable, but it also raises questions. To generate this pressure on the land, particularly when overseas colonization was sending mouths abroad, calls for a considerable rise in population. This rise has never been successfully demonstrated, and it is difficult to find exceptional factors which might have caused it then, and not at other times in antiquity. Secondly, some argument has been made that hoplite warfare—the style of the heavy-armed infantryman—is known to the *Iliad*. Finally, ancient Mediterranean societies give us plenty of examples of armies of massed infantry serving extremely stratified and hierarchical societies. Even though these near eastern armies had different weapons, and armies were organized differently from those of the Greeks, there is no need to suppose a "democratic" impulse inherent in military activity depending on armed foot soldiers. Greek propaganda derogating the quality of the "slave" armies of the Persian king can be taken with more than a grain of salt when we take into account the efficiency of Persian troops in so many wars.

The emergence of the materialist theory in contemporary historical writing focuses attention on the importance of the city-citizen phenomenon in Greek history, and the difficulty in explaining the emergence of this unusual form of government. The geography of mountainous terrain, isolating Greek communities from one another and making land communications difficult, is obviously not enough of an explanation. While parallel situations seem in a few instances to have encouraged similar kinds of communities, such as the Berber villages of the Atlas Mountains, there is no regular pattern of isolation producing the kinds of city-citizen involvement characteristic of Hellenism. In Greece, the force of the interaction between members of the community and the political structure was extremely strong, and wherever we have adequate evidence for details of development, this interaction was a major influence on events.

At Athens, citizen expectations and political machinations interwove to continue turmoil after the departure of Hippias, as the Alcmaeonid politician Cleisthenes came to the fore. Both Herodotus and Aristotle tell of a reform program in the last decade of the sixth century, but only the *Constitution of Athens* gives the details. There seems to have been a thoroughgoing reform of the constitutional structure: the four family or tribal groups providing the validation of descent and membership in the broad Athenian body were divided into ten. The council, or *boule*, was now made of 500 members, 50 from each tribe. The individual citizen was in future to be identified by his geographical district—his deme—rather than his father's name for political purposes and for registration as a citizen. The geographical demes were also now used for political organization, as groups called trittyes were formed by creating 30 individual segments. These were made of demes combined along geographical lines, so that there were ten trittyes from the shore area, ten from the city and ten from the interior, with one trittys from each area in each tribe (Herodotus says that there were ten demes in each).

This is a complex redistricting, and there has been a lot of ink spilled in modern times trying to explain its purpose and its effects. There is also a lot of debate over another reform attributed to Cleisthenes. The sources claim that he introduced a law instituting a procedure called ostracism, a popular vote producing a kind of election in reverse, with the politician with the most votes consigned to a ten-year banishment, but with no loss of status or property. Modern historians doubt that the law was really the work of Cleisthenes, since the first ostracism did not come until the beginning of the next century, but a reluctance to believe that Athenians waited so long to apply ostracism is probably inspired by the attractions of using such a procedure on modern politicians. There is also doubt about the sequence of events in which Cleisthenes struggled with his major opponent Isagoras, who called in the support of the Spartans. The order of events is really not clear, but the tradition is consistent that Cleisthenes was involved in a political struggle with Isagoras, that Isagoras did call in the Spartans, that Cleomenes, one of the two kings of Sparta, tried to dissolve the council, which refused his instructions, and that Cleomenes and Isagoras, after taking the Acropolis and being besieged there for two days, finally were forced to evacuate Athens under a truce. During or after all of this, Cleisthenes' reforms were instituted, and when Isagoras and Cleomenes left, probably in 508/507, the new structure was in place and the style of government called by later Greek writers the "democracy," was firmly in the saddle. An attack shortly after this, led by the Spartans, with a thrust from the island Euboea in the east and Boeotia in the west, failed when the Corinthians, who supposedly had insouciantly joined the expedition without being told its target, broke off action. Demaratus, the other Spartan king, followed the Corinthians off the field, and that left the Athenians free to repel the Boeotian threat and then cross to Euboea to defeat the army of Chalcis and plant there some cleruchs—military settlers—to occupy the land of the rich men of that city. The new democracy of Athens was now secure externally as well.

The story of the Cleisthenic reform makes a puzzle, especially since Cleisthenes himself disappears from history after this one event. All sorts of far-seeing and sagacious purposes have been read into the actions, usually passing over explaining it in terms of baser political motives, which might have prompted the reforms as part of domestic political manoevres. With the Alcmaeonids back in Athens, their leader, Cleisthenes, was involved in the old game of seeking power. His major opposition came from the group of aristocrats who had once been led by Lycurgus and were now headed by Isagoras. Neither side could gain a clear victory: a third group could assure it. Cleisthenes turned to that group, the remnants of the supporters of Pisistratus, and the new immigrants who had come to Athens under the protection of the tyrants. We know that Cleisthenes supported the citizenship of those newly enrolled, and we may hypothesize that for their support he would, and did, promise them secure enfranchisement, and the thorough mixing up of the population assured this security. With a new form of identification and citizen registration, and the tribes completely jumbled, there would be great difficulty in challenging people registered in deme registers. Whereas Isagoras had been able to implement a disenfranchisement under the old arrangement, Cleisthenes' cancellation of that act was given permanency.

This whole reorganization of the state, presented in Aristotle's history of the constitution without much rationale and reported as a step toward democracy without much explanation, can thus be seen as a phenomenon arising from the continual political wars in the politics of Athens and many other Greek cities. It also focuses attention on the critical issue of citizenship or membership, which more than once in

Athens and elsewhere generated violent political upheaval. The fact that so elaborate a constitutional reform as that of Cleisthenes was in some way involved with citizenship and the franchise shows how far-reaching the implications of that status were for Greek society. In fact a good deal of political thought and activity in Athens before the advent of formal philosophical teaching dealt with issues of participation, membership in the state and the balance between public and private interests.

For most people, the structure of everyday life depended on membership in the civic group, at least during the period of vitality of the typically Hellenic political unit the Greeks called *polis* and we call city-state—perhaps better—citizen state. Not only were the rights to engage in debate on policy or to cast votes for officials at issue, but membership also provided the protection of the common group represented by access to the court system, and countless other big and little privileges. Citizenship entailed participation in civic religious activities, with all the advantages those brought. For the most part, marriage of children or dependent relatives was practicable only within the civic group. In return for the life provided by the laws, as Plato put it into the mouth of Socrates, obedience and conformity were expected. That meant a considerable practical requirement in the course of everyday life. The obvious demand was service in war, and as conflict was endemic in Greece, military service was often a serious drain on the ordinary citizen's time and resources. Those who were more than ordinary citizens had more obligations. They provided funds for religious festivals and rites, they paid for civic entertainments, they underwrote the costs of major military and naval equipment, and of course, they assumed public office and performed official tasks sometimes time-consuming and onerous. In return for dedicating the larger part of their time and a good deal of their wealth to public activities, the social culture of honor and reward assured them of prestige and social power. It would be fair to say that as much as the wealthy leaders of Athens contributed to the fabric of society by their expenditure of money and time, they also owed their continued economic dominance to the status and power bought by that contribution.

The high point in the history of Athenian power and the expansion of the influence of the lesser elements in the population came during the fifth century B.C. As the Athenian democracy developed, greater weight in the state passed beyond those who could afford to outfit themselves with weapons as heavy armed infantrymen to those of even lower economic status. The predominantly aristocratic writers of Greek literature repeatedly cite the developed Athenian democracy of the late fifth century B.C. as a constitution under which the "worst elements" controlled the state, and it is certainly true that in Athens of that time, the non-owning classes seem to have done better for themselves than they did anywhere else or at any other time in antiquity. The attacks on leaders of the "demos"—the masses who should not control affairs, in the view of aristocrats—make it clear that the advances in power of the populace owe a great deal to the ambitions of those who chose to use popular support to advance their own positions. When Aristotle, who was certainly not fond of radical democracy, rates as best the state which has as its lowest citizen class the yeomen farmers who are too busy to take part in politics, he is deploring the activity of the restless sailor-citizens who were so influential in politics in Athens.

The Athenian experience in the fifth century B.C. was one of rise to empire and fall from power, the consummation of a Herodotean cycle in a single century. The restlessness of Athenian ambitions emerged at the beginning of the century with Athenian help sent to Ionian cities in revolt against Persia, and was obscured by the triumph of allied Greek forces, led by Athens and Sparta, in repelling two punitive Persian invasions, one in 490 and the other sent reeling in 480 and 479. The Athenians used the opportunity of the success of their leadership to build a naval league of Aegean cities as a defensive alliance against Persia, and by mid-century had converted their role as first among equals to that of unconcealed control. It was only a long war with Sparta, stretching, with interruptions, from 431 to 404, that finally brought Athens down, and even then, only misfortune in a major thrust to Sicily and the Persian support of Sparta finally forced the imperial democracy to her knees.

Imperial, yes, but democracy too, a combination which misled liberal idealists of the enlightenment and later to excessive praise, or induces modern pacifists and anti-imperialists to blind condemnation. To Greeks looking at the Athenian experience, the pertinent question was the competence of radical democracy in times of crisis, and as aristocrats they reliably found Athenian institutions wanting. But the issue was a practical matter in part, and where it was moral it related to Athenian treatment of others, not their internal constitutional arrangements. There was no challenge to the basic ideological assumption that all members of a society should share to some extent in the control and the benefits of that society. Where aristocratic historians and philosophers faulted Athens was in its balance of powers: too much allocated to the landless and wealthless.

The exploration of that balance was the work of Athenian politicians and intellectuals of the fifth century. At the heart of many of the works of Athenian dramatists lay the assumption that there was legitimacy on the part of all demands, and that public morality was, essentially, the allocation of priorities. As tragedy put it, even the most serious disturbances of the moral order were matters of political determination, and Aeschylus, writing in the first half of the fifth century, devoted a trilogy, the *Oresteia*, to a dramatic presentation of the manner in which cleansing the community of the pollution of murder moved from divine retribution to human judicial process. His three-play work is not only one of the great literary accomplishments of the ancient world, it is also brilliant illumination into the modes of thought dealing with the role of citizen in the state. Aeschylus has tied into the *Oresteia* many issues of human life, like the relative values of male and female prerogatives, tension between family and state, the obligations among the individual members of the family, and finally, the controlling theme of human justice and its divine sanction. In the first two plays, each character in turn interprets divine law. In the first play, *Agamemnon*, King Agamemnon's wife kills her husband to exact punishment for his sacrifice of their daughter. Then in *The Libation Bearers*, Queen Clytemnestra's own son Orestes kills his mother, at the god Apollo's behest, and the cycle of vengeance seems to go on as the furies sweep down on Orestes and pursue him screaming from the stage. In the final play, *Eumenides*, Orestes comes finally to Athens, after a visit to Apollo at Delphi. The case is to be heard by the goddess Athena, who is to decide which of the two other divine forces, Apollo or the furies, has the greater right. Athena does not make the decision on her own, but shares it with a jury of men whom she appoints as a court of homicide, for this case and for all cases of killing in the future. In the particular case of Orestes, with justice tied up with divine orders and traditional retribution, she shares the responsibility for judgement with the jurors in a complex voting scheme giving equal weight to the divine and human spheres, but in the future, the humans are to be on their own in rendering justice.

The trilogy is more than an accounting for the existing court of the Areopagus in Athens, and it goes far beyond questions of support for or opposition to the prerogatives of that court. It is part of the Athenian sense of transition from family to public law, the shift from a social structure in which conduct was regulated by tradition and family authority to one in which rules and judgements were more impersonal, more public and political. It is the same theme implied by some of the legislation attributed to Solon—legislation like the law permitting wills, shifting inheritance from being a completely family matter to one in which courts have authority to adjudicate in some cases. The assumptions of the trilogy about the nature of this court, however, go even deeper into the Athenian political and social stucture. Aeschylus' jurors are the good burghers of Athens, so to speak, and the court of the Areopagus appears in its fifth-century aspect, made up of the ordinary citizens of Athens. They are qualified to judge merely by their membership in the civic body, for, as the tradition has it, Solon had opened membership of courts to the large body of citizens with the least financial qualification. And the Athenian court system had by the fifth century evolved into a critical part of the democratic structure, a justification for seeing Solon's reforms as tending toward increase in democracy. Since officials were accountable in a formal assessment at the end of their tenure of office, and charges of impropriety could go before courts, the access to judgement was a political weapon, and officials would always be aware of the potential of the lowest classes for political action through law.

Thus membership in the court system merely through citizenship was another way in which the Athenian system tended to broaden the distribution of political power. Ancient commentators on Athens seem to think that for a good part of the fifth century, the overall democratic system seemed to work. Herodotus, in his account of the Athenian demos dealing with diplomatic issues before the Persian Wars, and then with the actual conduct of war, leaves no room for implications that the democracy was erratic or self-indulgent in the ways that Thucydides paints it during the Peloponnesian War in the last quarter of the century. The citizens in the choruses of Aeschylus' plays show sober and conservative, even if banal, wisdom, and Sophocles, writing in the last half of the century, gives us the same kinds of citizen groups in his plays. The growth of professional teaching for middle and upper class citizens represented by the sophists also emerges from an environment in which the broad mass of citizens are regarded as capable of reasonable, and even virtuous, decisions on public matters. The background to Socratic thought, if we understand it right, is one of acceptance of the legitimacy of the influence of the lowest classes in public debate, and the import of Socrates' insistence on concern for the goodness of the individual soul is a philosophical ratification of a democratic, as against an aristocratic ethic. The aristocratic ideal is older than Homer, and glorifies family connections, wealth, personal strength and prowess in sports and battle, and physical good looks. Only the members of aristocratic families could aspire to this kind of goodness, or *arete*, for only they had the long traditions of generations, the wealth, and the leisure to pursue the physical skills required. The ideal was still dominant in some Greek communities in the fifth century, as the poetry of the Boeotian Pindar shows, and even in Athens the aristocrats held on to it as long as they could. Socrates' idea that goodness was not prowess and not physical, but intellectual and spiritual, was a radical notion, and it was possible only in a community slipping away from the grip of aristocratic ideology.

The realities of late fifth-century Athens are not very clear in our sources, because their aristocratic leanings lead them to obscure what was happening in the ideology of participation in Athens. There, as the war continued to be fought and the city pursued a naval policy, the burdens of the state were carried more and more by the large numbers of people who staffed the vessels and were away from the city for periods of time. These people, in turn, depended upon their pay as sailors, for even those who had small plots of land were unable to profit from them as Spartan armies repeatedly ravaged their farms. Ultimately, a decision was carried to provide each citizen who needed it a minimum daily income, a "dole" as it is described by modern historians who have been for the most part prosperous gentlemen or well-paid middle-class professors. The ancient aristocratic writers also despised this halting step toward economic egalitarianism, and found in it one of the causes of Athens' ultimate demise. Thucydides' history of the war with Sparta not only imposes a moral judgement on the Athenians, he presents a narrative that can only lead his readers to conclude that the radical democracy was incapable of waging a sustained war. There are changes of mind, like the revoked decision to kill or enslave the population of Mytilene after this ally was forced to abandon its revolt. Thucydides makes it clear that the change was not a matter of pity for the people who had been consigned to destruction to terrorize the other allies, but a revision of the demos' idea of its self-interest, convinced in a new debate that so drastic a punishment would mean that future cities in revolt would never surrender. Thucydides' descriptions of the activities and military success of the demos-leader Cleon—demagogue, to us, with all of the connotations Thucydides made for the word—ensures our dislike and disrespect of this popular politician and general. Thucydides' text also ensures that we see the reluctance of the populace to accept Spartan overtures for peace after the first decade of war as the product of the lightness of mind of the citizens in assembly and the ability of popular leaders to draw the population to bad decisions.

Thucydides' political judgements on the largest portion of the populace emerge in historical narrative. The next generation's Plato imposed them in philosphical essays explicitly drawing an analogy beween the many citizens of the body politic and the unrestrained emotions and passions of an out-of-kilter human being. And Plato's student, Aristotle, taking the long view of the evolution of the Athenian democracy toward the fulfilment of that form inherent in it, saw the development of extreme democracy as the excessive aggrandizement of the lower classes beyond the reasonable allocation of power to them. However, even the adverse judgements on the Athenian democracy issued no challenge to the fundamental idea that those classes which were abusing their powers nevertheless should be fitted into the power structure in some appropriate way.

The central question in Athenian politics, and for that matter in most Greek cities, was never the choice of constitutional structure. The theoretical discussion of monarchy, aristocracy and democracy presented by Herodotus as he recounts a putative debate in Persia after the overthrow of an illegitimate ruler was just that—theoretical. Athenians would never have considered instituting a monarchy, and the institutional structures of courts, magistrates, council and assembly allowed for a greater or lesser democracy only insofar as limits were placed on the number of citizens involved in the institutions. An oligarchic revolution of 411 was short lived, and the government of 30 "tyrants" instituted by Sparta after the victory of 404 was intended to yield to a moderate oligarchy (or democracy) of 3,000 citizens granted voting rights. So the central issue was the number of members of the citizen body with the right to participate in operating the system. While Athens at the height of her power was extreme among Greek states in the numbers involved in political activity and in the scope allowed that participation, that aspect of Athenian politics was always subject to challenge even by Athenians.

Probably the best insight into the Athenians' sense of themselves comes from a speech Thucydides put into the mouth of Pericles, the aristocratic popular leader who was pre-eminent at the onset of the Peloponnesian War. At the end of the first year, Pericles delivered the traditional speech in honor of those who had died in battle, and the text Thucydides gives to us shows the historian's view of patriotic Athenian rhetoric. Athenians were to be lovers of their city, dedicated to maintaining the power and glory built by their ancestors and fathers. The speech praises the style of Athenian political life, its openness and its quality of lively debate: "We do not think that discussion is in any way harmful to action, but that damage comes from not considering in advance in words what is needed in action." The Athenians, in the words attributed to Pericles, make state business a priority: "each person is concerned for public as well as personal affairs, and even those primarily occupied with business are not uninformed in political matters, and we do not, like others, consider a person who takes no part in politics to be minding his own business, but we consider him useless."

The ideal is one of participation and involvement, and the breadth of that among the citizens is enhanced by an absence of wealth or social restriction: "The name we give our government is democracy, because it is at the disposition of the many, not the few, and under the law everyone has an equal standing in private disputes. In public appointments, a man gains standing by his ability, not his social position, nor does poverty hold him in obscurity if he has anything good to do for the public." The passage, if not the whole speech, has long been cited with approval by liberal political thinkers, and it is still a valid ideal for those who think of human worth primarily in political and social terms. That is one of the fundamental values of Athenian thought. Arising from the concept of membership and participation in benefits, Athenian ideals substituted subordination to public aims and a value system based on social and political service for personal and private gratification.

Athenian values and institutions were by no means unique among the Greeks, even if they represented a stronger commitment to the scope of their application. While we know much more about Athens' formal constitutional structure and the actual practice of political activity there than we do for any other Greek city, there is still enough information for some generalization. Sparta is probably best known after Athens, and we do have names for her internal bodies along with some information about their procedures. There are some direct parallels with Athens. To the Athenian *boulé* or council corresponds the

Spartan *gerousia*, and the Athenian assembly had its counterpart in the *apella* of all male Spartan citizens, who in that body had the right to approve or withhold approval of all major decisions. At Sparta as at Athens there were administrators: two kings, supposedly descended from Heracles, who were advised by, and often controlled by, a board of five supervisors, called *ephors*.

Ancient writers concentrated on the restrained sense of political activity at Sparta and the intense concentration on maintaining a high quality of military spirit and ability, while modern comments focus on the highly elitist nature of Spartan values. As modern historians often portray Sparta, the population was made up of three broad groups. There were, at the bottom, helots, descendants of some of the people in the area around Sparta and also of the inhabitants of Messenia, a large area to the west of Sparta which Sparta had subdued in early times. The helots were in a sort of serfdom, required to live on and work specific plots of land alloted to the ownership of Spartan citizens. Above the helots were free inhabitants of all the countryside and towns of Laconia, the general area of the Peloponnesus in which Sparta was located. These Laconians were free, but paid taxes and served in the army, without participating in the political life of Sparta or the social and political life reserved for the citizens of Sparta itself. Members of this top group, often known as the Spartiates, made up the citizen body eligible for participation in the apella and for political office. The peculiar Spartan system is generally thought to have come from the need to create from a very small citizen body an army of superb quality in order to keep the large number of helots subject. Male Spartans participated in the highly communal military training, separating boys and fathers from families, and the system imposed an austerity limiting their economic possessions severely, outlawed luxuries like jewelry and precious metals and allocated the subject lands in rough equality. When Sparta went to war, Spartans always led the armies, which were made up of far more Laconians and Peloponnesian allies, and the elite Spartan citizen-troops took the place of honor on the right wing.

In the Spartan view of society, however, their society was anything but elitist. The citizens referred to themselves as "the equals," and their relationship with one another was based on the ideal of social equality, with even the kings only first among equals. The difference in interpretation of society is a difference in the delineation of the group. Unlike Athens, where citizenship extended to all the residents of the villages of Attica to create a very numerous citizen body scattered over a wide territory, for the Spartans there was never any idea that the membership in society could ever go beyond the residents of the town of Sparta itself—a relatively small place with a small population. Furthermore, economic and social values at Sparta discouraged the entrepreneurial spirit which at Athens expanded the core city of Athens and her port and brought in new residents who were on a few occasions added to the citizen rolls. However, beyond the fact that the notion of the group was very limited and the number of members accordingly small, the Spartan concept of the relationship among the members and their privileges vis-a-vis one another was not very different from that of Athens and was in fact highly egalitarian: by membership, the citizens were equal, had equal rights in approval of public policy and, economically more egalitarian than Athens, were expected to be content with roughly equal lots. The Athenians would find the inequality in Spartan society in its discouragement of debate and policy direction by public assembly, which was limited to approval or rejection of decisions made by the few members of the ephorate or *gerousia*, and would be surprised to find that the same basic assumptions about citizenship and society had created so different a pattern of behavior as the Spartan.

The basic constitutional structures we find at Athens and Sparta were repeated all over the Greek world. Corinth, for example, after domination by an aristocratic Bacchiad family and then a sequence of tyrants, developed constitutional government directed by a board of eight from a council of 80. In the west, after tyranny, fifth-century Syracuse operated as a moderate democracy, with close parallels to Athenian institutions. There was an assembly and a council called a *boulé*, as well as other councils with roles less well known today, and annual officials known as *strategoi* or generals. There was even a short-lived recourse to the practice of ostracism, called *petalismos* at Syracuse.

At Syracuse also, the issue of membership was critical, although there, unlike as at Athens, after the fall of the early tyrants, political manoevring did not bring the tyrant's new citizens permanency in the group.

Like Syracuse, in the fifth century and later, many Greek cities operated a system which was a democracy of some sorts. Athens imposed this government on the resisting oligarchs of some cities, as at Samos, but for the most part, all over the Aegean and in South Italy and Sicily this was the prevailing form of government. Examples are found all the way west and in Bosporus and Black Sea areas as well. "Moderate" democracy was probably the prevailing form of government in the Greek city in this period, because for those times it answered best to the deep-seated conviction of the right to sharing for all members of the group. Later ancient political analysts like Aristotle and Polybius used the fifth-century experience to develop the notion of an ideal "mixed" constitution, with the elements of monarchy, aristocracy and democracy combined in a blended balance to provide fairness to the different interests and stability to the group as a whole.

These patterns of government were idealized in later times, as in the renaissance and the enlightment, and they were identified with the government of the Roman Republic to justify efforts at political autonomy and self-government at times when some individuals and societies were trying to break away from the grip of medieval and modern emperors and kings. The times were different, and the goals could be expressed with slogans like "liberty," with meaning very different from the *autonomia* sought by each big and little Greek city, until something like the ancient attitude has re-emerged in the ideals of the modern era. The differences show sharply in slogans of the two great revolutions of the eighteenth century. The right to "life, liberty and the pursuit of happiness" of the American revolution is an idea of its own time, caught up with political freedom and the liberty of the individual from authoritarian oppression or interference. The "liberté, égalité et fraternité" of France has something of an Athenian (and Spartan) ring to it.

The fundamental attitude that membership in the society entails political and social rights was the same in most in Greek communities. It determined the nature of the Macedonian monarchy as much as it provided the impetus to Athenian democracy. Oligarchs made their mutual arrangements in assumptions of its validity, and usually allowed for it in their relations with their social or economic inferiors. Even tyrants—unlawful autocrats by definition—conformed to these principles by exercising political domination but not usurping too much of the general wealth, and there were some instances, at least, in which tyranny served the interests of the lower classes. These attitudes survived the fifth and fourth centuries, when cities governed along these lines exercised most of the power in the Greek world, and they influenced philosophical and political attitudes when the influence and potential of communities like this were severely curtailed. It is, no doubt, the effects of this attitude in framing the attitudes of formal and popular philosophy that lay behind feelings of social dissatisfaction in the centuries when it was no longer very practicable for those who exercised real power.

3 "We Know How to Be Greek"

In the third century B.C., when Egypt was under the rule of a Macedonian dynasty and Greeks and Macedonians were the dominant members of society, a native in the countryside complained that he was being insulted because he did not know how to "hellenizein." Modern historians have debated the meaning of this word and this complaint, because it goes to the heart of our understanding of the relationship between the ruling Greeks and others. Did the Egyptian mean that he was being insulted because he did not know how to speak Greek, or is the better translation "behave like a Greek"? This little note on papyrus is one of the few direct pieces of evidence for racial or cultural attitudes on the part of Greeks, and it comes after a long history of interrelations of Greeks with other peoples.

During the Mycenaean period, before 1000, Greeks had been in contact with many of the different cultures in the Mediterranean. There had been close contacts with Egypt and the civilizations along the coast of Syria and Palestine, and off the shores of Anatolia there had actually been some settlement of Greeks. As the eastern Mediterranean fell into turmoil in the period after 1300, the Greeks on the Greek peninsula turned toward the west, seeking with contacts in South Italy and Sicily to make up for the economic losses in the east.

The two or three hundred years after the destruction of the Mycenaean centers is largely a gap in our knowledge. The period saw a change in Greece itself, at least in terms of distributions of speakers of the different Greek dialects. In the Bronze Age, wherever the clay tablets with the Linear B Mycenaean script turn up, we can tell that the dialect was east Greek. Central Greece, and all of the Peloponnesus, show this dialect. But later, after 800, the speakers of western dialects, notably Dorian, turn up throughout peninsular Greece, where they are identified by their literary works and inscriptions. By that time many of them had also settled overseas, along the southern coast of Turkey, on some of the islands off that shore, and in the far west in South Italy and Sicily. Their arrival in Greece is called by some modern writers "The Dorian Invasion," and is often related to the Greek account of the return of the sons of Heracles to reclaim the Peloponnesus as their inheritance. Whether the Dorians themselves were responsible for the destruction of the Mycenaean centers, whether they shared in them, or whether they took advantage of some yet unidentified troubles that destroyed Mycenaean power and allowed them to filter in unopposed, they spread throughout the peninsula and left only a few pockets of east-Greek speakers. A few of these stayed up in the hills of Arcadia, while others seem to have emigrated to Attica, where they settled and formed a comparatively large population.

Beyond the dialect change, however, there is little to show the presence of new people. What we can learn from archaeology seems to show gradual change: using the evidence of pottery found at those sites preserving a continuous record of inhabitation, art styles shift smoothly from the Mycenaean and post-Mycenaean into the styles of the next period and then on into those of later times. We have no artifacts we can identify as "Dorian," and we have only the legends and history recorded by later Greeks to help us reconstruct events, at least as far as the development of society and politics is concerned. We can, however, derive from archaeology and from art history some clues about the broader activities of the people who lived in the Dorian-speaking areas in the eighth century, when they led the Greeks in a great expansion of international activity. This is the period of the so-called "orientalizing pottery," a style of pottery painting making a radical departure from its parent geometric style. The bright, multicolored decoration of the new style, with its multitude of designs and representations deriving from the traditions of the East, first appears in the pottery of Crete, Corinth and the areas around Sparta, then spreads among the other Dorian centers like Megara, and then finally reaches Athens and Ionia.

This orientalizing pottery shows the expanding horizons of the Greeks in this period, not only because the very heavy influence of eastern motifs demonstrates an intensifying contact between Greeks and their eastern neighbors, but because these wares, identifiable by city of origin, turn up all over the Aegean during this period. It is, in fact, by determining different syles of pottery that we can tell something of the histories of early cities like Smyrna, a commercial center in Ionia and one of the few early Iron Age sites to have been excavated to any great extent. Smyrna, on its small peninsula jutting out to sea in the center of the Turkish coast, was at its start occupied by Greeks speaking an east Greek dialect, Aeolic. Even in its earliest period, however, Smyrna had connections with Attica, and the site shows some broken pieces of protogeometric pottery similar to that in Attica about 1000. Through the ninth century, influence from the neighboring speakers of the Ionic dialect increased until at the beginning of the eighth century, the small, crowded city of some 450 households was thoroughly Ionic. The city seems to have expanded after 700, after some catastrophe, and luxury items and foreign imports begin to turn up. While there had been some importing of fine pottery during the eighth century—both Attic and Corinthian—during the seventh century Corinthian pottery was in common use. This illustrates a rather general phenomenon in the Greek world at this time: Corinth as leader joined by cities of Crete, as well as Megara and others, trading extensively in the Aegean and eastern Mediterranean.

By this time, also, the colonizing movement had scattered Greeks east and west in the Mediterranean. This period of colonization was utterly unlike anything the world had ever seen before or would ever see since, and the colonization itself was carried on in a manner unique to the Greeks. The colonies were not, as colonies have been in modern times, outposts of empire promoting economic or political expansion. They were new, independent cities, tied to their founders by bonds of culture or religion, but not subject to the political control of the mother cities. When a city planned to send out a colony, it planned an act of separation, in which a group of citizens would leave the city to create a totally new and independent entity, a physically new city and citizen body. It was a deliberate act, and one with religious as well as social overtones, and in fact there are instances of colonies being sent out on instructions from oracles which came to the founders unsought. If, however, some god did not command the foundation in the first place, it was still necessary for a divinity to endorse the undertaking and act as divine leader. So oracles were consulted, and when the replies were affirmative, colonies would be sent out. Each new city thus looked back to the approving god as founder, along with the human founder, or *oikistes*, who was appointed by the founding city to lead the colonists. In some cases, the colonists would go out in a single group; in others, there might be successive sailings. In almost all cases, the colonists were all citizens of a single city, although they went with a variety of skills and social and economic backgrounds and on arrival might intermarry with native women.

There were all sorts of reasons, one supposes, for the selection of sites for the new foundations. Good, arable land, available water, good harbor facilities, proximity to commercial sailing routes, distance from hostile natives—or hostile Greeks—some or all of these must have determined the choice of each specific spot. The reasons for sending out colonists must also have varied, and modern historians have proposed many reasons to explain the phenomenon: overpopulation, political unrest, trade, search for resources, shortage of land. There are explanations of specific colonizations reported by ancient writers in some cases, as, for example, drought at Thera leading to the colonization of Cyrene in North Africa, reported by Herodotus, and shortages at Chalcis prompting the dispatch of the colony to Rhegium according to Strabo. The resources of the city sending out the colonists often determined the potential of the colony, which would, naturally, require numbers and resources before it could stand completely on its own and begin to control its own fate. Thus the powerful Dorian cities of Corinth and Megara played a leading part in the whole movement, while the larger Ionian centers like Miletus were equally important. Cities developed their own areas of particular interest in some cases, as, for example, Miletus scattered colonies all through the Black Sea area from the first half of the eighth century on, where she and her daughter colonies were ultimately responsible for perhaps a hundred Greek settlements in that area and the Propontis, the small body of water at the entrance to the Black Sea. Other Ionian cities also sent colonies there in the late seventh and in the sixth centuries, as did Megara, to put some Dorians there. The Propontis was heavily colonized by Ionians, with Miletus again important, as well as Dorians from Megara, while the Hellespont and the coast of Thrace also received their share of settlers.

In the west, colonization began when the Euboean cities, Ionian in dialect, of Chalcis and Eretria planted new cities on the island of Ischia off the Italian coast near Naples, as well as on the toe of Italy and on Sicily. Greek traditions place all these colonizations in the last half of the eighth century. The Dorians played a major part in colonizing this whole area, with Corinth and other Dorians founding the major center of Syracuse. Megarians, Cretans and Sparta founded other colonies in Sicily in South Italy, while Corinth herself secured the routes to the west by heavy colonization on the west coast of Greece itself and by displacing Eretrian settlers on Corcyra and planting her own colony there. Many of the cities in Italy and Sicily were to become great in later times, influencing important events for both Greeks and Romans. There was Rhegium, the colony of Chalcidians at the very toe of Italy; there was Sybaris, a colony of people from Troezen and the Achaean areas of the Peloponnesus. Sparta founded Taras at the site of the best harbor in South Italy, and there was Neapolis—Naples—and Cumae far up the coast toward the Etruscans and what was to become Rome. On Sicily, besides Syracuse, and inclined to give her trouble, were Leontini, Catana, Zancle, Naxos and Segesta, and the Dorian colonies of Megara Hyblaea, Selinus, Gela and Agragas.

Discoveries moved Greeks beyond Italy and Sicily. At the very end of the seventh or beginning of the sixth century the Phocaeans from the west coast of Turkey founded Massilia (modern Marseille) at a harbor in a land to become famous for its olives and wine, and Massilia in turn sent out its own colonies to other sites along the coast of southern France and on to Spain. And across the eastern Mediterranean, on the African coast, Cyrene, founded by the Dorians from Thera and colonizing other points along the coast at Barca and elsewhere, became a major center and one which was to play an important part in the history of the Greeks in that part of the world. In Egypt itself, at the invitation of the king the trading center of Naucratis was founded toward the end of the seventh century.

All these colonies were established with the basic institutions of the Greek city, showing that these structures and the ideology framing them had been implanted among Greeks long before these characteristics showed up at Athens in the sixth century. Although particular institutions might vary with the structures of the founding cities, the colonizers carried with them to their new homes the concepts of group cohesion and participation by its members according to the patterns which they used before leaving their old cities. The nature and even genesis of the whole colonizing movement depended in large measure on the very existence of the originating cities in the characteristic Greek form, for without the pattern of polis society among the Greeks, the forces which impelled the movement would probably not have been present. The great number and diversity of the colonies surely owe their existence to the multitude and diversity of the founding cities, all of which acted independently of one another and perhaps even in competition in their profligacy of foundations. And in many ways, the colonizing movement is another expression of that particular Greek attitude toward social structure and government of which the most outstanding expression is the polis itself.

The vast majority of colonizing efforts took place in areas without the influence of a central authority with which the Greeks would have to contend. So there was a lot of activity in the west, in the areas of Sicily and South Italy outside Carthaginian influence, and not far enough north in Italy to encounter the Etruscans. The Black Sea area was more or less open, since the Scythian nomads did not resist the planting of Greek colonies, and in fact found them a source for the luxury goods of the Greeks which the Scythians themselves wanted. However, despite the hundreds of foundations in these areas and the relative freedom with which the colonists could communicate with the varied indigenous peoples, there seems to have been practically no influence impinging on the colonies from the environment in which they were placed. Any influences went the other way, as in the case of the Scythians acquiring some taste for Greek goods.

On Sicily, as the Greeks placed more and more colonies on the coasts of the eastern part of the island and the Carthaginians did the same for the west, the native peoples retreated to the interior. The Greeks had relatively little contact with them, and their relationship with the Carthaginians and the Etruscans was primarily of hostility. In political terms, the western Greeks also had their period of tyrannies, although there the tyrannies held on longer and the movement to democracy was less vigorous. There is no indication of any non-Greek influence on the new foundations, and in fact, the architecture of Sicilian and Italian centers provides some of the best preserved and earliest examples of Greek construction. In a plain south of Naples, for example, at Paestum, stand three great temples of Doric style, the earliest good examples of this architectural order found still largely intact anywhere in the Greek world, and on Sicily a number of sixth-century temples still stand. Sicilian and Italian Greek cities maintained close commercial and cultural contacts with old Greece. The development of philosophical and religious ideas accelerated at the end of the sixth century with the emigration to Croton of Pythagoras from Samos in the Aegean. Pythagoras' religious society at Croton led the city to supremacy among the Achaean towns in Italy, and the mathematical, philosophical and religious ideas of Pythagoras had a great impact on fifth-century Greeks.

In both Sicily and Italy most of the middle of the fifth century was taken up with local matters, both internally in the cities with successive changes in government and among the various states as one or another attempted dominance in its area. The most notable achievement of Hieron, brother and successor to Gelon in the Syracusan tyranny when Gelon died in 478, was his great victory over the Etruscans in a naval battle off Cumae in 474. The Etruscans had been pressing the Greeks of Cumae in order to maintain their own trading access to southern Italy, and Hieron's victory as an ally of Cumae stopped any further threat which the Etruscans might have presented to the Greek cities. In southern Italy itself, the resistance of the Italians in the interior impeded the ready expansion sought by many Greek cities there. This was a particular problem for Taras (Tarentum), which was badly defeated by Messapian tribes in the mid 470s. The conflict between the native population and the Greek cities precluded much interchange of cultural influences. Among the Greeks themselves, there were rivalries separating the major cities of Taras, Locri, Croton and Rhegium, with Taras showing the greatest strength as Croton weakened after the middle of the century.

The most important event in South Italy was the refounding of Sybaris and then the founding of Thurii when that failed. It was probably around 443 that, near the site of the old Sybaris, a new city was founded, called Thurii, a project made pan-Hellenic by design of Pericles, the Athenian leader. Ancient tradition reports that Hippodamus of Miletus, who had laid out plans for the Athenian port city of Piraeus, was commissioned by Pericles to apply his system of town planning to Thurii. There is no reason to doubt this tradition, although it is clear that the so-called Hippodamian system, laying out regular blocks of structures separated by streets intersecting at right angles, was something known in Sicily and Italy and was used to a greater or lesser measure in laying out a number of cities there well before the time of Hippodamus. Also somewhat ambivalent is the tradition with regard to the constitution of Thurii, for some report that it was Protagoras of Abdera, another associate of Pericles, who set up the laws for the city, while credit is also given to Zaleucus, the early lawgiver of Locri, and Charondas, lawgiver for his native Catana and other western cities. The special nature of the foundation of Thurii is stressed by the much later Sicilian Greek historian Diodorus, who lists the ten tribes of the foundation, reflecting the origins from Arcadia, Elis and Achaea in the Peloponnesus, from Boeotia, the Delphic amphictyony and Doris in Central Greece, and then finally the Ionians, the Euboeans, the islanders and the Athenians, the last of whom provided the founders. The foundation of Thurii is one of the events for which Pericles and the Athenians are given special credit, as leading but not dominating other Greeks in a venture that carried a sense of unity among Greeks at a time when such sentiments were rare.

In Sicily, the early fifth century is marked by a period of turmoil associated with expulsion of tyrants in the major cities. The period after this is marked by the achievements of a native Sicel leader, Ducetius, who gathered a following among the native population. About 460 he mustered the support of Syracuse to gain control of Aetna, the former Sicel town of Catana which had been taken over by Hieron. In subsequent years he gained control of most of the interior of Sicily and created a Sicel federation with a new-built capital of Palice. He ran into trouble with the city of Acragas and his former friend Syracuse when he began encroaching on the Greeks, and by about 450, he was accepted as a suppliant by Syracuse and sent off to Corinth to live. He returned in about 446, unobstructed by Syracuse, and built a new city, called Cale Acte, between Messana and Himera. If Diodorus' account is to be believed, this was the cause of a falling out between Syracuse and Acragas, producing a battle between the two won by Syracuse. After the battle there was peace between the two cities, and nothing further was accomplished by Ducetius, and he died in about 440, leaving a vacuum among the Sicels which the Syracusans tried to fill as best they could. The episode of Ducetius illustrates the absence of any permanent connections or influences of the native people on the Greeks, and in fact, natives seem to have been able to play a role in the politics of the area only insofar as they fitted themselves into Greek patterns. The Greek cities of Sicily and South Italy had their connections, cultural, economic and military, with other Greek cities, whether one another, their own colonies, or old Greece. What commerce there was with non-Greek areas was extremely limited, and was essentially a matter of import into the Greek sphere and transshipment to other Greek areas, like the metal trade with the Etruscans, rather than an on-going and close commercial relationship.

The situation in the Black Sea area paralleled that of the west during most of this period. In the area to the northwest of the Black Sea the Greek cities had to contend with the group of Scythians known as the Royal Scyths, a kingdom the importance and power of which had been clearly established at the time they successfully turned back an invasion by the Persian king Darius. In the last years of the sixth century, Darius had marched northwest across the Danube into Scythia, leaving some of his Greek subjects to guard the bridge behind him. Herodotus tells an exciting tale of the Scythians retreating before him, stopping their wells, destroying their crops and baffling his attempts to bring them to battle. Finally Darius was forced to bring back his harassed and depleted army to the bridge which had almost been destroyed as a result of mutinous sentiments among the Greeks.

The Scythians seem to have been an Iranian people, who dominated large tracts of territory reaching back into the hinterland from the crescent of the north shore of the Black Sea. By the early fifth century the Scyths were heavily influenced by the Greeks of their area, and one of their kings, Scyles, was allegedly killed for his tendency to Hellenize in matters of customs and religion. Some of the Greek cities on the north shore of the Black Sea were tributary to the Scythians, and the trade which the Scythians of this area, the Kuban, carried on through the Greek ports and probably directly as well, made some of the Scythians leaders wealthy. In spite of the essentially tribal nature of Scythian society, in the fifth century the Scythian kingdom had an organized administration, with taxation and governors to whom the tributary Greek cities made their payments. Despite their political subservience to the Scythians, those tributary Greek cities remained part of the Greek world, and did not "Scythianize," and maintained their connections and cultural affinities with the independent Greek cities of the area and the older cities of the more southerly Aegean regions. There is an exception to this in regard to the important cities of the Crimea and South Russia, such as the Milesian colonies of Olbia and Pantipacaeum, and Tanais, founded by Pantipacaeum in its turn. Settled as they were among the vigorous Scythians, they developed an artistic tradition showing strong influence from their Scythian neighbors. There was a close connection between the Scythians and Greeks of the area. Greek luxury items are found in profusion in Scythian tombs, and enough was known about Scythian religion and customs that Herodotus on his travels could find out the names of their gods and some of their religious and funerary rites. But what was known was not adopted. Although the Greeks of the area might follow some Scythian modes in art, there seems to be no impact in other areas. Nothing was taken over of the elaborate burial practices of the Scythians, with their mounds full of valuable goods, nor does there seem to be an impact on the cults even of deities who were thought to be the same as those worshipped by the Scyths, so that there is no particular prominence given to Hestia, the Greek version of the pre-eminent Scythian goddess Tabiti. Regardless of how close the connections were between Scyths and Greeks, even extending at times to Scythian domination over one or another Greek city, there is little Scythian influence on the Greeks outside the realm of of art, and no indication of any other kind of cultural, literary or religious borrowing.

Another non-Greek locus of power in the north was that of the Odrysian Thracians, who ruled the area from the Hebrus River to the Danube in southern Thrace along the coast of the Black Sea. There, a kingdom "founded," according to Greek tradition, in the period 480-460, controlled the territory stretching up from the Bosphorus past Salmydessus and down again to the Aegean. The opportunity for the Thracian rulers to enlarge their domains must have been created by the contraction of Persian power after the great victory of the Greeks over Xerxes' invading armies in 480 and 479, and in fact, the first appearance of the Thracians on the political scene comes in the context of a treaty with the Scythians, suggesting Scythian expansion south after the withdrawal of Persian forces. The power of the Odrysian Thracians grew steadily during the fifth century, so that by the time of the outbreak of war between Sparta and Athens in 431, their king Sitalces could play a role of some importance in Greek affairs. Like the Scythians of the Black Sea area, the Thracians became Hellenized to some extent by the influence of Greeks settled near them, but they did not have any effect in transmitting their own cultural tradition to the Greeks who had contact with them.

The development of the Black Sea and northern Greek colonies, and their relationships with their neighbors and trade with Greece itself were strongly affected by the impact the Persians made in the area, but the effects of Persian expansion were felt much more strongly by the Greek cities of Asia Minor. There, the expanding kingdom of Lydia had absorbed all the cities of the west coast of Turkey, until Lydia itself fell to the westward thrust of Persia before the middle of the sixth century. The Greek cities of the coast were taken as the spoils of victory, and were incorporated into the Persian Empire and administered as part of the province which included Lydia itself and the entire western part of Turkey.

None of this had been disturbing to the Greeks of the motherland. When their colonies and fellow Greeks fell to Lydia in the seventh century, they took that as no threat and no interest to themselves, and when Persia in turn became the neighbor to the east many of the trading entrepreneurs found some convenience in that superpower's control of the vast reaches of Asia as well as Egypt in the northeast corner of Africa. There was a market in Greece for some of the products of the Far East, as well as for African ivory, and, now that a few people wrote and read books, for papyrus grown and manufactured along the Nile. The eastern motifs of orientalizing pottery show how Greeks had always been open to the east, and some of the concepts and ideas of religion as well have been thought to have emigrated to Greece from eastern peoples. Hesiod's eighth-century work, *Theogony*, or *Generation of the Gods*, has its eastern parallels, and there may be others for parts of the Greek mythic tradition. With Persia in control of all of those areas, access was easier, for the Persians did not interfere with Greek merchants, few as there were. Thus many Greeks had no fear of the Persians, and when Darius moved Persian armies into Europe along the north coast of the Aegean, he was unopposed by Greeks, and in fact, most of the peoples of northern Greece were quite friendly.

At the beginning of the fifth century, the future seemed to belong to Persia. In 500, the dominions of Darius reached from the Indus River in modern Pakistan westward to Thrace, and included all the great empires earlier in control of parts of the east—Egypt, Media,

Babylonia, Assyria. Persia now took in the wild lands of the central Asian steppe, like Bactria, Aria, Sogdiana—the Afganistan that modern Russian armies did not find easily controllable. Persian power reached up along the shores of the Caspian Sea and the Black Sea, and Persian officials governed the old lands of Palestine, Syria, Anatolia, and Lydia with the Greek cities of the coast. Even some of the the islands came under Darius' sway, as the Greeks of Samos, Lesbos and Chios submitted.

Only the Scythians had succeeded in checking Persian expansion, and the Greek cities in western Asia reacted to that check with revolt. That the mighty Darius could stumble must have played some part in the willingness of the Greek cities of Ionia to risk war, even though Herodotus credits personal motives for the outbreak of revolt. In his account, Histiaeus, tyrant of Miletus, was invited down to Susa by Darius, who was suspicious of him and therefore kept him in honorable captivity in the Persian capital. This left his son-in-law Aristagoras in command at Miletus, and he soon found himself worrying about his position vis-a-vis the Persians as a result of the failure of an expedition against the island of Naxos into which he had inveigled the Persian governor Artaphernes. While that had been going on, Histiaeus, restless at his confinement, concluded that the best way out would be to create unrest in Ionia, so that Darius would send him back to settle affairs. Accordingly, he sent a message to Aristagoras, calling for revolt, using the now-famous strategem of the man with the shaved head; he shaved the hair from the head of the messenger, wrote his message on the scalp, and then when the hair had grown back over the writing he sent him off to Aristagoras at Miletus with only the message, "Shave my head." The man arrived when Aristagoras was pondering his awkward position after the failure of the Naxos expedition, and that was enough to determine him on the course of revolt.

Many modern commentators have noted that there must have been important economic, political and even psychological factors behind the readiness of the Ionian leaders to embark upon the dangerous path of revolt against so powerful a king. Even if we are content to note that Herodotus did not feel the need for such explanations, and that as a writer he could expect his readers to follow the mental set of the personal explanation, we can readily see the political and economic impact of the revolt and its failure. The Ionians looked to the homeland for help, and after the Spartans refused, they turned to Athens, which did send a contingent of 20 ships, joined by five more from the city of Eretria on Euboea. Initially the Greek forces were successful, to the point of the capture and sack of the provincial capital of Sardis in 498, but soon the action turned against them, especially when the Athenians failed to carry their participation beyond the first year of campaigning. First the Persians reasserted control of the island of Cyprus, where Greek cities had joined the revolt, and then after 496 the Persians turned their attention to the west, and the Greeks there were soon on the defensive. One city after another fell, until in 494, the remnants of the few remaining cities in a supreme final effort gathered a great fleet of ships at Lade, an island just off Miletus. The battle was hard fought, but the Greeks lost, and the coast was not only open to Persian depredations but the Greek cities were now isolated from one another. The victorious Persians first besieged the ringleader Miletus, and the city fell, its people to be dispersed into captivity, the city and its holy sanctuary of Didyma to be plundered and burned, ending the campaigns of 494. Nothing was left but mopping up operations to complete in 493. Aristagoras, who had turned over command at Miletus and gone off on an adventure to Thrace, was killed while attacking a Thracian city, and Histiaeus was captured in 493 and put to death. The Persians had regained everything and had rid themselves of some ambitious Greeks into the bargain. Darius could now look to a thrust at Greece itself to punish Athens and Eretria for their help to the Ionians.

The revolt from Persia marks a watershed in the history of eastern cultural relations with the Greeks. Earlier, influences could move without much hindrance through Iran and Asia Minor; the Persian dominions of Egypt, Syria and the Levant could transmit a myriad of ideas; the Persians themselves could be a source of information and new concepts, and their advent on European soil had been viewed by many Greeks with no alarm at all. The revolt changed all this, beginning an era of hostility during which things Persian were regarded with suspicion and friendship with Persians was regarded as treason, "medism" as many called it. The war which the Persians brought on Greece in revenge was the final rupture, and there would thereafter always be an ideology of hostility towards Persia in at least some Greek quarters.

Herodotus saw the importance of the conflict, and wrote his *Histories* both to detail its course and to explain its genesis. His generation was the last to have known Greeks who had lived under Persian domination, and no Greek of his own time or after acknowledged authority emanating from Susa or Persepolis. Although from Herodotus' time on, Greeks might deal with the Great King and his satraps as allies or even friends in political terms, none would any longer see in Persian administration the agency controlling their political, economic, social and perhaps even cultural futures. The agency of Iran as a medium of transmission of ideas from the east effectively stopped.

The flow of ideas was now seriously constricted, if not completely ended. Although there were points of contact, they were not numerous. A few of them were colonies which had served for some time as centers of interchange between Greeks and non-Greeks, but they do not seem to have brought much direct influence. For most Greeks there was little need to know much of the non-Greek cultures and no need at all to learn other languages, Most Greek cities, even the distant colonies, carried on the bulk of their trade within the Greek-speaking communities of cities. While we do not know much about the patterns of long-distance trade, such as, for instance, the spice trade, crossing many language and cultural borders on its path through the Persian Empire from east to west, it seems clear that such trade entered the Greek world through a very limited number of entrepots, in a manner which did not require of the Greeks much ability to negotiate in foreign languages. Much the same could be said about the trade in other items, such as amber, which came from outside the Greek area. None of it forced Greek cities to become multicultural centers.

There were, however, special cases, exceptional cities which did not follow the usual pattern of colonies, and served much more as trading centers. The most famous of these is Naucratis. Established in Egypt in the seventh century during the reign of Psammetichus, Naucratis was exceptional because it was not the colony of a single city. One tradition credits twelve Ionian cities with its foundation, while another makes Miletus largely responsible, but there is no doubt that the first settlers were a melange of Greeks from a number of separate cities. In its early years Naucratis and its residents probably served almost exclusively the interests of the Egyptian rulers, but by the fifth century, it was well known to Greeks. By the end of the sixth, in the reign of Amasis, the great *Hellenion* had been founded by nine cities, to create a religious center in the city to serve those so far removed from other Greek bonds, and the city itself had been granted its particular status by Amasis. It was the only *emporion*, or market, in Egypt, and all international commerce was required by edict to pass through it.

When Herodotus visited Naucratis in the mid fifth century, the city was the beneficiary of a rich and varied commerce. The international aspect of the city remained, for the founding cities had the right to appoint the magistrates of the market. By this time, the great Egyptian revolt against the Persians, in which the Athenians had participated until their great defeat and disaster of 454, had come and gone. The city had seen and had probably supported Greek armies for the first time, but the Persian victory meant that it would remain under Persian control for a century longer. Despite Athenian support for the Egyptian revolt, Naucratis survived as a Greek center in Egypt, and was allowed to continue its connections with the Greek world.

Naucratis is one of the few places where interaction between Greeks and the surrounding culture can be shown to have taken place. Clearly, the Naucratites retained their Greekness, in such shrines as the *Hellenion*, or the single shrines founded by individual cities, like that of Hera by the Samians, or Zeus by the Aeginetans, and Apollo by the Milesians. Excavations in the late nineteenth century and early twentieth have revealed the remains of five Greek sanctuaries at Naucratis, as well as many pieces of broken pottery inscribed with dedications to Hellenic deities. On the other hand, Greeks in Egypt very early began to worship local deities as well. There is a dedication to the Egyptian goddess Isis, in the Ionic alphabet, as early as the late sixth century or early fifth. Excavation of Naucratis has revealed the essentially Egyptian character of most of the architecture. The familiarity with the Egyptian gods which Herodotus shows illustrates the extent to which information about Egyptian religion had penetrated the Greek community by mid-century, when he was in Egypt. The identification of Greek with Egyptian deities was well established. "Isis is in Greek, Demeter," Herodotus could write, or "the Egyptians call Zeus by the name Ammon." Whether this familarity with matters Egyptian extended beyond the area of Naucratis we cannot tell, but that city would at the very least have provided a base for such developments.

Naucratis, although doubtless the strongest community of Greeks in Egypt, was not the only one. In earlier times, Psammetichus had established two settlements for his Greek and Carian mercenaries, one on each side of the Nile, called the *Stratopeda*, "camps." From these camps, inhabited for "much time," according to Herodotus, King Amasis later moved the inhabitants to the city of Memphis, where they settled and formed a separate community. When the Greeks were first in the camps, Psammetichus sent Egyptian youths to learn the Greek language, and these formed the nucleus of the corps of interpreters Herodotus knew in his day. It is interesting, and significant, that we hear of Egyptian interpreters, but nothing of Greeks taking on such professional skills.

Of much greater importance to Greeks everywhere, although not a Greek settlement itself, was the great oracle of Ammon in the Oasis of Siwah in the Libyan Desert. Although the Siwans seem to have been ethnically different from the Egyptians, the oasis was under the control of the Egyptians long before it became known to the Greeks. That familiarity must have begun no later than the founding of Cyrene on the Libyan coast in the seventh century; certainly the oracle itself was known and respected in the Greek world by the sixth century, and in the fifth century many Greek leaders consulted it on matters of importance. For such consultations the priests must have learned Greek or had interpreters. The former was probably the case. There is a story that the fifth-century Spartan general Lysander tried to bribe the priests at Siwah to obtain an oracle favorable to him becoming king at Sparta, but the priests sent some of their number to Sparta to accuse him, an embassy which would seem to call for use of the Greek language. In the next century, certainly, the oracular priests used Greek, for Plutarch's story about Alexander's consultation of the oracle has the priest, to show friendliness, address the king in Greek, but with an error that seemed to address the conqueror as the son of Zeus—*pai dios* in Greek. Again, however, these are instances of foreigners learning Greek, rather than the other way around, but they do attest the ability of Greeks and the priests of Siwah to communicate with one another. There indeed, if they wished, Greeks could learn of the great god Ammon and other powerful deities of Egypt, and there too they could see the imposing monuments of Egyptian architecture.

Finally, out in the desert, there was an isolated community of Greeks, settlers from Samos. In the so-called "Great Oasis," or Karga Oasis, about 250 km. west of the Nile, deep in the Western Desert. According to Herodotus, again, there was a city there called Oasis City, seven days journey from Thebes on the Nile, occupied by Samians of the Aischronian tribe. When they went there, or why, we have no idea, and in fact all we know about them is their bare existence, but they do form another exceptional group of Greeks who, in the fifth century, had been established far outside the normal perimeter of Greek activity. That Herodotus knew of them indicates some communication with the rest of the Greek world, however tenuous, and perhaps only through Egypt. How Greek they remained, and how much they might have passed on of their environment to other Greeks will surely never be known.

Also remote from the Greek world was the city of the Branchidae, settled by Milesians early in the fifth century. When the Persian king Xerxes was returning from Greece after his defeat at Salamis in 480, the Branchidae, priests of Didyma, the re-established Milesian sanctuary of Apollo, betrayed the temple to ingratiate themselves with the king. Then, in apprehension of retaliation by their fellow-citizens of Miletus, they asked asylum of Xerxes, who resettled them far to the east near the Oxus River in remote Sogdiana. There they remained, until Alexander the Great came upon and destroyed their descendants in revenge, 150 years later. By that time, according to Curtius, who described the later events in some detail, they had shown the effects of their barbarian surroundings: "They had not yet broken away from their ancestral customs, but were bilingual, having gradually departed from their own language under the influence of foreign speech." It is the only instance of Greeks in any number known to have been bilingual. The text is very clear in this regard, calling them *bilingues*, and it is significant that the ability to speak a foreign tongue is seen as a departure from one's own speech.

How early in the fifth century this bilingualism was established remains unknown, but it is likely to have been early in view of the exigencies of the situation. The maintenance of Greek language and institutions, combined with the ability to communicate with locals, gave this far eastern settlement an exceptional potential for the transfer of oriental influences to the west. However, such a transfer would at best have been sporadic, and insofar as it could have affected the west at all would have depended on trade and the occasional traveler.

Another group of Milesians had been sent east, by Darius, at the time of the sack of Miletus which ended the Ionian revolt. According to Herodotus, those of the Milesians who were captured were sent off to Susa, and thence, settled unharmed at Ampe Polis at the mouth of the Tigris on the Arabian Gulf. The city, the name of which in the text of Herodotus is taken as an error for the correct Aginis, was a place of size and importance before Darius sent the Milesians there, and the site was mentioned by later Greek and Roman writers. The city had a harbor and good commercial location, and the Greeks who found themselves there thus had, as Herodotus says, "no other harm done to them." We know, however, nothing of what became of them, or whether they survived for any period as a Hellenic community. They represent, for however long or short a time, another enclave of Greeks who in the fifth century would have had close contact with a non-Hellenic environment. An even more obscure group of Greeks, probably not a true community, are the Greek laborers at Persepolis of whom we learn from an inscription. Whatever became of them, they must have had some authoritative insights into the Persian world.

A much more influential group of Greeks were those located at Al-

Mina, or Posideion, as it was known in Greek, on the northern coast of Syria. That trading port at the mouth of the Orontes River had long served as the terminus of an overland trade route from the east, and an enclave of Greeks had been established there as early as the ninth century. Toward the end of the sixth century, in about 520, the Greek activity revived after a gap of a few decades or after after the physical renovation of the site and its structures. In earlier periods, East Greek or Cypriote or Rhodian pottery had been dominant at one time or another, with occasionally some admixture of other Greek wares. Now only Athenian pottery is found. Perhaps even more significant, while the large numbers of coins of small denomination are of the sort one might expect to turn up in an east Mediterranean port under Persian domination, all the coins of larger denomination were silver tetradrachms coined at Athens or struck locally on the Athenian standard and in imitation of Athenian types. The Athenian affinities carry on right through the period of the bitter fighting of the Persian attack on Athens and the invasion of Greece, and continue on into the later fifth century as the Athenians were establishing their control over former Persian territories in Asia Minor and were carrying the war farther east to adventures in Cyprus and Egypt. Even if the Athenian wares and coinage do not prove the presence of Athenians themselves, but only show the victory of Athenian pottery and coin in distant markets, there is no question that the Greek traders flourished without interruption at Al-Mina despite the prolonged hostilities between the Athenians and the Persian overlords of the site.

Despite the long and active history of Greeks at this port, of which fifth-century Greeks were well aware, there seems to have been little of the local Semitic culture that crossed into the Greek ambit, either in the business port or in the—presumably—residential town on a nearby hill. Certainly no pottery or similar artifacts demonstrate any influence of this sort. Yet there is no doubt that there was a great deal of communication between Greek and non-Greek, not only in the immediate vicinity of the city, but also over the expanse of the eastern lands abutting the Mediterranean. There were Persian coins, of minor denominations, from Cyprus and nearby Sidon; there was glassware from southern Syria. And one must surely assume that filling the blocks of warehouses in the town called for continual contact with the caravans coming down to the sea with goods from distant eastern regions.

It is not so easy, however, to know what commerce the warehouses did serve, or with what easterners the Greeks of Posideion would thus have come into contact. We do know from reasonably well-preserved structures of the early fourth century that the merchants had in store metalwork from the Caucasus, glass amulets from Syria or Egypt, quicksilver which probably originated in Spain, and a variety of Greek, Syrian and Mesopotamian weights to deal with the geographic range of the commerce. The direction of trade cannot, of course, be established with certainty, but some Greek comments of the period cast light on the matter. Athens, at least, was portrayed as an importer. A famous fragment of a now-lost fifth-century Athenian comedy gives some sense of the situation: "Silphium comes from Cyrene, along with ox-hides. Mackerel and salt fish comes from the Hellespont. There is spelt and ribs of beef from Italy; slag for the Lacedaemonians from Sitalces the king of Thrace; there are whole shipments of lies from Perdiccas of Macedon. Syracuse sends figs and cheese; Egypt sails and papyrus; Syria ships incense. Crete sends cypresses for the gods, and Rhodes raisins and sweet-dream-bringing dried figs. Pears and fat sheep come from Euboea, and from Phrygia come slaves. Arcadia sends mercenaries, Pagasae slaves and branded thieves. From the Paphlagonians come chestnuts and almonds, from Phoenicia dates and fine flour, while Carthage ships carpets and colored pillows." Even with allowances for the desire of the comic poet to intrude jokes and satire into the list, it is clear that the trading activity alluded to is exclusively that of importing to Athens, and that there are very few manufactured goods involved in the trade: sails and papyrus from Egypt, carpets and pillows from Carthage. All the rest are people, raw materials and agricultural products. The mention of dates and flour from Phoenicia gives us a hint of what must have been in at least some of the warehouses at Posideion.

For trade such as this, even in some volume, one need not assume very much contact in depth. The use of the weights and measures found at the site does not call for much sophisticated conversation, and the laying out of the required amounts of silver on the table is an adequate explanation of the price offered for anything. The quantities of Athenian coin at the site show that the Greeks there served a primarily Greek market, for had they been selling to locals or caravan traders in any quantity, they would have taken in larger denominations of Persian coin in such transactions. They were, mostly, buying for resale to Greece, and in that role had no need to develop marketing skills in eastern languages, or seek out markets or purchasers for their goods among the peoples of Syria. In the fifth century, at least, the contact between Greeks and their neighbors in the locale of Posideion does not seem to have been of the quality to generate much cultural influence, either on the Greeks actually resident in that area or through them, on the Greeks of the homeland.

Active trading centers like Posideion and Naucratis differed from most Greek colonies in that they were planted, not among unsettled and semi-nomadic peoples, but in the territories of well established cultures with histories and traditions of their own. They had the opportunity to develop close ties with their neighbors, and although they do not show any influences on their own Hellenism from their surroundings, they had the potential of providing a continuing source of information about and possibility of influence from eastern civilizations. So too did the more remote Greek settlements, like those planted by Darius and Xerxes or the apparently voluntary emigration of the Samians to the Karga Oasis. Our information about these groups is so meagre, however, that we cannot draw any conclusions about their activity, apart from acknowledging the evidence of a rare example of bilingualism among the Branchidae. Finally, there are some unusual examples of colonization in which the Greek colonists incorporated some natives into the settlement. Such was the procedure followed in the founding of Crouni and Bizone on the west coast of the Black Sea. Most such were small, inconsequential and therefore little noticed in antiquity, and it would take an earthquake like that which at some time destroyed Bizone to prompt writers to refer to them very much. We have no knowledge at all of the effects or implications of such cofoundations in which Greeks and natives were involved; they represent opportunities for a cultural interchange which may have occurred, but also may well never have taken place.

All in all, the fifth century offers us practically no evidence of cultural influence from non-Greek peoples—"barbarians," as the Greeks called them—affecting even the centers in or close to those alien peoples. The influences of the ninth, eighth, seventh and even sixth centuries, which can be traced in the pottery of eastern Greek cities and in some literary or religious takeovers, and most notably, in the Greek adaptation of the Semitic alphabet, are not carried forward in the fifth. Neither in sculpture nor in painting, where those influences showed so clearly in the "orientalizing" period, is there any trace of an oriental impact on the ateliers of the Greek centers of the east. The evidence seems to show that these Greeks kept their Hellenism pure, free from any infusions from the strong cultures around them.

There is no doubt that the major reason for this was the strength of the sense of what it meant to be Greek. Although the strong local loyalties which stress service to one's city meant that Greek cities were often in conflict, bitter conflict, there remained some forces of cohesion which gave Greeks a sense of community and superiority to the rest of the world. Community of language was one factor of course, but more than that, the unifying factors of the great pan-Hellenic religious festivals and centers at Olympia and Delos and elsewhere always led Greeks to an awareness of a cultural and religious unity. Only Hellenes could compete at Olympia and elsewhere, and the unity represented by the various sets of games was emphasized by the cessation of combat among Greek cities when the games were on. Besides these obvious features of life, the community of thought represented by the tradition of myth and epic intensified the feeling that to be Greek was to be something different and special. The Homeric epics were the basis of education for Greeks from the the sixth century on, if not before, and throughout the history of Hellenism it was Homer if nothing else that appeared in a Greek library, so that all Greeks shared a single awareness of the remote past, and the mentality of all Greeks was affected by the interpretation of human and cosmic forces inherent in the story of Achilles. To the Greeks, everything else was alien, just as to the British of earlier centuries, "the wogs began at Calais." There was, to Greeks, some inferiority implied by the word barbarian; it was not just that those people spoke languages that sounded like "bar-bar-bar." To be Greek was to be part of the superior culture. The notion is clear in Aristotle's reluctance to allow that Greeks who happened to be slaves as the result of capture in war could in any way be considered "naturally" slavish, and there is a tradition that the philosopher provided Alexander with an ideology that encouraged his march against the eastern inferiors.

With all of this feeling of superiority, however, there was still contact with barbarians, a great deal of contact, even if it did not produce significant effects on Greek mentality. A great deal of information about other cultures reached educated Greeks of the fifth century, even if the routes do not seem to have been the expected avenue provided by Greeks overseas. Knowledge of the world came, in the fifth century it seems, from people who deliberately set out to acquire it. Of the results of this, we are fortunate in having the complete work of the man who was one of the most intelligent, the most investigative, and one of the best traveled of all Greeks of his time. Herodotus of Halicarnassus was born in a city in the southwest part of Asia Minor in the early decades of the fifth century and lived until about 430 or 425. He wrote to explain the significance, in many senses, of the great victories of the Greeks over the Persians, and to record for posterity the great things done then and before. To achieve his objective he fashioned a complex narrative to enlighten the reader not only about the specific military events of the wars, but would demonstrate the importance of those events against the perspective of earlier times. To make his meaning clear he provided an account of the early great empires which fell, one by one, into the clutches of the Persians. To learn and understand, he traveled to see and traveled to enquire. He looked at dedications and inscriptions at Delphi, at ziggurats in Babylon and pyramids in Egypt, at the landscape, and the animals and the people who populated it. He spoke to Chaldaeans in Babylon and priests in Egypt, and specifically mentions the use of a translator who interpreted an inscription on the great pyramid of Cheops. The Greeks, Persians, Egyptians and Lydians who served as sources were legion, and Herodotus sought them out everywhere in his travels, in Athens and other cities of Greece, as in Asia Minor and to the east, in lands still satrapies of the Persian Empire.

His travels were very extensive. He made several individual trips during his lifetime, visiting many of the major cities and nations described in his text, and from those descriptions we can tell something about the voyages themselves. He went to Egypt, perhaps returning to Greece along the coastal route to visit Tyre and other cities of the Levant. In Egypt itself, he saw much of the Delta, including Naucratis, of course, and traveled south to see Memphis, the Fayum, and the pyramids, and then up the Nile to Thebes and on as far as Elephantine. He also traveled to Babylon, either at another time or as part of the trip to Egypt. He was also familiar with Asia Minor and its peoples, not only those on the coast but those inland as well. At another time he coasted from west to east along the south shore of the Black Sea, reaching as far as Colchis just south of the Caucasus Mountains. He made a similar trip along the coast of Thrace. At Athens, according to a tradition which need not be doubted, he presented recitations of his work, and he was well enough known to the playwright Sophocles to elicit the epigram the poet created for him. His knowledge of Greece and Greek history came not only from people there but also from the citizens of other Hellenic cities which he visited, and his knowledge of North Africa came from a voyage to Cyrene and the Libyan coast. His experience of Sicily and South Italy was probably due to his migration to the Athenian colony of Thurii.

Herodotus' description of Persian and the Persian domains, as well as Greek and eastern history, shows what a fifth-century Greek could learn. He gave details about customs and from that drew general conclusions about foreign peoples and their religions. He enquired about Egypt from the Egyptians themselves, and noted that his information about the early history of Egypt comes only from the Egyptians and their priests. He had more confidence in his information about events from the reign of Psammeticus and after, because from that time on there were Greeks in Egypt who knew what was happening, from whom he could "learn precisely everything from the time of King Psammeticus on." He clearly felt a difference in the quality of sources when he could converse in Greek, and in Babylon his choice of the Chaldaeans as sole sources may not just have been because he mistakenly thought they were priests, but also because they could talk to him in Greek. He had detailed familiarity with Persian affairs, and some of his information must have come from written materials, even if these would have to have been in Greek, the only language he knew.

Much of what he saw and reported was mere description; of animals, temples, monuments; and although Herodotus' eyes might occasionally have been deceived, many of his observations were scrupulously gathered and provided the Greek world with an accurate and permanent account of many of the most significant works of the non-Greek world. Although the central theme of the triumph of Greeks over Persians would have been enough to make the work interesting to Greeks, the collection of geographical and historical curiosities shows what interested him and what he thought would interest his readers. A whole book is given over to Egypt, which played no important part in the story, but had always fascinated Greeks for its antiquity and its oddities, and he goes into lengthy digressions on other remote places. Although he was aware that customs and even morality are relative to culture, his text would have presented no problems of orientation to Greeks who thought that the non-Greek world was full of oddities and peculiar people, customs and ideas.

Some of Herodotus' information must have come from Greek predecessors, and their existence shows he wrote in a tradition which already had developed some information abut the east. Although he does not mention any Greek sources by name, we know some who existed, although their chronology is uncertain and the understanding of their work depends in part on interpretation of Herodotus' own work. There were Xanthus of Lydia, Charon of Lampsacus, Dionysius of Miletus, Hellanicus of Lesbos, and Hecataeus of Miletus, all of whom dealt with eastern history or geography and might have been consulted by Herodotus. The kind of information which Herodotus might find would vary from author to author, but we know at least what could be obtained from the text of Herodotus itself. There is geographical data about the locations of cities and temples, and valuable information about the distances and travel times between places. There is a great deal of what we would call "anthropology," detailing Persian customs and practices, often in precise detail, if not as extensive as he could offer from his own observations in Babylon and Egypt. There is an interesting summary of Persian religion interspersed with a description of Persian customs, a summary as interesting for its misconceptions as for its accurate information. Overall, the account fits reasonably well with what we know of religion in western Iran in the mid fifth century, although in certain respects, such as the use of the name Mitra (Mithra, a male deity) for the female divinity Anahita, he is clearly in error. He certainly does not give any of the main themes of Persian religion, perhaps from lack of interest or sympathy, but he must have been told and misunderstood some of them, as we can see from his stress on the Persian veneration of truth and abhorrence of lies. This is a surface manifestation of the sixth-century Iranian prophet Zoroaster's doctrine of Truth as part of the essence of the Supreme Deity, with the world the arena of conflict between that Truth and its opposite, the Lie. Although Herodotus claims that he knows what he reports "certainly," that certainty must refer to his own state of mind and not to the facts themselves. Whatever the intermediary or intermediaries who explained Persian religion to him, they led him into some error, and failed to enlighten him on more than the observable aspects of religious behavior. The sources were probably Greeks familiar with Persians, rather than Persians themselves, for Persians would not have made the mistake about Mitra. In any case, Herodotus shows us quite clearly the quality of information about Persian religion available to Greeks. It was not very high, not very subtle, not always accurate.

The nature of his Persian history is somewhat different. It is comprehensive, in that it traces the growth of Iranian power from its beginning with a Median dynasty, through the takeover of power by Cyrus, the expansion of empire by Cyrus, Cyrus' successors and their vicissitudes, and finally the revolt and reorganization of the administration by Darius. Much of this history is condensed, but Herodotus is aware of the main themes, such as, for instance, the fact that Cyrus' success shifted control of the empire from the Medians to the Persians. It is, however, not clear in all respects. There remain important questions about the genealogies of both great Persian kings, Cyrus and Darius, when Herodotus' text is compared to other ancient evidence. The details of the campaigns of Cyrus and Darius are also open to some question. More important, the account shows the effects of the kinds of oral sources Herodotus was forced to depend upon, and many modern scholars see the influence of different traditions—Greek, Egyptian, Median, Persian—on these. For example, the story of Cyrus, who is said to have been the grandson of the last Median king, Astyages, whom he actually overthrew, is seen by some as influenced by Median accounts, and may actually reflect propaganda by which Cyrus claimed a sort of legitimacy. Then again, the hostility shown Cyrus' successor, Cambyses, can be attributed to the impact on Herodotus of sources among the Egyptians, who are thought to have been hostile to Cambyses because of his alleged disrespectful treatment of Egyptian religion.

These biases may exist among the sources, and Herodotus' Persian history doubtless owes a great deal to many different traditions and many different groups through whom the information passed. But it is important to recognize that none of it requires direct contact on Herodotus' part with any but Greek sources. All the information in the narrative makes sense in Greek terms, and much of it shows the effects of Greek styles of historical thought and approach. The semilegendary stories of the earliest kings of Media bear resemblances to the qualities and actions of kings in the early days of Greek cities as recounted by Greek sources. Similarly, the story of the youth and victory of Cyrus could easily have been told of a Greek. Cyrus' grandfather, Astyages, had dreams which according to soothsayers meant that Astyages' daughter, Mandane, would bear a son who would supplant him. He tried to avoid this by his choice of husband for her, and she then produced Cyrus. Cyrus' boyhood was promising, and his leadership was recognized in such a way that Astyages thought that his being named "king of the boys" meant that the dream had been fulfilled in a safer way than expected. Astyages, no longer fearing for his throne, brought the boy down to the palace. In the outcome, Cyrus overthrew Astyages; the original interpretation had been correct. All this is evocative of themes in Greek legend like the Oedipus story, and would not have seemed the least foreign to Greeks.

Traditional accounts like these could easily have come to the Ionian Greeks from a variety of sources in the east, through Lydian, Median, Persian or Babylonian narrators. So too could have come the large amount of accurate detail recorded by Herodotus, often mixed with almost fanciful tales. We should compare, in his account of the successful revolt which brought Darius to power, the story that among a group of co-conspirators, Darius became king because his horse was first to whinny, with the fact that Herodotus names the six who co-operated with Darius, and five of these are confirmed by Darius' own list in an inscription found far to the east at Behistun. But again, this information, no less than the stories of a more imaginative nature, could have been communicated to and preserved by Greeks on the fringes of the Persian empire, available to the interested or the curious from Persians who would know these names because of the continuing importance of their families. All in all, there is every likelihood that all of Herodotus' Persian history came to him from Greeks, that none of it represented contact with Persians on his part, and that the Iranian history, ethnology and religion in the pages of Herodotus are indicative of the level of knowledge Greeks had of the great empire immediately to the east. For all the regular contact many Greeks must have had with Persians during the near-century of Persian rule of Ionia, Hellenic knowledge of Persia remained at a very superficial level.

Virtually the same phenomenon can be observed in Herodotus' description of the Scythians. Although it does not always coincide with what we know from other sources, his overall conception of the geography of the area seems sound, his knowledge of the customs and religion of the people conforms with what we have learned from archaeology, and his careful distinction of the true Scythians from the other nomadic peoples of South Russia is unusual for a Greek. What he tells us, however, about the burial customs of the Scythians, for example, would have been known to the Greek residents of the area, and the names of the Scythian gods, which Herodotus gives in most cases in the native language and in Greek, would have been known to local Greeks.

Herodotus' narrative can exemplify the very best that a fifth-century Greek could accomplish in developing knowledge of other cultures, and his work was the best overall account of the east available in his own time, and probably ever, in the Greek world. In many ways he framed what Greeks were to think of their eastern neighbors, providing both light and limitation for Greek understanding of eastern ideas. His life and his work provide the clearest indication of the ways in which Greeks would come into contact with other cultures and learn of their habits: some travel, some reading, and some conversation. There were others who would do this, although not in so comprehensive a manner nor with so great an impact. We learn of writers who dealt with eastern regions, but have no evidence of early extensive writing about the great empire of Carthage, not to speak of the less citified peoples of Italy or southern France. Whatever contact there was between Hellene and non-Greek in the western regions, with all the prosperity and cultural interests of the Greek cities of Sicily and South Italy in the fifth century, the written word played little part in that communication, either for the Greeks in the western cities or those in the home peninsula.

There was another way Greeks could meet non-Greeks and learn something of their ways. Some foreigners traveled to Greece itself, or settled in Greek cities. Perhaps the most famous of those who did that in the fifth century was the Persian noble Megabyzus' son Zopyrus, who fled to Athens in the latter part of the century after his involvement in a rebellion against Artaxerxes I. Herodotus himself mentions the presence of this Zopyrus at Athens. Many today believe that it was from the Persian that Herodotus learned what he set down about Darius' capture of Babylon, for Zopyrus' grandfather of the same name tricked the Babylonians into entrusting him with their forces by mutilating himself horribly and presenting himself to the Babylonians as so harmed by Darius, so that he could then betray the city to his king. If we can imagine Herodotus learning Persian history from this man, Athenians too could discover the same and much more from him during his sojourn in the city.

There were many such in Athens, and they had come both willingly and unwillingly. By midcentury, the population of metics—resident aliens—had swelled to enormous numbers. The commercial activity of the port of Piraeus, serving as it did not only the needs of Athens but many other Greek cities for whom it acted as a trading centre and focus of exchange for the importing of goods from all over the world, was a magnet for sailors and merchants from all places. Some would stay only while their ships were in port, while others would put up at inns and similar establishments for an entire trading season, and beyond these, a great many came to settle and make Athens their permanent home. All these people brought their religions and rites, their costumes and their food preferences, and almost any language could be heard on the streets.

The Athenians encouraged this settlement, and gave these metics most of the privileges of full citizens, so that in general they held the same economic position as the rest of the Athenians. They also met the same responsibilities imposed on citizens, serving in the army or with the fleet, paying the same contributions and taxes as were expected of citizens. In this the Athenians were very unusual among the Greeks, extending a kind of membership in their society to those who had no birthright to it. By the latter part of the fifth century the numbers of these foreigners, it has been estimated, reached a total of 45,000. The majority of them were Greeks, of course, but there were barbarians among them, and in an overall number so large, their numbers would be great. There were Lydians, Phrygians, Egyptians, Persians, Babylonians, Phoenicians—natives of virtually every part of the world with which Greeks had contact—and they lived out their lives in Athens and died there, as their gravestones show. They not only engaged in commerce but worked alongside Athenians as tradesmen and craftsmen, as we can see from the building records of temples on the acropolis. Their loyalty to Athens and their sense of participation in her life shows in the proud epitaph of a Phrygian who died defending Attica against Spartan invasion in the first year of the Peloponnesian War: "The one who was the best of the Phrygians in the broad lands of Athens, Mannes, son of Orymaios, this fine monument is his. I never knew a better woodsman than myself, by Zeus. He died in the war."

In addition to all these foreigners who had freely emigrated to Athens, there were the slaves, tens of thousands of them. The number and role of the slaves in Athenian society is vexed and much discussed, but there is enough agreement on some of the main lines of the subject that the social impact of those from non-Greek lands can be suggested with reasonable assurance. Unlike the predominantly Hellenic metics, most of the slaves were barbarians. They had been captured in wars and raids along the perimeter of the Greek world, so that the slave markets of the Piraeus and elsewhere teemed with Syrians, Lydians, Phrygians, Carians, Scythians and others. They were all jumbled up not only in the markets but in the households in which they finally found themselves. We have inscriptional evidence for this, like the lists of property confiscated for sacrilege and destruction of the sacred statues which were the expression of the god Hermes' protection of the roads. For example, the property of one of those convicted, Cephisodorus the metic, included 16 slaves, and of these, there were five Thracians, three Carians, two Syrians, two Illyrians, one Scythian, one Lydian, one from Colchis at the east end of the Black Sea, and one from a city probably to be identified as Cappadocian. In other similar confiscations there were also slaves from Macedonia and Messenia as well as three born in the owners' houses.

The slaves worked at the same tasks as other Athenians, citizens and metics alike. We find wage payments to slave owners along with the others in the same gangs of craftsmen and master-masons who built the temple to Erechtheus on the Acropolis in 409, and the work—stonework, column fluting, carving—as well as the pay, is the same for each, citizen, metic, slave. The slaves also worked in large numbers in manufacturing, as in the production of shields in a factory owned by Lysias at the end of the fifth century. He had 120 slaves, he tells us in his oration *Against Eratosthenes*, the majority of whom must have been workmen. Elsewhere slaves worked along with free men as potters and as pottery painters, in the large and small workshops of many trades characterizing the cottage industry of antiquity. We need only pause for a moment to be able to imagine the workshops and the streets of fifth-century Athens, filled with a jumble of languages and accents, slaves and metics shrugging and gesticulating to communicate with one another and the native Athenians, barbarian amulets swinging from necks, wrists and ankles, images of foreign gods tucked into corners or on shelves all over the place, scenes of ritual and worship depicting the rites of Scythia, Egypt, Babylonia, Lydia and much more, all this a daily occurrence and easily observed by the Athenians and anyone else who cared to look. And, although Athens offered the most of all this, such scenes were re-enacted continuously in all the major centers all over Greece.

If we add the impressions brought by slaves and metics, the information recorded and available in the writings of Herodotus and other reporters of history and geography, the reminiscences and tales of merchants and travelers, and finally the acquaintance with surrounding cultures gained by those in the settlements abroad, the total offers some idea of the nature of cross-cultural communication open in the fifth century. Although the Persian Wars stopped the role of Iran as an important, if not vital, element in the transmittal of oriental influences, as the century wore on, Iran's place was filled by a wide range of actors playing increasingly more vigorous and influential parts. Communication was there, and it passed more than it had through Greek intermediaries or took place in Greek environments, so that influences were more subtle and much more difficult to identify. Whatever concepts were coming from the east in this period were refashioned in Greek modes as they passed through the overseas settlements, through the mind of Herodotus, or were expressed by resident foreigners and slaves who were now functioning in Hellenic environments. For gods and goddesses whose power and ritual were accepted, Greek names were found, the so-called *interpretatio Graeca* by which a deity with a foreign name is interpreted as the same deity as that known by a Greek name.

Concepts too became Hellenized, or were expressed in terms the Greeks could understand. The elevated ethical import of Persian monotheism or dualism could only be understood in the pragmatic terms of "the Persians abominate liars," for the notions of a supreme deity imbued with an essence of truth and good was still so far from Greek modes of thought that simple translation of Persian language would be almost meaningless. Such concepts could and would be rendered, however, in terms of practical human behavior in day-to-day affairs. In a similar way, Egyptian religion is understood more in Hellenic terms, with the animal representation of deities largely passed over in favor of cult focused on anthropomorphic forms; so too the deep stratum of magic which, in Egypt unlike Greece, is characteristic of official religion, is passed by in favor of reports of mysteries, parallel to and even, allegedly, the derivation of the Eleusinian mysteries of Demeter. In the same way, the careful and accurate description of embalming procedures ignores the theology behind the activity and fails to mention even the all-important Book of the Dead, because there was nothing in Hellenism through which the significance of these concepts could be grasped.

There were, then, many contact points between Greek and barbarian during the fifth century, but they acted as much as barriers and filters for barbarian influence as they served as media of communication. The attitude of Greeks in far lands was different from what it had been one, two or three centuries before, when they struck out into the world as isolated bands from single cities, and then were often overwhelmed with wonder at the new things encountered. Once they had been receptive to the ideas, visual and intellectual, so far as they could understand them, of other peoples. In the fifth century, after the great victories over the Carthaginians and the Persians, there was some sense of a unifying Hellenism, and a strong sense of its superiority. Greeks were aware of their common bonds as well as their divisions, and they could meet the influences of other cultures ready to reject as inferior anything different from their own institutions and beliefs. Many Greeks could be very aware of barbarians and their institutions, but with all that familiarity could have very little interest in or knowledge of anything but the most superficial aspects of the culture, belief or religion of people with whom they had daily contact.

In this, they may have laid down a pattern for western culture. Europeans have traditionally regarded their culture as superior to those with which they came in contact. "The wogs begin at Calais" is an English exclusion of everything foreign to the island, but the rest of Europe is no different in regarding its own society as the best that humans have devised, and all together, they have made "western civilization" the standard against which others are judged. Greeks of antiquity would probably have been as derogating of the great civilizations of China and India as were the European colonists of the last few centuries, and the literate Chinese would have been called barbarians along with Persians and Egyptians. No doubt, the great self-satisfaction which Greeks took in their culture and institutions helped preserve them against the strong influences of older civilizations. It may also be that the conviction which Greeks had of the merit of their culture persuaded even the Romans, who had certainly proved themselves more adept at war and politics than the Greek cities had been. Apart from a few sour conservatives, Romans were inclined to accept the Greeks' self-valuation, to the point that Virgil's national epic of Rome allowed that the Romans would not be known for their contribution in the plastic arts, science or letters.

However all this may be, a fundamental characteristic of Greeks was their existence in cysts of culture, as it were. In a way, that is a cultural parallel of the political systems which Greeks generally adopted. As each city was its own closed society, limited in membership to those who could claim citizenship by family connection, and limited in size, for the most part, by the physical city and its surrounding terrain, so any group of Greeks, in the far-flung colonization, closed in on itself and maintained its Hellenism. They might learn something of the surrounding peoples, but never studied them very deeply, and their interest in them was usually antiquarianism and curiosity. And whatever they did learn about other civilizations was never absorbed into their own, so that Hellenism remained much the same for centuries.

4 Greek Imperialism

Although many of the other cultures with which sixth-century Greeks dealt were territorial powers or empires, Greeks initially had no ambitions to rival them or try to reproduce that form of political organization. The small Greek political units were still more concerned with adjusting the conflicting demands of citizens internally, or dealing with the seemingly perpetual antagonism of other Greek cities. As anyone might expect, during the three or four centuries that these small communities were developing, they would hardly have had the resources to support an attempt to extend their power beyond their immediate neighborhood. Apart from Sparta's permanent territorial conquests, we hear of only obscure and limited wars before the end of the sixth century. There is, no doubt, significance in the fact that Thucydides, cataloguing wars before the Peloponnesian which might have rivalled that in scope or importance, skips from Mycenaean times and the Trojan War right to the Persian Wars at the beginning of the fifth century.

What the situation might have been in Mycenaean times is mostly a matter of guesswork. While the physical remains of palaces and the bureaucratic information in the linear B tablets suggest rulers of some significant resources, nothing gives us much idea of the territorial reach of any of them. At Pylos, in the southwest corner of the Peloponnesus, there are some uncertain geographical references suggesting connections with a broader area around the palace, and the appearance of the tablets on Crete after 1500 suggests the arrival of mainlanders there. This presents at least the possibility of dominion by some mainland center, and in Greece itself, one ruler may have dominated others. On the other hand, those on Crete may have been an independent group, not politically related to anything on the mainland, and the different centers on the mainland may well have also been completely independent of one another, even if they had some limited territorial scope. There is really no way to tell.

After the fall of the Mycenaean centers, a century or more passed before we have any indication of political or territorial aggrandizement. Athenian traditions of the heroic age give some notion of what Athenians thought about the establishment of the political unit taking in all of Attica. There was a King Codrus who saved Attica from Dorian invaders by sacrificing himself because an oracle had foretold the success of the Dorians if Codrus' life were spared. More significant, the national hero Theseus, who performed feats like the slaying of the Minotaur on Crete, after he became king was able to perform a unification of all the communities of Attica under the headship of Athens, which thus became the political center of a fairly wide region. This unification is historical fact, although the date of its occurrence is a matter of speculation. By the time we have written documents from Attica, this unification had already taken place and all the affected Athenian institutions were in place. The union, however, was not one of territorial domination, but the acceptance on an equal basis of the population of a territory wider than that of most Greek cities.

Spartan development was different, and perhaps unique. It shows the characteristic Late Bronze Age culture of the Peloponnesus, with characteristic "Mycenaean" material represented at Sparta itself and in nearby places, while a short distance south at Vaphio a beehive tomb produced magnificently worked gold cups, among the most famous objects of the period. The Spartan area, Laconia, unlike Attica, was Dorian in historical times, but Sparta had an experience similar to Athens in its absorption of villages. The Spartan expansion was different in most respects, as it depended for the most part on force. The union of a few closely neighboring villages made up Sparta and the Spartan citizenship, and that relatively small entity controlled the rest of the Spartan dominions. The union of villages made possible the subduing of all the rest of the Laconians, who paid taxes and army service even though free. From that base of power the Spartans were able to conquer Messenia to the west, although the effort was a long drawn-out series of campaigns probably lasting from the end of the eighth century well into the seventh. By the sixth century Sparta was consolidating her position as a land power, with wide territories in the southern Peloponnesus, and was the leader of a confederacy with the other independent cities in the north of the Peloponnesus.

By the beginning of the fifth century Athens and Sparta were the two most powerful Greek cities, by virtue of a greater land or population base. Most other cities were single political units, although a few, like Corinth, had an external commerce that produced revenue and supported a strong army and navy. Groups of cities also formed leagues, like an early Achaean league in the north of the Peloponnesus or the tribal organization of Aetolians in west central Greece. Finally, some cities had intermittent success in dominating their neighbors, as had Thebes in her continual effort to control Boeotia. But these were strictly local affairs, and had little impact on the rest of Greece, except insofar as alliances brought them into contact with other cities. Even the Spartan and Athenian territorial states were limited to contiguous territories, so that until the fifth century, there was nothing that could be called imperial in the sense of the political expansion that some non-Greek powers had achieved. Only Sparta's conquests, and her emerging dominance of the Peloponnesus at the end of the sixth century, had any resemblance to imperialism.

All this changed as result of the Persian Wars. When Darius began his attacks on Greece, he set in motion a series of events that made the fifth century one of imperial conflict. Having suppressed the Ionian revolt, Darius decided to expand his dominions into Greece itself. In the spring of 492 he sent his young son-in-law (and nephew) Mardonius to the Aegean with a large army and fleet. Mardonius first disposed of the remaining tyrants in the cities of Ionia, proceeded across the Hellespont and on through Thrace, where, caught by a storm while rounding the promontory of Mount Athos, his fleet was badly mauled by weather and by the natives when survivors struggled ashore. Mardonius was forced to return with the remains of his force, having himself suffered a wound from the Thracians. Two years later, another fleet was ready, this time under the command of two generals, Datis and Artaphernes, and aimed more specifically at the punishment of the two cities who had abetted the Ionians in their revolt, Athens and Eretria. The fleet sailed out from Samos, took Naxos, which this time offered the Persians no resistance, moved through the Cyclades taking the surrenders of the major island cities, and landed on Euboea just south of Eretria. The Eretrians shut themselves within their walls, but only held out for six days; on the seventh, two of the leading citizens betrayed the city, and the Persians entered, pillaged and burned everything, and took the people captive. Then they turned toward Athens.

There is not much indication of how the Greeks viewed all this. That the Ionians had been restive under Persian rule is obvious from the fact of the revolt, but the lack of sustained support for them on the part of Athens and Eretria, let alone the other Greek cities, suggests that there was no feeling of common danger or mutual interest in resistance to Darius. "The freedom of the Ionians," or intervention in Persian affairs, as Darius certainly saw the actions of Athens and Eretria, was not yet a popular cause. According to Herodotus and other Greek writers, Darius had by this time sent emissaries around Greece "demanding earth and water," an expression we are led to believe was symbolic of surrender, and had met with success in many places. The Athenians and Spartans had refused, but enough cities on the mainland had yielded to create problems of unified resistance. Acquiescence or resistance to Persia was undoubtedly woven into the pattern of Greek inter-city politics, as in the case of the "medism" of Aegina. There had long been hostility between this powerful naval state and Athens, and in fact the two were at war at the very time that Darius' representatives were making their rounds. The island was near Attica and had a good harbor, and its accession to the Persian side posed a threat. In fact, as Herodotus tells the story, domestic politics at Aegina turned on this issue, while internal affairs at Sparta were in a turmoil over the question of how to deal with pro-Persian elements at Aegina. The two

Spartan kings, Demaratus and Cleomenes, disagreed, and Cleomenes went so far in his efforts to restrain medism at Aegina as to suborn the Delphic Oracle in order to remove Demaratus from the kingship on the grounds of illegitimacy. He succeeded, Demaratus was replaced by Leotychidas, who cooperated with Cleomenes in his Aeginetan policy. The two went to the island, seized ten of the medizing leaders and deposited them at Athens in order to assure Aeginetan adherence to the Greek side. Although Cleomenes soon lost his own position as a result of his swindle at Delphi, and killed himself, leaving his position to his brother Leonidas, the treatment of Aegina was effective. Athens was encouraged to renew her hostilities, and although her success was indifferent, Aegina in the outcome did not side with the Persian fleet when it arrived. These events, occupying the months immediately before Darius' expedition crossed the Aegean and landed on Euboea, left the Athenians free to face the Persian threat.

After the destruction of Eretria, the Persian force under Datis and Artaphernes crossed the narrow strait between Euboea and Attica and landed at Marathon. The Athenians reacted quickly. They dispatched a force of 10,000 heavy-armed infantry to Marathon, sent a runner to Sparta to ask for help, and called for reinforcements from the neighboring allied city of Plataea. The Plataeans hastened to pull together a force of about a thousand, and sent it quickly to Marathon. The Spartans replied that they would send their army as soon as the moon was full, an event still six days away, for religious law precluded military operations during their festival of Apollo. Persians and Athenians faced each other in the plain of Marathon. Among the ten Athenian generals there was disagreement on tactics. Taking the lead and urging an immediate attack was Miltiades, who had recently returned from the Chersonese in the north, where he had become familiar with the Persians. Miltiades was able to convince the president of the board of generals, who in his casting vote tilted the decision toward attack. Of the generals, each of whom led a contingent from one of the ten tribes of Athenian citizens and took a daily turn at command of the whole force, five yielded their days to Miltiades. It happened that he was in command on a day when the Persian cavalry, usually an inhibiting threat to the Athenians, was off the field, and Miltiades raised the signal for a dawn attack.

The battle was fierce, but in the end the Athenian wings, stretched to match the Persians and then strengthened, overcame their opponents and were able to wheel and catch the Persian center from behind. The Persian cavalry, finally back on the scene, was not able to play an effective role. Defeat turned into a rout, and the Persian troops fled to the shore. They made good their escape to their ships, losing only seven of those, and set off to sail around Cape Sounion to land at the city itself. Miltiades, however, took the army quickly back to Athens, and the Persians found it there, blocking any possibility of landing. The fleet left for Asia without attempting any further operations. When the 2,000-strong Spartan vanguard arrived the next day, after marching some 225 kilometers in three days, the Athenians could show them the field of victory, littered with Persian dead, proudly accepting Spartan congratulations for their almost single-handed triumph. The defeat of the Persians at Marathon, to the Athenians, was their finest achievement. For generations after, they pointed to that day when they (with the Plataeans) stood alone against the Persian hordes, and sent them reeling back to the east. They had earned the gratitude of all other Hellenes, and regarded themselves as the saviors of Greece.

There is no doubt that Marathon was important. It is true that the western Greeks had been untouched by the Persian threat, and the eastern Greeks were unaffected by the Persian defeat. Nor did the defeat discourage Persian support on the Greek peninsula, for the Thracian cities remained faithful, as did King Alexander I of Macedonia and the dynasts of Thessaly. Still, Marathon, if Marathon did not "save" Greece, proved that Greece could be saved, and could resist the might of the Persian king. It demonstrated the efficacy of Greek infantry against Persian, and established with firmness a bond between Athens and Sparta which would be needed again, and it may have encouraged some of the internal upheavals the Persian empire was to face in the coming decade. But perhaps most important of all, it encouraged an Athenian self-confidence affecting Greek history for a hundred years.

We have little or no information about the state of mind and the view of Persian intentions at Athens immediately after Marathon. The interpretations of modern writers are colored by the fact that we know that the second assault by the Persians was to come within ten years, and also by the account of Herodotus, who also knew how it all came out. Herodotus tends to interpret political events after Marathon in Athens and elsewhere in Greece in terms of the Persian threat, and modern historians incline more or less to the same view that political activity was marked by divergent views of the appropriate response to Persia. This may be so, but it also may not be, and Athenian actions, at least, seem more consistent if they were not based on the primacy of the Persian issue. After the failure of a naval expedition to the islands under Miltiades, leading to Miltiades' trial and conviction and subsequent early death from a wound, politics at Athens may have focused purely on domestic matters for a few years. This would certainly make sense in terms of what we hear about the political quarreling, carried on intensely for every year until the actual arrival of the second Persian force.

In this period, ostracism became an important political tool. Ostracism called for a preliminary decision whether to hold a vote, and later, if the first decision was affirmative, an actual "election" of someone who was thereby selected to remove himself from Athens for ten years. No permanent penalties were inflicted, although the political disability is obvious, and life-expectancy for adults being short, in my view, many would not survive a ten-year period. The procedure was not unique at Athens, although it was unusual among the Greek cities, and it has attracted a great deal of comment and interpretation among ancient Greeks as well as modern writers. There is much we do know about it, including an alleged date of the establishing of ostracism by Cleisthenes, but the major interpreter of ostracism, Aristotle, consistently saw ostracism in constitutions as a feature tending to prevent the development of extraordinary political power. It certainly seems to have been used in this period by the political factions at Athens as a means of cutting down opposing leaders. As Aristotle details events, first Hipparchus, son of Charmus, a leader of those still friendly toward the followers of Pisistratus, fell to ostracism. In the next year it was the turn of Megacles, a member of the Alcmaeonid family, and in the year after that, another "friend of the tyrants" was ostracised. Then in 485/4 Xanthippus, son of Ariphron, another Alcmaeonid and the chief accuser of Miltiades, "won" the vote and was removed from the political arena. Finally, probably in 483/2, Aristides, formerly an associate of the Alcmaeonid Cleisthenes, and who had served as one of the ten generals, joined the group of distinguished politicians who had been ostracized. The only important political figure who remained on the scene was Themistocles, who, at about the same time as Aristides was ostracized, carried a motion in the assembly for the use of new funds from silver mining resulting in the building of a modern fleet of triremes, ships available when the Persians invaded again.

Many modern analysts see all this as reflective of a struggle between aristocracy and democracy, while others envision political combat between partisans of Persia and elements in favor of resistance. Aristotle, who deals with the internal affairs of Athens in this period more extensively than any other writer, certainly does not see attitudes toward Persia playing any role, and gives an account which can be interpreted most consistently in terms of personal and group political rivalries. Such apparently was the case in other Greek cities for which we have any information for this period. At Sparta, for example, although the chronology of the struggle between Demaratus and Cleomenes is uncertain, it was certainly over within the year after Marathon. Thus the implications of conflict over policy towards Persia reflected in the establishment of the Aeginetan hostages at Athens cannot be carried on into the years after Marathon. Immediately after Cleomenes' death, the Aeginetans sent to Sparta complaining about Leotychidas' participation in the deposit of the Aeginetan hostages, and the Spartans responded by a judicial condemnation of the king, who ended the affair by asking the Athenians to return the hostages. We hear nothing of Spartan attitudes toward Persia, nor indeed of any other Greek city, until the Persian forces are at the gate again.

It is hardly surprising that the Greeks should neglect a possible threat, for the Persians had been having a difficult time of it. Although Herodotus reports that Darius reacted to his defeat with preparations for a new invasion, and turned his empire upside down for three years as he got ready, nothing in fact seems to have happened in the west, for the revolt of Egypt in 486 was a much more serious matter for the Great King's attention. It was dangerous, much more so than the defeat of an expedition with less staked on it than Darius' Scythian expedition, the failure of which Darius had not followed up either. The loss of Egypt was closer to home, represented a serious financial loss, and showed a sustained and successful opposition to Persian power. Darius died before he could recover Egypt, and his son Xerxes, who mounted the throne in late 486, was left with the problem. He turned to Egypt with a personal campaign in 485, and by the following year the country was once again under Persian control. From this time on, we are told by Herodotus, Xerxes prepared for a renewal of the attempt to conquer Greece, induced by the aggressive and ambitious Mardonius, his cousin and brother-in-law, who used the advice of Greeks present at court to urge the possibilities of invasion in face of Greek disunity. For three years, workers labored to dig a canal through the isthmus of Mt. Athos, to preclude the disaster which had overtaken the first fleet sent around the point. The river Strymon, in Thrace, was bridged at its mouth, and food depots were established along the Thracian coast and into Macedonia. At the Hellespont, preparations were made to cast floating bridges across to expedite the transit of the huge army that was planned.

All this activity, moving forward from 484/3, might be thought to have excited a frenzy of counter-preparation on the part of the Greeks. If it did, we hear nothing of it from the sources, for they report no such action until Xerxes' army was actually on the move. Greeks in central and southern Greece certainly must have heard about it, but they probably also heard about the difficulties Xerxes was having with Babylon, and may have assumed that they were safe for the moment. That revolt, in 482, was crushed rather quickly, and Xerxes was finally ready for the march west. The army moved out from Susa in the spring of 481, filled by contingents from 46 peoples in numbers so staggering that Herodotus does not even attempt to give them, joined by a fleet of over a thousand ships. By the spring of 480, after wintering in Sardis, the force was on the move again, crossed the Hellespont, traversed Thrace with some difficulty, and was into Macedonia by summer.

To these events the Greeks reacted. In the autumn of 481 representatives from all the Greek states who were committed to combined action against Xerxes assembled at Sparta. There they established a formal Congress, structured to administer the league to be known as "the Greeks," meeting regularly at the Isthmus to plan religious, military and diplomatic strategy to meet the invasion. Delphi discouraged them in the religious sphere, with dire warnings of the outcome for Athens and Sparta, and their negotiators met little success among Greek states who already had submitted to or were fearful of the Persian advance. But they persisted, and ultimately there were 31 of them to be inscribed on the victory monument dedicated to Apollo at Delphi. The offering was a golden tripod resting on a base made up of three intertwined serpents, on the coils of which were inscribed the names of the peoples who made up the alliance: Lacedemonians, Athenians, Corinthians, Tegeans, Sicyonians, Aeginetans, Megarians, Epidaurians, Orchomenians, Phliasians, Troezenians, Hermionians, Tirynthians, Plataeans, Thespians, Mycenaeans, Ceans, Melians, Tenians, Naxians, Eretrians, Chalcidians, Styreans, Eleans, Potidaeans, Leucadians, Anactorians, Cythnians, Siphnians, Ambraciots and Lepreats. Although the Congress by no means included cities from all parts of Greece, its representation was remarkably diverse. In addition to Athens and her associates, and the Peloponnesian states, whose adherence to Sparta could be expected, and those from central and west Greece who had some hope of turning the Persians aside, there were some in more exposed positions. There were islanders, whose shores lay open to the huge Persian fleet, and even Potidaeans, whose character as colonists of Corinth might have been thought to be outweighed by their isolation in Chalcidice among the medizers of the north.

The campaigns lasted for two years, and the federal congress handled both tactics and strategy surprisingly well. Although forward positions were first taken up at Tempe, north of Thessaly, they were abandoned, probably for sound military reasons, and the subsequent decision to stand at Thermopylae meant that any possibly support from Thessaly was given up, as the cities there, now open to the Persians, made their submission. Then, as the line at Thermopylae, the narrow pass from Thessaly to central Greece, was turned, with the loss of the entire Spartan force and the Spartan king Leonidas to fulfil the Delphic Oracle's prophecy, central Greece lay open and fell. The Athenians evacuated their city, save for a small rear-guard force on the Acropolis, and the Persian army swept in and burned everything in vengeance for the destruction of Sardis twenty years before. The Athenians, who had ferried their women and children over to the island of Salamis and had embarked on their ships as a result of Themistocles' interpetation of Delphi's puzzling statement that they would be safe behind their wooden walls, saw their city, their port, their farms and their sacred places either destroyed or occupied by Persians.

The outcome was decided by the two great battles of Salamis and Plataea, the first at sea in 480, and the next on land in the following year. The initial plan of the Congress to withdraw the fleet from the waters near Athens was averted, and Xerxes was drawn into battle in late September, due, we are told, to a secret message from Themistocles warning him that the Greeks were planning to withdraw. The message induced him to fight in unfavorable waters. In the battle itself the Greek fleet was completely successful, probably due in some measure to the Athenian familiarity with the currents in the tricky and narrow straits between the island of Salamis and the mainland. The Persian fleet was not completely destroyed, but the casualties, 200 sunk and others captured, according to the later author Ephorus, were severe enough to prompt Xerxes to withdraw his navy. His decision was again assisted, as the story goes, by the wily Themistocles, who sent another message after the battle, warning the king that the Greeks were planning to break the bridges at the Hellespont. In council, Xerxes decided to accept the proposal of Mardonius that the army be left in Greece under his command, while the king himself could return to Asia, following the fleet he had already sent home. Xerxes marched with the army to Thessaly, left most troops there under the command of Mardonius, and departed, ending the campaigns of the year.

In the course of the winter, Mardonius and his generals maintained their forces and deterred any Greeks who might leave the Persian side. Attempts to detach Athens from the league were unsuccessful, even after a second invasion of Attica with further ravaging of the countryside and more burning of anything still standing in the city. The Athenians, who had decided to attack the Persians from their base on Salamis and were calling for the defense of Attica in Boeotia, sent to the Spartans to demand support, warning that they might make a separate peace with Persia. The Spartans finally responded, and the allied Greek force began collecting near the Boeotian city of Plataea, where the Persian force was encamped. The two armies settled down to a waiting game of about three weeks, during which the Persian cavalry harried the Greeks, who were suffering also from shortages of supplies and water. Then, finally, the Persians decided to attack, and the Greeks, warned by King Alexander of Macedonia, shifted their line, a tactic that was met by the Persians. After a day of Persian cavalry attacks and a shift of position by the Greeks to come closer to Plataea, and confusing marches during the night leaving the Athenians out of the main action, the great battle was finally fought. It was a disaster for the Persians, and when it was over, Mardonius himself had died in the main battle, and all but a small contingent which managed to make its way north had perished in the slaughter in the Persian camp, where the troops had fled in disorder from their broken battle line.

It was September, and there was no threat of a renewal of operations in that year. The Persians were, in fact, never to come again to Greece, and the Greeks were already carrying the war to Persian territory. The Greek fleet, having moved across the Aegean earlier, had landed a force at Mycale in Ionia, and in a battle fought there on the same day as Plataea, annihilated the Persian force and burned its ships. The Greeks could control the Aegean now, and the Ionians were breaking away from Persian domination and joining them. The fleet then sailed to the Hellespont to break down the Persian bridges, which in fact had already been washed away. The Spartans went home, but Xanthippus and the Athenian contingent laid siege to Sestos. They were finally successful later in the winter, and in the spring of 478 they sailed home to Athens in triumph, bearing with them booty from their victory and the cables from Xerxes' bridges. It was, at least in the account of Herodotus, who concluded his history with these events, the end of the Persian invasion of Greece.

The fifty years after the victories of Salamis, Plataea and Mycale saw the development of the first Greek imperial structure, as Athens assumed first leadership and then control over a formally reconstituted alliance against Persia. It is a period for which the only contemporary ancient account, that of Thucydides, is extremely condensed and is meant to focus moral and political judgement on the actions of the Athenian democracy, which became more responsive to popular will in those years. Later writers, like Plutarch with his biographies of Athenians prominent at the time, or the Sicilian Diodorus, whose account, part of his universal history, is less pointed than Thucydides,' supplement Thucydides' narrative and preserve details in the works of other historians. Differences between these accounts and internal inconsistencies in Thucydides' own text have generated a great deal of modern investigation and analysis, creating a body of writing far exceeding that left to us by the ancient writers. On many disputed issues of chronology and events there is still no modern agreement, and some of the points of contention are not so minor. Each modern writer is faced, for example, with deciding whether a history of the period should or should not include a reference to the so-called Peace of Callias of 449, mentioned by Diodorus but not by Thucydides. The scholarly controversies have focused on matters not only of fact but of interpretation, and have often highlighted questions of political goals, civic ideologies and the attitudes of statesmen and poets. Any modern account of specific events is interpretive as much as factual.

This said in warning should not detract from the solidity of our overall knowledge. The direction events took, the dominant national purposes of the main actors in the drama and the effects of international affairs on the development of the leading states are by and large agreed today, although variations in the treatment of specific events and causes naturally have influenced the understanding of why some things took place, and modern biases have played a significant role in making moral judgements on the actions of individuals and states. Modern writers are not alone in this, for the ancients had their own opinions and drew their own conclusions, and in fact, the whole history of the period often turns on the attitude of one or another ancient writer. Some of these events were frequently cited to enlist recruits in moral causes. Others were presented as justifications or condemnations of later policy. The exercise of power marking the period was often used, in short, to point a lesson in morality, a lesson, however, sometimes confounded with an an attack on Athens' broadly based democracy.

The creation of the first great imperial structure in Greece could not have been predicted from the beginning, and Sparta did not resist the decision of the Ionians to create an alliance with Athens as leader. The Ionians did not want to accept a Spartan proposal to transplant them west across the Aegean, and so accepted an Athenian offer of support. The initial agreement was a mutual defense association whereby the Ionians agreed to have the same enemies as the Athenians, and vice-versa, with each of the signatory Ionians to contribute to the common military effort a specified sum of money or number of ships and men, levied at the outset by Aristides, the Athenian most acceptable to the others. The total of the first assessment was, according to Thucydides, 460 talents, an enormous sum, and it provided the allies the wherewithal to carry the war to Persian domains and to extend the orbit of the league itself. The treasury was established on Apollo's sacred island of Delos, where it remained for 25 years, supervised by Athenian-appointed *hellenotamiai*, "Hellenic treasurers." The league fleet, in fact largely Athenian, was financed in great part by the contributed funds, a procedure making it possible for Athens rapidly to dominate the eastern Aegean and outstrip her major naval rival of Corinth.

In the first decade after the Persian defeat the league consolidated the independence of the maritime states. Some cities, like Carystos in Euboea, were forced to join the alliance or were actually rescued from Persian control. In those years it was made clear that there was no leaving the alliance, for an Athenian siege forced Naxos to rejoin after an assertion of secession. Thucydides described this action by Athens as the first instance in which the original agreement was broken and an ally was "enslaved," beginning his brief account of the steady progress of Athenian domination of other Greeks. In these first years the Persian War generation of generals, Themistocles, Aristides and Xanthippus, passed from the scene, either by death or political destruction. They were replaced by Cimon, who had paid the fine levied on his father, Miltiades, and had won the allegiance of a large number of his fellow citizens. Sometime about 467 Cimon demonstrated the quality of his military leadership, as he sailed along the southern coast of Turkey against a Persian squadron preparing to move into the Aegean. At the river Eurymedon, first the Persian fleet, and then a land army, were destroyed. The victory was a great one, for it demonstrated the superiority of the forces of the Athenian alliance, and it was more impressive by being followed by another naval success off Cyprus, and then soon after that, by Cimon's clearing the Persians from the Chersonese Peninsula in the northeast Aegean.

In 465 the Persian world was disrupted by the assassination of Xerxes and the subsequent murder and replacement of his older son by the younger one, Artaxerxes I. Another brother, satrap of Bactria, rebelled, and following the suppression of the revolt the king had all his remaining brothers killed. There were other rebellions to disrupt the beginning of the reign, but the most serious was that of Egypt, which began in 460. The movement was led by the Libyan dynast Inarus, and it had wide popular support among the Egyptians, including that of one Amyrtaeus of Sais who was probably of ancient royal lineage. The initial rising in Lower Egypt was quite successful, and the Egyptians and their mercenaries defeated both land and sea forces of the Persians. The Persians, however, were not ready to give up so easily, and a large force remained in the country, supported by a sizable fleet on the Nile. Inarus, accordingly, needed allies, and he looked to Athens with her traditional interest in Egypt and hostility toward Persia. Athens was a promising ally at this time, for she had just concluded a long, and ultimately profitable, campaign in the north Aegean against Thasos.

That war shows the effectiveness of Athens as an imperial power, and is also associated with the beginning of the split between the Athenians and the Spartans. The war against Thasos, begun in 465, had many vicissitudes, including serious defeats of Athenians at the hands of mainland Thracians when the Athenians tried to settle the so-called "Nine Ways" at the Strymon River. In the end, however, the Athenians forced Thasos to harsh terms, bringing not only revenue to the Athenians but also the Thasian navy as well. In the course of the war, Thasos had appealed to Sparta to help, and, according to Thucydides, Sparta agreed and would have sent help if she had not been involved in her own troubles. After her withdrawal from leadership of the Greeks because of her own and others' displeasure with the actions of Spartan generals in the years immediately aftre the Persian War, Sparta bent her efforts to maintaining her position as leader of the cities of the Peloponnesus. There was some trouble with Argos and Tegea, but Sparta maintained her supremacy by a victory in the later 470's. In the next decade she was badgered by a serious revolt of the Messenians and the combination of her enemies to the north, a force only overcome by the superiority of her infantry in a hard battle at Dipaea in mid-decade. The town of Sparta suffered badly in 464 when an earthquake demolished many of the buildings and killed thousands, prompting an onrush of helots, just barely held off by the citizens standing hurriedly to arms amidst the ruins. Retiring from Sparta itself, the helots gained support from *perioikoi*, non-citizens dwelling in the area, and from the Messenians who had rebelled earlier. They established themselves in the towns of the Laconian countryside and carried on a full-scale war with the Spartans. The situation was so desperate that the Spartans sent one of their number to Athens to sit beside the altars of the gods as a suppliant. Opinion at Athens was divided on the question of whether to help. The democrat Ephialtes was opposed, but Cimon, maintaining his policy of cooperation with Sparta, was able to carry the assembly with him, and led out an army of Athenians and Plataeans to support the beleaguered Spartans.

Most of the details of these events are very obscure. Much of what we do know about them comes from Plutarch's *Life of Cimon*, which is weak on chronology if nothing else. Thucydides alludes to these events only briefly. Plutarch tells of two occasions when the Spartans asked for help and Cimon persuaded the Athenians to send a supporting force, the second coming some time later, when the Messenians and helots were holding out on Mount Ithome. Diodorus differs in mentioning only one such episode, and his chronology is at variance with that preferred by most modern writers in that it places the earthquake and the events associated with it in 469.

It is from Diodorus, however, that we learn much of what we know about the other Peloponnesian cities in this period. Argos, badly weakened by her defeat at Sepeia at the beginning of the century and had lost control of the Argolid, the area around her as a result, began to show a resurgence. Themistocles' activities and residence at Argos in the late 470's and early 460's suggest that he recognized her renewed potential against Sparta. Themistocles had always had suspicions of Sparta, ever since the Spartans had urged the Athenians not to rebuild their walls after the Persian War and Themistocles had led an embassy to Sparta to stall an answer while the Athenians frantically built. At some time in the 460's (early, according to Diodorus, but tied in after the confusion at Sparta at the time of the earthquake) Argos crushed Mycenae, enslaving her citizens and razing the city, an event associated with her re-establishing control over the Argolid. By this time also (471/70 according to Diodorus' chronology), the small and numerous towns of the Eleians had united to create a single city named Elis, forming another strong center in the Peloponnesus.

Thus when, sometime between 463 and 461, Sparta finally subdued the rebel helots and Messenians, she had suffered an exhausting war, a terrible natural disaster, and confronted new centers of power in the area she was accustomed to dominate. The Spartans also faced a radical change in their relationship with Athens. Cimon's Athenian force had been sent back, unused, by Spartans suspicious of Athenian intentions, and the result was the discrediting of Cimon's policy of friendship with Sparta. In hostility, Athens immediately consummated an alliance with Argos and Thessaly, and in 461 ostracized Cimon, marking the end of any sentiment for cooperation with Sparta among Athenian politicians.

The new mood allowed for policies freeing Athens for imperial activities which would come directly into conflict with Sparta's allies.

The political situation in Greece was part of the complex of broader international relations, especially once the Egyptians revolting from Persia had gained Athenian support in that conflict. There were 200 vessels of the league fleet in the waters off Cyprus when the call from Inarus came, and they crossed to Egypt and sailed up the Nile. Together, the forces of Inarus and the Athenians defeated the Persian fleet, taking or sinking 50 ships and killing the commander. The Persian land force, however, held on to the fortress of Leucon Teichos, and the Great King turned to supplement his military forces with the weapon of gold, hoping that he could use such inducements to bring Sparta into action against Athens. In 460, the Persian ambassador Megabazus arrived in Sparta to finance an invasion of Attica. Although the idea was reasonable, in the context of Greek affairs, and Persian money was spent in Sparta, no invasion proceeded, and Megabazus finally returned to Persia with what money he had left. King Artaxerxes now equipped a large force under Megabyzus, the son of Zopyrus, and sent it to Egypt against the Athenians and Egyptians in the spring of 455. The Persians now defeated the Egyptians and their allies, drove the Athenians out of Memphis and besieged them on the island of Prosopitis for 18 months. Finally, diverting the canal waters protecting one side of the island, the Persians marched across now-dry land to victory. Thus in 454, after fighting in Egypt for six years, as Thucydides says, the Athenian expedition to Egypt was destroyed. Almost all of its members perished, only a few escaping across the Libyan desert to Cyrene. Inarus was captured and crucified, and all Egypt, except the marshland under Amyrtaeus, which the Persians could not take, was back under Persian control. The Athenian disaster increased in magnitude when a fifty-ship squadron, unaware of the recent events, arrived at the Mendesian mouth of the Nile and was overwhelmed by a joint land and sea attack, again with few escaping.

The destruction of the Egyptian expeditionary force left the Athenians seriously weakened at sea, and around this time, fortuitously or by honest apprehension of the Persians or using the opportunity to present an excuse, the Athenians transferred the treasury of the league from Delos to Athens. There has been a lot of modern controversy focused on this event, conventionally dated by most scholars to 454, and the issues raised include motivation, relationship to other events, and date. That it happened there is no doubt, nor is there any question that the transfer radically affected the relationship between Athens and her allies. From then on, Athens had the assets of the League directly under her control, and could and did use the monies for her own purposes and as a nest egg to establish her own security.

Events in Greece over the preceding few years would have heightened the advantage of this action, and it certainly must have come as no surprise to the other Greeks. A number of cities had been fighting the Athenians for some time, and the hostility between Athens and Sparta had finally broken out into open war. The division between the two had been clear at the time of the rejection of Cimon's force during Sparta's conflict with the helots. Sparta's inability to hold her own allies showed almost immediately with Argos' making the triple alliance with Athens and Thessaly. Other cities continued to go their own way. Megara, in conflict with Sparta's major naval ally Corinth, defected and became one of Athens' allies, and took an Athenian garrison into the city itself and into Pegae across the isthmus on the Corinthian Gulf. At the same time, Athens built long walls connecting Megara with her port of Nisaea to make the city safe from land attack. Corinth responded to this, and to the need of Aegina, just recently at war with Athens and under siege as a result of a major naval defeat, and with Epidauros sent a small force to Aegina. More or less at the same time, a force of Corinthian and allied troops was held to a drawn battle near Megara, but 12 days later, a force of Corinthians who had returned to the scene to set up a trophy were destroyed to a man by the Athenians.

In the next year, 457, a large army of Spartans and their allies were in central Greece, apparently not seeking hostilities with Athens but rather to settle a war between Doris and Phocis in favor of Phocis. The Athenians, however, moved land and sea forces to cut the Peloponnesians off from their route home, and the denouement of all the activity was a Spartan victory at Tanagra in Boeotia, fought with heavy losses to both sides. The Spartan army, though no longer strong enough to attack Athens, was now able to return home, and did so, ravaging the territory of Megara on the way. With the Spartans gone, the Athenians returned to Boeotia in a couple of months, defeated the Boeotians at Oenophyta and swept into control of all the cities in the area, and followed up with the taking of hostages to secure Phocis and Opuntian Locris. The solidification of Athenian control of central Greece was capped by the surrender of Aegina, so that by the end of 457 Athenian success on land and sea was unrestrained. The war continued unabated for two more years, with forces of the Athenian fleet, some elements now led by Pericles, showing success after success around the Peloponnesus, in western Greece, and in the Gulf of Corinth. The various naval cities of Greece, like Corinth, Sicyon, Thasos and Aegina, had failed to unify their opposition to Athens, and had been picked off or damaged badly one at a time, so that Athens was left unquestionably supreme among Greeks at sea. Only the naval contingents of the Persians could represent a threat.

In the years following the transfer of the treasury to Athens, while Pericles was making his way to political supremacy among the Athenians, the other Greek states were jockeying for position in relation to one another and to the imperial power Athens was now able to exercise in the Aegean. Sparta did not intervene directly in these events, and the war between her and Athens first lagged, and then was suspended for five years by a truce arranged in 451. At about this time Argos moved away from Athens, and concluded a 30-year peace with Sparta. Argos seems thus to have been free to play a somewhat greater role in Greek affairs, as we find from an inscription found at Argos and in the Argive dialect, showing Argos acting as arbiter, probably in some sort of federal structure, for the cities of Knossos and Tylissos on Crete. The inscription is one of the few indications of the links between the Cretan cities and the mainland. Although Crete seems to have been able, by and large, to avoid entanglement in the political and military struggles of the peninsula and the Aegean, she had clearly not lagged behind most of the rest of Greece in development. The famous law code of Gortyn, a mid fifth-century text carved on twelve columns of a circular wall at Gortyn, an inland city of central Crete, exhibits a social and legal development not out of line in comparison with what we know of the state of such matters in mainland Greece at this time.

In central Greece, the period of truce between Athens and Sparta seems to have afforded an opportunity for a struggle between Phocis and Delphi for possession of the great sanctuary, with Athens and Sparta supporting opposing sides, although without coming to direct blows in violation of their truce. In 447, however, the circumstances of Boeotia changed radically. Exiled oligarchs regained control of some places, and the Athenians, marching in to head off an overall overturning of their control, were overwhelmed in battle. Negotiations for the ransoming of the captured Athenians led to the Boeotians' extricating themselves from the Athenian alliance, and they then established their own confederacy under the leadership of Thebes, The new league was to play an important part in the affairs of central Greece, and was able to act as an independent force for almost a century. Thebes, as leader, quickly rose to a position among the major Greek states, and like Athens, at times found herself at odds with confederate cities restive under her hegemony.

The loss of Boeotia was a blow at Athens, and made Pericles and the other expansionist politicians at Athens more amenable to accommodation with Sparta, and so in 446 negotiations for a permanent peace were successfully concluded. The agreement of a thirty-years' peace, the details of which are not reported by the sources, seems to have divided Greece into Spartan and Athenian spheres of influence. So far as we can tell from later events and allusions to the peace, the allies of each were named and were not permitted to switch allegiance, while uncommitted cities could join either alliance, apart from Argos, allowed to join neither but permitted to be friendly to both.

The peace held for 15 years. During that period there were attempts on the part of some of Athens' allies to leave the league, but none were successful. Earlier revolts on Euboea were now ruthlessly suppressed. Another notable failure at rebellion was an attempt by

Samos, which refused Athenian demands for reconciliation with Miletus, and opened negotiations with the Persians in the course of a revolt which was suppressed and then erupted again. It took a nine-month siege lasting into 439 to subdue the island. Byzantium, in the north, had joined Samos in that revolt, and Athens had to turn there after Samos and force Byzantium into line as well. The league, by now easily be seen as an empire, required regular attention and control.

Sometime after the Samian revolt was over, the Acarnanians and Amphilochians, on the west coast of Greece, called in Athens to help recover Amphilochian Argos from the Ambraciot co-settlers who had seized control of the city. The Athenians were successful and enslaved the Ambraciots, and concluded the campaign with a treaty of alliance with Acarnania. Since the westerners so far had been allies of neither side, the treaty did not clash with the peace of 446. The alliance did, however, bring the Athenians further into the area considered by Corinth to be her sphere of influence. At the time of the peace of 446, Athens' only real base in the Corinthian Gulf had been her ally Naupactus, where the Athenians had helped the helots and Messenians settle in 461, when they left the Peloponnesus as part of the terms ending the great revolt against Sparta.

In 437, Pericles decided to assert Athenian influence among the Greek cities along the coast of the Black Sea. Until then, the area had remained clear of the conflicts of Greece, but in that year Pericles sailed out with an impressive fleet to cruise the Propontis and the Black Sea. There were at the time no firm alliances with Athens in the area, and the fleet moved along the coast establishing Athenian colonists and connections with the Greek cities. On the southern shore, the fleet expelled the tyrant Timesialus from Sinope and established 600 Athenian citizens there, who would occupy the lands formerly belonging to the tyrant. A little further east, more Athenian colonists were landed at Amisus, and the name of that city was changed to Piraeus. Pericles then sailed north to the so-called Cimmerian Bosphorus, the Crimea, and in all likelihood it was then that the Athenians gained Nymphaeum, a fine port in the area. Pericles also concluded a treaty of friendship with Spartocus, a Thracian mercenary commander who had just got control of the Crimea, beginning a durable dynasty. The Athenians had now drawn the peoples of the Black Sea firmly into Greek politics, and the success of that expedition was soon followed by the founding of Amphipolis, on the river Strymon in Thrace, in 437, at long last bringing to success the Athenian effort to establish a base in the area.

By 435 almost the entire Greek world was involved in greater or lesser degree with one of the two great rival alliances of Greece. Although for ten years both Athens and Sparta had studiously avoided any renewal of conflict, Athens' and Sparta's maritime allies had been steadily increasing their involvements with cities far from the center of the Greek world. Athenian commercial and trading activities prompted her to protect and expand her sea lanes, and the same was true to a lesser degree of Corinth and then Megara. Finally, in 435, in the extreme northwest of Greece, began a series of events leading to a rupture of the Thirty Years Peace.

A fierce civic disturbance disrupted the Illyrian coastal city of Epidamnus, a joint colony of Corinth and the island city of Corcyra, herself a colony of Corinth. Corinth took the side of the democrats in Epidamnus when Corcyra failed to help them, while Corcyra supported the oligarchs, and in 435 a large Corcyrean fleet defeated an almost equally sizable Corinthian force with great losses to the Corinthians. Epidamnus surrendered the same day, all naval prisoners taken by Corcyra were killed except the Corinthians, who were imprisoned, and the settlers who had been placed in Epidamnus by Corinth were sold into slavery. It was the start of serious war, and Corinth began preparations which were to take two years. By 433 she had isolated Corcyra from the Peloponnesian cities and had built and manned 90 ships, actions prompting Corcyra to send to Athens to request an alliance. Urged on by Pericles, after a brief hesitation the Athenians agreed to help Corcyra with a defensive alliance, but cautious about sending an excessively provocative force, they sent two successive squadrons of 10 and 20 ships to aid the Corcyreeans only as a defensive force. In August of 433 a battle fleet of Corinthian ships with their allies overwhelmed the Corcyreans off Sybota, and was preparing a landing when the second Athenian squadron arrived. The reinforcements discouraged the Corinthians from renewing battle, and after brief negotiations in which the Athenians defended themselves against Corinthian complaints of aggression by stating that they would act only to defend Corcyra according to the terms of the treaty, the Corinthians withdrew. They had won the battle but had not succeeded in conquering Corcyra, which could now serve as a base for Athenian naval operations in the west.

The Athenians followed up this success with further pressure on the Corinthians and their allies. In the winter of 433/2 the Athenians ordered Potidaea, in Chalcidice, originally a colony of Corinth but now a member of Athens' league, to dismantle the defenses protecting her from assault from the sea, to deposit hostages at Athens and to dismiss and not accept in the future the magistrates which the Corinthians had traditionally always sent out to her colony. While Potidaean protests were being discussed at Athens during the summer of 432 and the Potidaeans were sending for help from the Peloponnesians, the Athenians enacted another decree: they banned Megara, their former ally but now an adherent of Corinth, from every port in the league. It was not only a provocative attack on Corinth via Megara, it was a demonstration of the autocracy Athens was prepared to exercise in governing her maritime empire. Soon after, an Athenian force sent north against Potidaea found an extensive revolt there, fomented by King Perdiccas of neighboring Macedonia. Archestratus, the Athenian commander, joined forces with two rival claimants to the Macedonian throne, and forced Perdiccas to channge sides and ally himself with Athens. The Athenians could then turn to Potidaea, and after defeating a force including some Corinthians and others from the Peloponnesus, they settled down to besiege Potidaea.

This was the situation when the Spartans, in response to complaints from Corinth, called a general meeting at Sparta to air accusations of Athens. Representatives of Corinth, Megara and other states spoke, as well as some from Athens who happened to be there. The Corinthians in particular urged action against a relentlessly ambitious and aggressive Athens. After hearing from all, the Spartan assembly voted that Athens had broken the Thirty Years Peace and that Sparta should support her allies. The congress of Sparta's allies met later that autumn, and decided for war. Sparta sent to Athens, demanding the end of the siege of Potidaea and that autonomy be restored to Aegina, and stating that war could be avoided by the revocation of the Megarian decree. Athens refused to negotiate on these terms, and responded to Sparta with counter demands, but suggesting arbitration. There were no further communications between the two, and war broke out in the following spring, in 431.

Thucydides, at the beginning of his history of the war, reports the words of the speakers at the Peloponnesian congresses and at Athens in response to Spartan embassies. While he could have listened to Pericles in Athens, the speeches of the Corinthians and others at Sparta at best could only have been reported to him. His filling out of the account allows him to present in speeches an assessment of the Athenians and the Spartans, and his portrayal of Athens through Corinthian words and then through the words of Athenians themselves allows a general characterization of Athens and her empire. The Corinthians describe the Spartans as moderate in judgement and slow to act, while the Athenians are ever-restless, seeking new acquisitions always, resentful if they don't gain what they set their minds to, individually prepared to sacrifice themselves for the power of their city, and a threat to all as they grow in power to a point at which it will not be possible to oppose them even in unison. The Athenian self-description to the congress at Sparta takes credit for the success against the Persians, and claims that it was in the first instance defence against Persia that led them to build their alliance. Thucydides uses the word "rule" as the Athenians' own word to describe their governance of the league, and has them argue that they had done nothing unusual in accepting power when it came to them and then refusing to give it up. Pericles, at Athens, urges steadfastness against the Spartans and gives the practical reasons why the Athenians can expect success. The mood for the ensuing war is set, and when, under pressure of events, the Athenians act ruthlessly—or Thucydides portrays them acting so—in their self-interest with regard only for power and none for justice, they are fleshing out the verbal description given them as the war begins.

War began with Athens' support of Plataea after Thebes tried to seize the city. King Archidamus of Sparta marched into Attica at the head of a great allied army and devastated the trees and standing crops in an operation Sparta would repeat almost every year. As the Peloponnesian army approached, Pericles gathered all the Athenians, with their women, children and possessions, within the walls of Athens, planning to avoid a land engagement, and depending on supplies arriving by sea. Pericles' strategy called for offensive actions at sea, maintainance of control of the sea lanes, and the use of land forces only when there was no risk of defeat. The strategy made sense not only in terms of Athenian resources and strengths, but also because the Peloponnesians could not touch Athenian sources of supply so long as Athens had control of the sea, while the Athenian fleet could inflict serious damage in hit-and-run attacks on the Peloponnesus itself.

Pericles held to his plans, and the Athenians stayed in the city when the Peloponnesians arrived to destroy what they could in Attica a second time, in spring 430. At that time, however, a plague broke out in Athens and held its grip on the population through 430/29, came on again in the winter of 427/6 and was not over finally until the end of 426. The mortality rate was extremely high; Pericles himself died, and the death rate among the troops may have reached as high as one third. Throughout these years there was fierce fighting in several theaters of war, among them the Corinthian Gulf, where Athens scored some notable early successes. Athens was able to put down a threatening revolt of Mytilene in 427, offering Thucydides the opportunity to reinforce impressions of Athenian ruthlessness. He reports Athenian debates about treatment of Mytilene after it surrendered. First the Athenians decided to kill all the males and enslave the women and children. However, a debate the next day changed their minds. The arguments put forth in the debate, which Thucydides gives at some length, had nothing to do with justice or mercy, but were merely differing positions on the question of whether so drastic a punishment would serve Athens' interests, or whether it would be beneficial to allow this city, and therefore future renegade allies, some benefit from surrendering. This pragmatic view carried the day, and a ship despatched to carry the second decision arrived just in time.

In 425 the war took a different turn. An Athenian fleet, heading off to Sicily in the course of operations there against the Spartan ally Syracuse, put in because of bad weather at Pylos, on the southwest coast of the Peloponnesus. Almost by chance the troops fortified the promontory on which they were encamped, and when they left for Sicily a general named Demosthenes remained with five ships. The Spartans then reacted, placed some troops on the island of Sphacteria across from Demosthenes' encampment, and proceeded to assault the fort without success. When Demosthenes called the main force back, the 420 Spartans on the island were cut off. The Spartans then made an armistice, putting their fleet in Athenian hands, but allowed to provision their men on the island, and sent an embassy to Athens proposing peace and an alliance in return for the freeing of the men on Sphacteria. The Athenian assembly refused, hostilities began again, with the Athenians keeping the Spartan ships on a pretext, and the Athenian force faced a difficult winter with wintry seas hindering naval operations and serious problems of supply for the men ashore. In those circumstances one of the political leaders at Athens, Cleon, made what Thucydides portrays as a vain boast that he could capture the Spartans in 20 days if he were given a force. The Athenians voted the expedition, and once there, with the aid of Demosthenes and a fortuitous fire which burned off most of the cover on the island, Cleon succeeded, contrary to the expectation of any reader of Thucydides. Within 20 days he was back in Athens with 292 prisoners, 120 of whom were Spartiates—Spartan citizens.

The stunning events at Pylos produced several Spartan peace overtures in the winter of 425/4, all rejected by Athens. Success followed success in 424, with the Athenian capture of the island of Cythera off the southern Peloponnesus and the seizure of Nisaea, the port of Megara. From this high point, however, things began to go wrong for Athens. First, a march on Boeotia failed, with heavy casualties, and second, in the north, the Spartan general Brasidas brought over some Athenian allies in Chalcidice and persuaded the citizens of Amphipolis to turn the city over to him, and then gained three more cities in the area. The damage to Athens was serious enough to interest them in peace, and they signed a one-year truce with Sparta to permit negotiations for a permanent peace. War resumed, however, in 422, with actions around Amphipolis, in which the most aggressive leader on each side was killed, Cleon for the Athenians, Brasidas for the Spartans.

Other leaders at Sparta and Athens were more inclined toward peace, and after several conferences the two sides agreed on a fifty years peace. The agreement was to be renewed each year, and provided that each side restore to the other all places captured during hostilities, with Athens also giving up Plataea but holding on to Nisaea, while the cities in Chalcidice were to be neutral and independent but still subject to the original assessment levied after the Persian War. When the treaty was submitted to Sparta's congress of allies the majority accepted it, but Megara, Corinth, Elis and the Boeotian League refused, in effect withdrawing from the Spartan alliance. The Spartans responded to this situation by invoking a provision of the treaty allowing Athens and Sparta to make changes in terms on their own, so they approached Athens and obtained a separate treaty and alliance whereby they would fight together against anyone who attacked either. The treaty further provided Athenian agreement to help Sparta in the event of a helot revolt. Thus the first ten years of war brought an accommodation between Sparta and Athens to divide the hegemony of Greece and support each other in their respective areas of dominance. Many of their allies, and particularly some of those of Sparta, were disenchanted with the outcome of all the fighting.

Despite the peace, Athens fought Sparta at Mantinea in 418, and mounted several diplomatic assaults on the political balance in the Peloponnesus. Corinth, in particular, demonstrated her resentment of Sparta and prompted Argos to lead the way in establishing a "third force" among the Greeks. By holding a treaty with Corinth on the one hand, and arranging a defensive alliance with the fellow democracies Mantinea, Elis and Athens, Argos arranged a somewhat complicated diplomatic position. The emergence of Argos left Sparta's alliance in the Peloponnesus severely truncated, but the Spartans took no action to improve their position until 418, the year after Argos began hostilities with an attack on Epidaurus. After a period of war, truce and renewed warfare, a decisive Spartan victory brought a fifty-year alliance between Sparta and Argos. In the following year the Spartans overthrew the Argive democracy, but the democrats gained control again and returned the city to the Athenian alliance. Thereafter, despite Spartan attacks, the Argives remained true to the Athenians until the end of the war, even to the point of sending a small contingent with the Athenians to Sicily in 413.

The involvement of the Athenians in Sicily, starting as early as the 450's, did not require the commitment of heavy resources until 415. Treaties with Rhegium and Leontini had been renewed in 433/2, just as Athens was on the brink of war with Sparta, and Athens had fought on the side of Leontini against Syracuse between 427 and 424, with contingents of 20 and then 40 ships, but with peace reestablished on the island the ships returned home. Athenian help was not called for again until the winter of 416/5, by her ally Segesta, then involved in a war with Selinus. This came in the same winter as Athens was subduing the small island city of Melos, an action Thucydides used to put into the mouths of Athenian ambassadors to Melos the cynical justifications of power with which the Athenians refused to allow the Melians their neutrality. The language sets the mood for the response to the request from Segesta, first in the Athenian dispatch of envoys to Sicily, and then, on their return in the spring of 415 with the mistaken report that Segesta had the financial resources to support an expedition, the decision to commit an exceedingly large number of ships and men with a great expenditure of money and material.

The two books in which Thucydides tells of the Sicilian expedition create an account as much political and moral philosophy as it is military narrative. The historian's thoughts about the meaning of the expedition include several themes, each of which is woven into the story and given prominence by its relationship to events. The story as a whole illustrates historical retribution for excessive ambition. From Thucydides' time on, the great three-year campaign, started with high hopes and expanded with a dangerously great commitment of Athens' resources, taking almost all the men and ships to death and slavery in agonizing defeat by the end of 413, has been used as a moral lesson by historians and politicians alike. Thucydides writes the story with a sense of inevitability which intensifies the dramatic effect and has made the Sicilian expedition stand out as one of the most memorable occurrences in Greek history. The outcome was not foreordained, however, and the fleet sent off with such excitement in 415 could in fact have brought mastery of Sicily. The objective was great enough and would have had such benefit for an imperial Athens that the risk entailed could be seen as reasonable. The failure was due less to flaws inherent in the plan than to mistakes, the avoidance of almost any one of which would probably have changed the result from failure to success.

Thucydides' portrayal of the decisions of the Athenian assembly makes it almost impossible not to perceive the Athenians as excitable, easy to stampede through rhetoric, impetuous and greedy. Democracy appears as unstable, unable to maintain consistent policy in adverse times as well as good, inclined to find scapegoats as causes of reverses instead of seeking better policies, or explanations in its own behavior. Democratic leaders are usually moved by purposes of immediate political gain rather than long range goals advantageous to the city. Thucydides' description of the debate and decision producing the expedition points this up, as he leads us through the rejection of Nicias' reasoned arguments against the expedition, apparently based on a long-range pereception of good strategy, overwhelmed by promises and great hopes by Alcibiades inspiring a populace that knew little of Sicily. Indeed, the whole career of Alcibiades is an example of the leadership problem, and the story of the mutilation of the statues of Hermes and the consequent trial and flight of Alcibiades illustrates the unreliability of the populace.

One night, just as the expedition was ready to sail, the little stone busts of Hermes, mounted on square stone pillars with protruding phalluses, and placed at doors and on the roads for protection of passers-by, were mutilated. No one knew who did it, and rewards were offered for information because of the expected bad fortune if the act went unpunished. Some sacrilegious acts of Alcibiades were reported, that he had mistreated other statues and had profaned the mysteries by burlesque imitation, so it was natural to suspect him in connection with the herm episode. Alcibiades challenged his accusers to put him on trial, but because they saw a better oportunity for conviction in the absence of many of his supporters who would be away on the expedition, the matter was left open and Alcibiades left for Sicily under suspicion. Then, when the force was actually in Sicily and operations were beginning, Alcibiades was recalled for trial, and mistrusting the justice of a population that was intending to execute him even though his name was not among those provided by an informer, he and some others being recalled escaped during the voyage home, and fled to Sparta. His subsequent advice to the Spartans proved valuable to them, and the fickle Athenians thus lost his much-needed services in Sicily, and later committed even more resources to the enterprise when the foremost advocate of the operation was no longer present.

By the time of the final destruction of the troops and ships in Sicily in 413, Athens had renewed hostilities with Sparta. In the spring of 413, responding to Athenian raids on Laconia in support of Argos in the preceding year, a Spartan army once again invaded and ravaged Attica. But this time, on the advice of Alcibiades, the Spartans fortified and left an occupying force in Decelea, within Attica, and thus denied the Athenians the use of their lands. This action, with the Sicilian debacle on its heels, began a series of Athenian disasters which was not arrested until Athens gained a number of naval successes in the Hellespont in later autumn of 411, capped by a great victory over the Spartan fleet at Cyzicus in the Propontis in 410. The setbacks she faced up to then were serious. Persia had finally entered the war and begun providing financial support to the Spartans, who could thus begin building a fleet. Athens also suffered some military reverses, but worse than those was a revolt of her allies, which began with Spartan encouragement and was widespread in the Aegean, and had spread to the Hellespont by 411. Perhaps worst of all was an internal upheaval at Athens in 411. In the city proper the democracy was overthrown and an oligarchic regime of 400 took over management of affairs, pending establishment of a new constitution with the franchise limited to a selected 5,000 Athenians. However, the main fleet of the navy, at Samos, maintained its loyalty to democratic institutions, and for a while the civic body was divided between two separate governments. This lasted almost a year, in fact, from autumn of 411 into the spring of 410, and at Athens control of affairs passed from the 400, who were deposed, into an oligarchy of 5,000 made up of the more prosperous citizens. Even the expanded oligarchy was anathema to the democrats of the fleet, however, and with the greatly increased prestige of the navy after the victories in the Hellespont and the destruction of the Spartan fleet at Cyzicus, the wishes of the sailors prevailed and democracy returned to Athens in June of 410.

The Spartan response to their losses at Cyzicus was an offer of peace, but Athens had no interest in their *status quo* proposal. Thus the war dragged on. Athens, even with the renewal of activity in her behalf by Alcibiades as general, was handicapped by lack of money, and it would be three years before Sparta could build another fleet, even with Persian aid. Alcibiades finally returned to Athens itself in 407, but when the Athenian fleet was dealt a defeat at Notium in early 406, followed by the loss of a stronghold on Chios to the Spartans under Lysander, people were more receptive to the complaints against him coming in from the allies and his own seamen. He was not elected as one of the generals for 406/5, so he fled Athens again, this time to his own personal redoubt in the Chersonnesus.

The year 406 also saw an Athenian victory as important for its aftermath at Athens as for its military implications. At the Arginusae Islands, off the Ionian coast, the Athenian fleet administered a stunning defeat to the Spartans, sinking 75 ships. The Athenians lost only 13 sunk and 13 disabled, but the personnel casualties were increased to the heavy number of 5,000, because a sudden gale prevented the rescue of the survivors from the sunken or disabled ships. Back at Athens, the council decided to arrest the generals; two fled and the others defended themselves before the assembly against the accusations of the ship captains. During the days of a festival intervening between this meeting of the assembly and the next, feeling against the generals was heightened by the awareness of those among the citizens who were mourning, and this feeling sharpened at the next meeting when many people appeared with shaven heads and other trappings of their grief. Emotions ran so high that a motion was presented to vote at once on the execution of the generals, taking all the cases together rather than judging guilt individually. There was even a man who came forward saying that he had only saved himself by floating on a meal-tub, and that those who were dying in the water asked him to report to the people and tell them that the generals had failed to pick up those who had served their country so well. The tumult was so wild that some of the Prytanes—executive officers—who had refused to put the question on the grounds that it was illegal, were cowed into submission. Socrates alone held out, stating that he would not act contrary to the law. Even a speech pointing out that one of the generals charged was in the water at the time failed to deflect the crowd, and the generals were condemned en masse and executed immediately. It was not only a *cause celebre* at the time, but a point of discussion for philosophers and a case to educate aspiring rhetoricians for centuries after.

The victory was Athens' last. The following summer Lysander, with a Spartan fleet newly reconstituted with Persian assistance, caught the Athenian fleet in the Hellespont, all but 20 ships drawn up on land at Aegospotami. The Athenians were taken completely by surprise, and the Spartans captured 160 ships in all. It was the end of the Athenian navy, and the end of Athens' ability to fight at sea. Of all the allies, only Samos remained faithful, and Lysander was able to expel the Athenians from all the places they occupied. He had executed some 3,000 Athenian prisoners at Aegospotami, and any others he took later he sent to Athens on pain of being killed otherwise, and the population of the city was thus swelled further as the Spartans settled down to besiege it late in 405. Sparta's terms for peace, which included the demolition of the long walls down to the port, were initially refused, although some of the citizens sent Theramenes off to Sparta to discuss peace. By the time Theramenes returned in the spring of 404, the situation was much more critical, and he with nine others was sent back to Sparta to get formal terms. At a meeting of the Peloponnesian allies, some argued for complete destruction of the city, and the slaughter of adult males and the enslavement of women and children, but Sparta held out for a more reasonable set of conditions. Athens could have peace if she would demolish the fortifications of the Piraeus and the long walls, release the empire, "letting the Greeks go free," take back her exiles, give up all territory but Attica and Salamis, and maintain a navy of no more than 12 ships. These terms the Athenians accepted, and Lysander arrived to accept the formal surrender. The war was over.

The end of the war was also the end—for a while—of the Athenian Empire, and also brought a short period of vicious oligarchy in Athens. The returning exiles brought with them the wealthy Critias and others who had participated in the oligarchy of the 400. With the support of Lysander the Spartan, moderate oligarchs like Theramenes gained the upper hand and set up an interim board of thirty. The Thirty, as they are called, took no steps toward the agreed broadening of participation, but secure with the requested Spartan garrison, they embarked on a reign of terror in which they executed not only their leading democratic opponents, but also any whose property they coveted. The citizen body was limited to the 3,000 of whose loyalty the Thirty felt confident, and even Theramenes, when he opposed the extremes, was struck from the list and executed. The events naturally led to opposition in force, and forces of democrats grew through the winter and by spring of 403 they were strong enough to control the Piraeus and wage a civil war against the forces of the Thirty in the city. Lysander arrived with a Spartan force to help the oligarchs, but luck was with the democrats, for the Spartan king Pausanias, a rival of Lysander, arrived with authority to supersede him. Pausanias' policy was one of reconciliation, and in the end, the democratic constitution was re-established, while the Thirty and their leading official partisan were allowed to withdraw to Eleusis. Athens remained weak for a long time, however, even though her democratic government prevailed, but her idea of rulership prevailed in other quarters. In the years after her defeat, other cities tried to exercise dominant power in one part or another of Greece and the Aegean, and the first half of the fourth century was a period of shifting alliances and balance of power politics.

As the century began the initiative lay with Sparta, and for the first time in her long history the great land power of the Peloponnesus tried her hand at an overseas empire. Opportunities were presented by confusion in the Persian domains of western Anatolia. Cyrus, the brother of King Artaxerxes, had died in his attempt to wrest the throne for himself, although his army of 10,000 Greek mercenaries had actually won the battle. Their victory and their success in winning their way back to the Aegean showed the qualities of Greek forces, and that may have encouraged Sparta to embark on war against Persia when the king ordered his governor, Tissaphernes, to move against the Greek cities of western Asia. Taking up the returned 10,000 mercenaries, the Spartan forces under a number of leaders were able to hold their own against the Persians in annual campaigns down to 394. Eventually, however, a coalition of Spartan enemies forced the abandonment of the overseas venture. Former allies, like the Boeotian League and Corinth, were joined by old enemies, Argos and even Athens, and so King Agesilaus had to bring his army back to Greece. In the spring of 394, the Spartans decisively defeated an allied force gathered in Corinthian territory, and then another major victory, won by Agesilaus on his way home, re-established Spartan supremacy on land.

The so-called Corinthian War dragged on for years, with Sparta's enemies supported in part by the same Persian treasury that had helped Sparta against Athens. The strange bedfellows of the alliance were primarily intent on preventing Spartan supremacy. By 388 it was clear that matters had reached a stalemate, and both sides were ready for peace. King Artaxerxes was also interested in peace, to end the interventions in Persian territory flowing from hostilities in Greece. In spring of 387 Artaxerxes issued a proposal for peace, on the terms that all the Greek states apart from three small islands subject to Athens were to be autonomous, and all the Greek cities in Asia were to be subject to Persia. All the Greeks except Thebes agreed, and even Thebes, though wanting to preserve her control over the small Boeotian cities, was forced to yield by the time all took the oaths in 386.

Sparta was now supreme in Greece, although it took Persian support to keep her so. Spartans now intervened freely in the domestic affairs of other cities in the name of the King's Peace, and ensured that their governments were friendly. Any opposition in the Peloponnesus was ruthlessly dealt with, and the congress of allies was reduced to rubber-stamp approval of Spartan proposals. By 379 all opposition there had been eliminated. In central Greece, where Sparta was at peace with Thebes, a Spartan commander named Phoebidas, on his way north on a campaign in 382, accepted the offer of some Theban traitors and seized the Cadmeia, as the Theban acropolis was called. The Spartans punished the highly improper action lightly by a fine, but accepted their good fortune by leaving their garrison in Thebes to control the city. Sparta was now really riding high. Although the Athenians were unfriendly, having accepted the refugees who had escaped from Thebes when Phoebidas seized the city, Athens was as isolated in central Greece as was Argos in the Peloponnesus. To the east, Sparta could count on the friendship of the Great King of Persia, and to the west she had managed to establish a good relationship with the only other great power in the Greek world, Dionysius of Syracuse. With no other Greek power in the Aegean with the strength to stand against her, Sparta seemed to have achieved what Athens had attempted: unchallenged hegemony of Greece, the ability to enforce her will on land and sea from Boeotia to the southern tip of the peninsula.

Sparta did not stay long unchallenged at the pinnacle of success reached in 379. In latter year, in fact, exiled opponents of the Spartans slipped back into Thebes, assassinated the governing officials, and with a force led by the Theban Epaminondas, forced the Spartan garrison to evacuate the city. The Athenians, who were sending a force to help, backed off when the Spartans showed their forces in central Greece, but Thebes held out nonetheless. Then the Spartan general Sphodrias made an attempt to seize the Piraeus, but failed, and the Athenians were enraged that the Spartan government did not punish this attack on a friendly state in time of peace. Subsequently, Athens supported Thebes in her war against Sparta. The struggle lasted four years, and occasioned the resurgence of the Boeotian League and a revival of

Athenian power, as Athens re-established her confederacy in a structure known today as the Second Athenian League. The Athenians began the diplomatic activity in the course of the early months of 377, and announced the terms of the new alliance in March. Any city not subject to Persia could become an ally of Athens, preserving its autonomy and with no payment of tribute, and with a guarantee that Athens would not impose a garrison. The structure was not unlike that of the Delian League of a century before, with a council made up of delegates from the allies, one vote to each member. The Athenian assembly had equal weight with the council of allies in setting policy, for no action could be undertaken without the agreement of both. Athens contributed money and ships, the council assessed contributions expected from each city, and administered the treasury of the alliance, kept separate from that of Athens. Although Athens was acknowledged as leader, or *hegemon,* of the alliance, and had executive powers usually exercised by Athenian generals, command was not exclusively an Athenian prerogative. The Athenians further, in order to reassure their allies, formally legislated against the acquisition of property in a member city either by Athens as a city or by her private citizens, and disavowed any claims to the property of any city in the alliance.

In developing these provisions, Athens was attempting to build an alliance structure without the features which had galled the cities of her earlier empire. When the Athenian political writer and rhetorician Isocrates later wrote criticisms of the manner in which Athens was dominating her allies in the second league, it was the treatment of the allies in the old imperial structure that he used as a parallel. At first, however, there seems to have been the intention to avoid those abuses, to encourage other cities to join. The alliance was clearly pointed against Sparta. The initial members made a list very reminiscent of the old league, and eventually there were 70 cities in all. The participation of Thebes, however, at the head of the soon reconstituted Boeotian League, was different, and it brought a great deal of strength in land forces. Athens and the alliance were free to throw all their resources into naval campaigns against Sparta, and accretions to the allied fleet and a series of successes brought dominance on both east and west coasts of Greece by 374. On land, the Thebans were able to keep the Spartans out of Boeotia in 376 and, on the offensive in 375, seemed about to dominate central Greece. However, when Thebes, with the new Boeotian League, subdued Athens' traditional friend Plataea and attacked Phocis, the Athenians were ready to see her successes stop. Accordingly, Athens sought an end to the war with Sparta, and in 374 concluded a peace on the terms of status quo—each side to keep the territories held at the time of the peace—and Sparta recognized the Athenian alliance as the body with which she signed the peace.

For the Athenians, the success was not enough. Within a year they were straining to finance a fleet in defense of a nascent democracy on the island of Zacynthus, they were accepting on the basis of sympolity—sharing of citizenship of two cities—refugees from Plataea, much to the anger of Thebes, and the allies were becoming doubtful of the wisdom of Athenian policies. By 372 Callistratus, the leading Athenian politician of the time, had persuaded the assembly to seek peace again, a circumstance that was opportune for the Persian King. Artaxerxes Memnon was still trying to quell a revolt in Egypt, and was interested in obtaining Greek help, at least in the form of mercenaries, and so he participated in a general conference held in Sparta in the summer of 371. Others besides the usual Greek city-states were represented, and in particular, Amyntas, King of Macedonia, was notable by his presence. Macedonia was interested in Persian attitudes toward the areas of the northern Aegean and was concerned about cities and districts adjacent to her own borders, so it was with Amyntas' consent that Athens obtained control of Amphipolis and the Chersonnesus when the dispositions of the peace were decided. Other terms focused on the independence of the Greek cities, in this second so-called "King's Peace." All garrisons were to be withdrawn from Greek cities, with supervisors appointed to ensure the removal. Any city violating the agreement was fair prey to any other signatory, and all were free, though not compelled, to aid any signatory attacked in violation of the peace. Sparta signed for the members of her alliance as well as for herself, while Athens signed alone, followed by her allies individually. Thebes signed, as a member of the Athenian alliance, but then, denied her request that she sign "for the Boeotians," so as to recognize her suzerainty of the Boeotian League, she withdrew from the peace, setting in motion a series of events of great consequence.

Thebes at this time was led by two outstanding military commanders, Epaminondas and Pelopidas. Both had led armies with great success as Thebes asserted her dominion over the rest of the Boeotians, and their presence among the Boeotarchs—the board of seven federal magistrates, three of whom were Thebans—was very influential in deciding league policy. Thebes could control the Boeotian League as much through the prestige of her two leaders as through her own near-majority of three votes of the seven in the league. Epaminondas had been one of the leaders who brought in forces at the time of the expulsion of the Spartans in 379, and Pelopidas had early established his reputation when, in 375, under his command the elite Sacred Band of 300 picked infantry routed a larger Spartan force.

Trusting in the quality of his forces, Epaminondas had the Theban delegates, whom he led, ask to have the name of Thebes removed from the list of signatories to the peace of 371. This accomplished, Thebes was outside the agreement, but only the Spartans were at the time inclined to do anything about it. Seizing on the chance circumstance that one of their kings, Cleombrotus, happened to be in Phocis with an army at the time of the signing of the peace, the Spartan assembly ordered him to attack Thebes immediately unless she agreed to disband the Boeotian League. Thebes, of course, would not agree to this, mustered an army only two-thirds the size of Cleombrotus' force, and faced the Spartans at Leuctra, about ten miles from Thebes. Epaminondas prepared for a pitched battle in the open—testing Theban ability to fight Spartans on the Spartan soldier's own terms—using the Sacred Band under Pelopidas. The Spartans were demolished, with Cleombrotus wounded mortally and his section of the line overwhelmed by the Sacred Band, and the whole right wing crushed by the troops under Epaminondas' command. Pressed by their allies, the Spartiates who had survived concluded a truce to recover their dead; on the way back to the Peloponnesus they met a second force, sent out at the news of the defeat, and reported the disaster graphically enough to deter the general from proceeding. The Spartan army returned and disbanded. Epaminondas and Pelopidas had done what none thought possible—defeat a larger number of Spartans in a set battle—and had ended Spartan pursuit of hegemony in Greece.

For the next 25 years, central Greece was the scene of continual and intensive fighting, as Thebes sought Sparta's old position and then Phocis tried to control her immediate area. Alliances were made and changed, citizens expelled and massacred fellow citizens, any number of treaties were struck and then broken. The first ten years of the period saw the supremacy of Thebes, not only in central Greece but in the Peloponnesus as well, and after that period came Athens' attempt to dominate her league again, ended only by a war with the allies that concluded in her abandoning the effort in 355. In central Greece, a long war centered on the Phocian attempt to control the Delphian sanctuary, an exhausting conflict begun in 355 with a short period of surprising success for the small Phocian federation, but which lasted until 346 and ultimately involved most of the Greek states. All this debilitating conflict was different from the disputes of earlier times because there was no consistency of alliances or of policy, and there were many causes behind it. Fear was an important ingredient—fear by each city or group that another city or league would become so powerful as to destroy autonomy. Another factor was ambition, both that of whole cities for power and hegemony, and that of individual citizens for political dominance. Financial considerations intruded as well, driving leaders and citizens in financial crises into actions undermining broader policy activity. And just plain human contrariness played its usual detrimental role, while bad luck often eliminated just the leaders who might have exercised beneficial influences on their societies.

Two such leaders were Epaminondas and Pelopidas. So long as they were both alive, Thebes maintained her military supremacy, although this entailed frequent war. Furthermore, Epaminondas, at least, seemed to be developing policy which, had he been able to implement it for the long run, might have stabilized power in Theban hands. Initially, when Thebes had so roundly defeated Sparta at Leuctra, Athens threw her support to Sparta out of fear of growing Theban strength, while Thebes was able to take advantage of anti-Spartan sentiment in the cities of Arcadia. There, a federal league developed, led mainly by the people of Mantinea, and supported by Thebes. Epaminondas conducted a number of campaigns in the Peloponnesus in this period, founded the city of Megalopolis in 369/8, and, after detaching Messenia from Sparta, also built Messene, with its great fortifications of enormous scope. Epaminondas was able to develop a Theban-Argive-Arcadian entente against which Sparta was able to do little, and Pelopidas gained the support of the Persian king. This time, however, the peace that Artaxerxes offered to impose in 366 was so favorable to the Thebans that her enemies immediately rejected it. By and large, Epaminondas' diplomatic initiatives avoided the extremes of domestic conflict so often associated with shifting alliances, so that when, for example, he was able to bring Sicyon over to the Theban side, the governing oligarchy did not change, and when he succeeded in bringing the Achaean League into the Boeotian group, the government and structure of that league remained the same. His arrangements did not always succeed, for Sicyon became a scene of strife after one of the oligarchs set himself up as tyrant, and when the Boeotians themselves changed the arrangements of Epaminondas in Achaea, the Arcadian League broke with Boeotia and rejoined Sparta. As to Pelopidas, he died in battle in Thessaly in 364, winning a great victory over the tyrant Alexander of Pherae in Thessaly.

In 363 and 362 Thebes' conflict with Athens and Sparta grew in intensity. In summer of 363, Epaminondas, with the newly expanded Boeotian fleet, cruised the north of the Aegean, and the Athenians did not challenge him. In the same year Boeotian diplomacy in the Peloponnesus collapsed, with the Arcadian League dividing in support of either Sparta or Thebes, and Epaminondas announced that he would march on Arcadia to enforce control. Mantinea, inclining toward Sparta, asked for help there and from Athens, Elis and Achaea, while Tegea, Megalopolis and other smaller Arcadian centers held to the Boeotian alliance. Epaminondas marched into the Peloponnesus in 362, and after some desultory fighting, in which he very nearly captured

Sparta and was only repulsed after fighting in the streets of the city itself, the two sides faced each other outside the city of Mantinea. Again a Theban victory was lost by the death of a leader. In a hard fought battle, which Epaminondas' generalship was winning for Thebes, the news of the general's death came just as his forces were breaking the enemy ranks. The advance halted, and the defeated enemy was able to escape and regroup. The outcome of the battle was a standstill, for nothing had been decided, and Xenophon, who ended his *History of Greece* with the Battle of Mantinea remarked that after this battle, which everybody expected to decide the future of Greece, "there was even greater confusion and uncertainty among the Greek cities."

That uncertainty affected the Athenian League, the one remaining powerful group. Even before the battle of Mantinea there had been some difficulties in the alliance. In 365 the Athenian general Timotheus was sent across the Aegean with 30 ships and a sizable force of mercenaries to support Ariobarzanes, a Persian governor in revolt from his king, but Timotheus chose to attack Samos, then held by a Persian loyalist. The Athenian victory after a ten-month siege was followed by the establishment of Athenian military settlers, or cleruchs, on the island, and Timotheus did the same after his capture of Sestos and Crithote later that year and Potidaea in 364. This was clearly a violation of the decree of 377, even if the cities affected were not members of the alliance when the cleruchs were installed, and the action signalled a return to the system of the fifth century.

After the Battle of Mantinea, an abortive attempt to create a general league of Greeks to maintain the peace failed to restrain Athens from the pursuit of her own interests and she mixed into Macedonian and Thracian dynastic quarrels. So far as Persia was concerned, after the death of Artaxerxes Memnon in 359/8 and the accession of Artaxerxes Ochus, there were some problems. Athens maintained a friendship with the rebellious Ariobarzanes, while some of her allies had close ties with the Persian loyalist Mausollus, governor of Caria. Finally in 357, the structure broke down. Athens was supporting the Euboeans, who had revolted from Boeotian leadership, had exchanged Amphipolis for Pydna under a secret agreement with Macedonia, and had taken over the Greek cities in the Chersonnesus under terms of a revenue sharing agreement with the mercenary captains serving the kings of Thrace. At this point, the close relationship of some of the Aegean allies with Mausollus of Caria paid off for the Persians, for Cos, Rhodes and Chios revolted from the alliance, beginning the so-called "Social" War, or War of the Allies. In the next two years, Athens failed in her actions in the Aegean, in her political manoeuvres calculated to push Artaxerxes into calling off Mausollus, but the king reacted to Athenian support of the rebel Ariobarzanes by demanding and obtaining Athenian withdrawal from Asia. Athens could no longer hope to subdue the rebel allies, and in 355 she made peace by recognizing their independence. The war was over, and so was the hope for a second empire, as only Euboea, the Cyclades and a few cities in the north remained as allies, while in Greece itself, only Sparta, beleaguered by Messenia and Arcadia, and Phocis were friendly.

Phocis would be of little help, for she was immediately faced in 355 with the Sacred War, which even in her episode of strength took all her resources. In 356, Thebes demanded that Sparta and Philomelus of Phocis pay the fines imposed for the Spartan seizure of the acropolis of Thebes and Philomelus' cultivation of sacred land. Thebes used the Delphic Amphictyonic Council as agent of the demand. The Phocians supported Philomelus, elected him sole general and provided him with 5,000 mercenary soldiers to help his occupation of the Delphic sanctuary. By October of 355 Thebes had piloted through the Amphictyonic Council a formal declaration of a "Sacred War" on behalf of Delphian Apollo. Philomelus immediately began using the temple treasury to hire 10,000 more mercenaries, and by spring of 354 had defeated the combined armies of Boeotia and Locris in one battle, and an army from Thessaly in a second. The little Phocian federation had defeated the prestigious Theban army with a force of hired troops. Phocis also had the advantage of the alliance of Sparta and Athens, who had supported her primarily out of hostility to Thebes.

The Sacred War was a wearing conflict. It cost the Phocians a succession of leaders and it was not resolved until the intervention of King Philip II of Macedonia. Philip was involved as early as 353, but it was not until a Macedonian conflict with Athens ended in peace in 346 that he was free to deal with the Sacred War. Once he could turn his forces against the Phocians they very quickly capitulated. The Sacred War was over, and the Athenians, who had refused to send forces with Philip against the Phocians, awaited his dispositions nervously, for he could now march into Attica with the Boeotians at his side. His settlement was reasonable, for instead of the massacre the Thebans proposed for the Phocians, Philip limited the penalty to an annual indemnity of 60 talents, the splitting of the Phocian towns into villages and the transfer of Phocis' two votes on the Amphictyonic Council to himself. The Macedonian king also received Athens' privilege of priority in consulting the Delphic Oracle, and was elected president of the coming Pythian Games. He supervised an agreement of the Amphictyonic Council for peace among its members, imposed no penalties on Athens, and after presiding at the games of September, 346, returned to Macedonia, leaving central Greece in peace and with some hope for stability.

Philip did not come out of nowhere. He had been king in Macedonia since 359, and his decade and a half of rule had seen him build Macedonia from a weak and divided kingdom to the most powerful political entity in Greece. While Athens had been building her second league, the imperial city could be a match for him, but once the league was lost in the mid 350's, she was hard put to impede Philip's expansion of his domains. Opposition to Philip was the political principle of Demosthenes, one of the leading Athenian politicians. We still have many of his impassioned speeches, calling on the Athenians to gather allies and forces against Philip, as the Macedonian king's ships moved freely throughout the Aegean, raided Athenian allies and even landed troops at Marathon on one occasion. The Athenians supported Philip's enemies in Chalcidice, but even with Athenian help the cities were unable to stem the Macedonian advance. After the peace of 346, Athens continued to oppose Philip diplomatically, and in 341 Athenian forces in the northern Aegean showed clear hostility to Philip, and Demosthenes delivered his third *Philippic*, or oration against the king, making it clear that he planned to commit Athens to open war with the Macedonians.

That war finally came in 340. The Athenians, without an empire, had to have support, and they followed Demosthenes' policies into a congress of Greek cities with an agreement to pool resources for a war against Philip. By this time, the imperial ambitions which had kept many cities militarily and politically active had passed away, and the initiative lay outside the orbit of the cities. Philip attacked cities controlling the Bosphorus, laying siege to Perinthus and the Athenian ally Byzantium. By 339, jockeying at the spring meeting of the council of the Amphictyonic League of Delphi had produced quarrels, riots, and ultimately, the declaration of another Sacred War, this time against the Locrians of Amphissa for sacrilege in cultivating sacred land and levying tolls at the harbor of Delphi. Philip, who had been involved in the decision for the war, accepted the council's invitation to lead the League's forces, and in late 339 marched south unexpectedly to Elatea, easily threatening Boeotia and only two days' march from Athens. During the winter, Philip and his enemies operated defensively in military matters and concentrated on diplomatic activity. Demosthenes led the Athenians in expanding the Boeotian-Athenian alliance and held the Athenians and Boeotians firm against Phlip's peace overtures. Then, in midsummer of 338, Philip moved his army into Boeotia and concentrated his forces at Chaeronea. There he faced a large Greek force in a strong position, experienced Theban troops and, a rare sight now, Athenian citizen-soldiers, inexperienced but standing together with Thebans instead of sending mercenaries. Philip's rout of the Greek force, a victory in which his son Alexander took part, was complete, with the Theban Sacred Band annihilated and the rest of the Greek force allowed to flee, unpursued. Thebes immediately surrendered, and Philip then disbanded the Boeotian League, set up an oligarchy in the city, and installed a Macedonian garrison. He sold any unransomed prisoners of war into slavery, and forced relatives to buy back the Theban dead. Athens was treated much more gently, for, after deposing the leaders of the faction intending to defend the city to the last, the Athenians treated with Philip and obtained peace terms. Athens agreed to disband her alliance, and Philip undertook not to send any troops into Attica. Athens held on to a few island cities, her prisoners of war were returned without ransom, and the ashes of her dead were escorted back to the city by a guard of honor led by Alexander. The war was over and, probably more obviously to us than the Greeks, so too was the era in which the city states, alone or in combination, could hope to dominate the affairs of Greece.

For the leading cities, all the attempts to dominate Greece had failed. The pursuit of domination also prevented a broad union of cities of the sort that had been achieved in some districts. For 150 years the major cities saw control of others as the route to self-protection, and the idea of power over others was the prevailing objective of external activity. Repeatedly, in any alliance, the impulse to cooperate for common goals stirred in the leader the ambition to control the rest, and the worst offender in this regard, Athens, saw that as the natural human pattern. The drive for power, as Thucydides observed, could lead to the worst displays of violence and brutality. When the Athenians defeated the Melians and slaughtered the males and enslaved the women and children, they perpetrated an act which even the strongest apologists for the Athenians deplore as an excess caused by war. They were, however, doing no more than they had initially voted in the plan to do the same to Mytilene much earlier in the war, and the focus Thucydides gives to these two episodes ensures our attention to the viciousness which empire can produce.

The sense of community existing among Greeks was always secondary to the particular ambition of each city, and cooperation among major imperial cities came only when one seemed so powerful as to threaten the others. Furthermore, the objective of inter-city power always expressed itself in terms of division of the *status quo*. That is, the aspiring imperial city would take from others or take over others, rather than find or create new sources of power, and not even the Athenian colonies planted as military outposts could be seen as generating Athenian power from new bases.

The Greek cities were a misunderstood ideal for the patriots of the late mediaeval and early renaissance north Italian cities. The imperialism of the Greek cities should also never be confused with the imperialism of Europe in the eighteenth and nineteenth centuries. The European venture, which was exploratory and commercial, carried Europeans into areas they thought of as backward and benighted, so that Kipling's "white man's burden" of civilizing the distant parts of the world was an attractive and believable self-deception. Greek imperialism never reached to the barbarian world to build Greek power on the production of weaker peoples. First, however "barbarian" non-Greeks might have been, they were not weaker, at least not weaker than the cities. Second, the imperial period began with great disproportions in power among the Greek cities, and there was always the inducement to pile up power by an accumulation of weaker fellow-Greek cities. Imperialism in Greece was not, in other words, adventure or expansion into new realms. Rather, it was the pure exercise of power by stronger over weaker, and it was never so well defined as it was by the Athenians themselves.

5 Civic Values

It is easy to see that when Greek cities looked outward and pursued objectives, they aimed either at mastery of others or at least protection for themselves against domination by others. Each city also had internal goals as well, goals that they sought to achieve within the walls, within their own territories and for their own citizens. These are not so easy for us to perceive, so distant in time as we are from them. They also differed from city to city, and with the paucity of information available to us, it is rare that we can make them out in places like Thebes or the island cities or the small cities of Phocis and elsewhere. Even in Athens and Sparta they are obscure because they were not always explicit to the citizens who acted to obtain them. Furthermore, the goals, or the means to reach them, may not have all been agreed upon by all elements of the citizenry, and political disagreement and even violent disorder may obscure or distort the nature of the goals which gave them rise. Finally, it is almost exclusively Athens for which we have information, and it is unwise to extrapolate too extensively from the Athenian evidence to the rest of Greece.

One major objective which we find in Athens seems, however, to have been common to all Greeks. The goal of social and economic stability, which was presumed as the desirable end of policy, is the basis of almost all political and economic thought and all writing of history. For us in the late twentieth century, thinking that we are turning away from from an ideology of expansionism, the goal of stability seems a good one at first glance, but a short examination of our real ambitions and values reveals how different we are from the Greeks.

A fundamental value of our culture is improvement. While we may debate whether bigger or smaller is better, we tacitly agree that we aim at better. We want better health care, better eduction, better music—whatever one may name. And we admire the new, aiming to promote our professors on the basis of their new ideas, not their faithfulness to what has been demonstrated to be good and reliable. Painters who are inspired to emulate their forerunners are "derivative" and authors who recall earlier literature are usually not published. We value invention and novelty, and the word "new" carries with it a sense of affirmation and desirability.

Not so among the Greeks. The Greek word "*neoterizein*," literally meaning "to do new things," used in political or historical writing, carries the sense of "engage in revolution." When Thucydides wrote the account of the Spartan hesitation to use the Athenian troops who had come to help them against the helots, the word Thucydides uses to describe what the Spartans feared of the Athenians is "*neoterizein*." Newness, in other words, was not a good thing in itself, and may be said usually to have had a negative sense if otherwise unqualified.

The idea that political and social change were undesirable comes through most clearly in the philosophers. Both Plato and Aristotle propose a fixed maximum number for a city, imposing a numerical stability as part of the ideal. Aristotle's *Politics* investigates the causes of change in constitution, as though aiming at controlling change through understanding it. Although Aristotle does have an idea of some constitutions being better than others, it is "destabilization" which is most to be avoided, and "bad" constitutions are undesirable for the most part because they are prone to being overthrown. There is certainly no idea that a given constitution, even a good one, can be continually refined and improved, becoming better than it was before by reform and change. Rather, the idea is that each type of constitution carries the seeds of its own dissolution and that the process of constitutional history is one of cyclical change. The concept is based, essentially, on the notion of a natural order, in which each political institution evolves according to its inherent form. This notion of a natural order and inherent form or nature comes to grief, even in Aristotle's own calculations, when he tries to deal with slavery. There, while proposing the idea that some people are naturally suited for slavery, he faces the problem and has no solution to the question of free citizens of Greek cities who happen to become slaves in war. He does not, however, advocate changing the established rules that allow them to be enslaved.

Plato's concept of an ideal state calls for a highly controlled society, based on the hypothesis that if it were possible to achieve a harmony of the elements in society, controlling the lesser elements by the wiser would maintain the balance. Again, a stable relationship is the goal, and, although Plato allows for the training of women and the offspring of the lesser classes with the necessary talents, he has no room for a notion that the inherently lower elements could be improved.

There is also nothing parallel to the modern idea of economic advancement, either personal or for the society at large. Aristotle will say that society is best when most citizens are neither very rich nor very poor, but his approach to trade shows that his fundamental assumptions disallow profit in exchange, as an unnatural expansion of value. When goods are exchanged for other goods or money, he argues, the values of property exchanged should be equal. The effect of unequal exchange will be destabilizing, and that, on his assumptions, is undesirable. This idea of Aristotle's is very deep-seated, not only in his writing but in society generally. Aristotle knew of the Spartan discouragement of trade, and the relatively long stability of Spartan government and society would have seemed to him a validation of Spartan customs in this regard.

The Spartans not only had the usual ancient disrespect for trade, they had unusual laws aimed at discouraging economic inequality among the citizens. Not only were jewelry and precious metals forbidden, citizens' possessions were limited to necessities. Even the kinds of coins used by other Greek cities were excluded from Spartan life. Heavy, awkward iron spits made up the currency, precluding an active commercial life and certainly discouraging hoarding or saving. In fact, the legislation peculiar to Sparta shows clearly that the Spartan ethos was not only hostile to change but also strongly devoted to the goal of equality among the citizens. The aim, as other Greeks understood it, was the creation of a highly effective, mutually committed body of soldiers, and that goal seems to have been achieved well before the Persian Wars. Spartan infantry was universally regarded as superior until it was defeated in 371 by the elite standing army which was Thebes' Sacred Band. Although it is generally agreed by modern historians that the Spartans were driven to these devices by the need of the small number of Spartiates to hold down the superior numbers of helots and Messenians, there was more involved than the mere pressure of enemy numbers. At work also was the basic desire to keep their society unchanged, even in numbers, with a reluctance to expand citizenship in the society even to the people of the free Laconian communities around them. The prevailing attitudes in Spartan society militated against the kind of citizenship expansion experienced at Athens or a commercial and economic expansion which would permit a paid army, so that the peculiar Spartan military egalitarianism was driven by Spartan assumptions about the good society and the goals of society.

Completely different were the attitudes at Athens. Why they should have been different is difficult, perhaps impossible to say, but the reason may go back to the experience of the union of Attica. That itself, and the willingness to allow the distant communities to share the citizenship of the central city, may have arisen from a feeling of community holding out against the wave of Dorian-dialect speakers lapping at the borders. In any case, the union must have taught Athenians by success, for there were periodic expansions of citizenship, and quite a different attitude towards the relationships among groups of citizens. By the time of the poetry of Solon, Athenians were dealing with the idea that some citizens were wealthier than others and would remain so, and they accepted the notion that having and gaining wealth was a good thing. The Solonian reforms also show the acceptance of the notion that the body politic legitimately interfered with the activities of citizens in the cause of protecting the community against adverse affects of private activity. Thus the law banned export of grain and basic foodstuffs, required that citizens participate in political affairs, and limited many activities in the quest for a stable and peaceful relationship among the citizens. The pursuit of gain was acceptable, for Solon's poetic homily acknowledges that his "desire is to have wealth, but not to have it unjustly."

Athens was unusual in the general acceptance of the idea that commercial activity was suitable to society and its leaders. The Alcmaeonid family, prominent in Athenian politics for at least two centuries, was commercially oriented as well as land wealthy, and one of the early stories about them has them involved in the temple rebuilding at Delphi on a contract basis. The state-owned silver mines at Laurium, which became an important political issue at the beginning of the fifth century, were let out to private entrepreneurs for exploitation, and as the Athenian empire expanded and the military establishment consumed more and more resources, those resources and the profits from their manipulation passed through the hands of private contractors. Non-military spending like temple rebuilding on the acropolis, along with the shipbuilding, armoring, equipping and provisioning fleets and land contingents, went through the accounts of private firms. The empire brought in the money needed to maintain it, and tradesmen earned enough from the "military-industrial complex" to elevate themselves to political prominence, or at least to have the time for political activity. Also exceptional, however, is that at Athens non-noble wealthy tradesmen were able to take over the political process. Cleon, much derided by conservatives, was a wealthy tanner. More unusual, the honest politician Cleophon died poor. Demosthenes, in the next century, came from a family of wealth made in sword manufacturing, and would have inherited the factory if his guardians had not cheated him.

The most explicit statement of Athenian ideals and goals comes in Thucydides' rendering of Pericles' funeral oration in 429, a speech which makes much of the ideal that citizens are not preferred to office for their wealth or family, but for their abilities. Pericles is made to say that the Athenians love beauty and philosophy, enjoy life with festivals and sacrifices and have a comfortable private life. They are courageous and capable in war without dedicating their lives to military training. They live in an open city, without excluding people for security purposes, and Athenian citizens are expected to take full part in public discussions of policy and do not think that full debate is an impediment to action. All of this describes Athenian habits in the most positive manner, and is presented to point up the differences between life at Athens and that at Sparta, but the underlying themes show something of the accepted civic goals of the Athenians. Thucydides makes them out to regard what we would call "culture" as a good thing, and the history of the activity in Athens before the outbreak of war shows a legitimacy to this. A good deal of public, even if league money, was spent on ornamentation, and although this was done in connection with religion and divine service, Thucydides' text suggests that it was carried out with a particular regard for artistic effects. It is without doubt the culture-consciousness of the Athenians that led to the development of Athenian tragedy, for the support of the plays had to come out of the funds provided by wealthy Athenians as part of their expected contribution to public activities.

The promotion of culture fitted with the advocacy of public awareness of political activity. In the fifth century, few cities besides Athens erected inscriptions recording decisions and public activity, and none did so in such profusion. However many Athenians or visitors to Athens were thought to have the ability to read, the assembly often voted to record its decisions in stone, and the revenues from the league were carved on stone blocks set up for all to see. The openness of which Pericles boasts was an encouragement to foreigners to visit, and the advocacy of public debate in the assembly created a market for purveyors of education, moral and rhetorical, so that late fifth-century Athens was a profitable base for foreign teachers. Access to them was open to any who would pay, and tradesmen as well as nobles sent their sons to the teachers to learn the skills that would make them successful in public life.

Private goals thus meshed with public. As Pericles claimed that no one was kept in obscurity because of poverty, those who could manage to do so, tried to equip themselves to live in the limelight. Public notice and public service were the criteria of worth, and Athenians with resources pursued those feelings of self-worth which came from public prominence. This pursuit of prestige could generate the weaknesses of the democracy which its aristocratic critics deplored, when they claimed that the politicians, seeking to hold on to status and power, pandered to the desires of the ignorant multitude in the assembly. There is no evidence that the multitude was, in fact, so ignorant, and even Thucydides has Pericles state that Athenians thought it was everyone's responsibity to be informed on public affairs. However, the internal political contests were waged with a ferocity that could be damaging. The recall of Alcibiades from Sicily was one such instance, and Alcibiades' response, indeed Alcibiades himself, were examples of political ambition gone wrong.

The Athenian desire to have the city and its activities run by the citizenry as a whole survived the fifth century, once the tyranny of the thirty had been overthrown and the democracy had returned. Aristotle's account of the constitution in his day, the mid fourth century, shows the institutional structure of the democratic constitution, with its councils, assemblies, and boards and commissions to oversee the running of the myriad activities of public works and administration of the city and the port. By Aristotle's time, also, the Athenian habit of inscribing public actions on stone had spread broadly, and the fourth century is the point at which we begin to see into other cities and into the private activities of their citizens. Those cities operating democracies of some form show some characteristics like those of Athens. The fourth century does, however, seem to experience some breakdown in civic dedication. The fact that the appearance of Athenian citizen-soldiers in the line at the Battle of Chaeronea in 338 was so noteworthy is significant in itself. Athens, like other cities, had fallen into the pattern of using mercenaries in her wars.

The emergence of mercenaries in the fourth century is an important phenomenon, and it tells a lot about civic goals and values. While the pursuit of power abroad still played a part in the politics of cities, individual citizens were less willing to commit themselves personally to the goal. The great increase of commercial activity in most of Greece after the fifth century meant a readier availability of cash for paid troops, and the pouring of Persian gold into Greece during the Peloponnesian War and after contributed to the money supply. Although the continual warfare among the major cities and their allies was debilitating for agriculture, it had little effect on mercantile capital. Indeed, since war preparations were carried on by private entrepreneurs for the most part, and there were frequent infusions of Persian money, we may suppose that for all the damage of war, there was a net rise in available capital during the fourth century. Money could certainly be made. A slave named Pasion went to work in an Athenian bank at the end of the fifth century. By the time he died around 370, he had his own bank and a shield workshop, had worked his way up to freedman and then citizenship status, and was the wealthiest banker and manufacturer in the city.

More important than all of this, Athens placed a value on the wellbeing of its citizens that is difficult to document elsewhere. Initially, this was the characteristic Greek idea that all members of a society deserved to share in the benefits coming to the group. As early as the sixth century there was an idea that the general populace had some rights as against the wealthy leaders, for Solon's poetry boasts that he dealt with an even hand, and neither gave the people more than they deserved nor subjected them to restraint. The history of the tyranny of Pisistratus seems clearly related to the existence of power in the hands of the poorer classes, for the tyrant is consistently reported as having their support in the latter part of his tenure. The sharing of public benefits also tells in the treatment of surpluses from the silver mines of Laurium. Until the discovery of the rich vein at the beginning of the fifth century, surpluses were simply shared out among the citizens, as in most Greek cities, and that would have been the treatment of the great increase if Themistocles had not succeeded in changing the pattern.

In the fifth century, however, as the poorer citizens benefited increasingly from the revenues of empire, the practice of providing income to citizens out of public funds became institutionalized. There was payment for service in public office and in the law courts. Pay for military service was instituted, and even though the levels were low, the long tours of duty in the fleet meant that the families of the sailors probably received the bulk of their income from the city. Both ancient and modern writers see this as the major motivation of the sailors' loyalty to the democracy. If this was seen as attracting people to fulfil their roles as participating citizens, it also had the objective of providing financial support to the poorer among them. That objective was approached more closely by the notable *diobelia*, or two-obol payment, a small sum paid on a daily basis to needy citizens. Again, that was good or bad according to how one looks at it: aristocrats and conservatives deplored it as political pandering to the masses, but it can be seen as a reasonable extension of payment as benefit rather than service. In the first decade of the fourth century, the practice of pay for public activity was extended to attendance at the assembly, and these policies continued even in Athens' financial straits later in the century. Ultimately, the practice of pay was an important means to the Athenian goal of providing economically for citizens, and a significant aspect of the democracy at Athens. It is especially important in view of the fact that Athens continued to rely on the wealthier citizens fulfilling liturgies—the furnishing of services or goods to the city at the citizen's own cost—to provide most of the city's requirements.

The increasing democratization of Athens came with another shift in values. From earliest times, the dominant values in Greek society were the aristocratic and personal which emerge as early as the Homeric epics. In neither *Iliad* nor *Odyssey* are there any important actors but kings, princes and nobles. A lowly commoner, Thersites, who expresses his opinion in favor of abandoning the war in the *Iliad*, is rudely beaten for speaking out of turn. Odysseus' servants show him the proper respect due from inferiors. The virtues of Achilles are the virtues of a young noble: courage, superior strength and martial ability, self confidence. The culture of the world of the *Iliad*, a so-called shame culture in which morality and custom is enforced by external marks of approval rather than personal psychological feelings, is an aristocratic culture in all its aspects. Even war is aristocratic in its character. The warriors do not lead and manoeuvre bodies of men, and we have no idea what it is that Achilles' myrmidons do or what he has to do with them. The warriors ride out to combat in chariots, meet their noble peers on the enemy side, and demonstrate their individual superiority in personal combat. It is war like the single combat of World War I fighter pilots, an aristocratic game in which Baron Von Richthofen was perhaps the most suitable player.

The ambience of the *Iliad* remained prominent in Greek literature and in Greek ideas, for the *Iliad* was the single most quoted work of Greek literature, and as the papyri of later time show, there were more copies of it than any other work. So the values of the *Iliad* remained influential. The self-willed Achilles, with his insistence on attempting to carve out of an uncaring or hostile universe a life-style and life-principle which would bring him happiness, or at least satisfaction, remained a figure comprehensible to all Greeks. He was the ideal for Alexander the Great. However, times changed, and brought challenges to the dominant aristocratic ideas. In the eighth and seventh centuries there were some demurrers to the prevailing ethos. In Boeotia, Hesiod expressed the sentiments of farming labor, even if he was not the poor peasant he makes himself out. There is an affirmation of hard work, even if not pleasure in it. Hesiod attacks at least some leaders for crooked judgements. Later, from across the Aegean, came a most un-aristocratic sentiment in a poem of Archilochus. Writing about fleeing battle, which surely Achilles would never have done, Archilochus dismisses the fact that he has lost his shield by remarking that he can get another one. This is certainly the reverse of the Spartan mother's injunction to her son to come home with his shield or on it.

The first real break from the aristocratic ethos which we can observe clearly is that associated with Solon. The legislation as a whole makes a shift from an aristocracy of class to an aristocracy of wealth. At Athens the class of citizens known as eupatrids, "well-born," seems to have been in control of what there was of government. Undoubtedly, most social issues were decided within families, although there were, by the sixth century, some inter-family institutions like the court of the areopagus and the magistracies, or *archontes*. Solon, or the sixth-century reforms associated with his name, gave membership in these institutions to the members of the wealthiest of four classes based on property qualifications, thus opening them to non-eupatrids of wealth and excluding eupatrids who did not qualify by property. The *boulé,* which now came to exist, prepared business for the assembly, and its membership, perhaps elected, was neither eupatrid nor even wealth-determined. Finally, the Solonian reforms undercut eupatrid control over public affairs in other ways. By establishing a *boulé* to provide business for the citizen assembly, the reforms took the assembly away from domination by the areopagus, which had been entirely eupatrid and was still probably primarily so by the wealth qualification. Then, the provision of appeal to the courts, on which even the poorest citizens could serve, gave some control over magistrates.

It is only at Athens that we can see evidence of formal constitutional weakening of aristocratic control, and even there, the institutions of property qualification for certain offices meant that the aristocrats would still retain the power of their wealth. Elsewhere, sixth-century poetry gives us some insight into what was happening. At Megara, Theognis complains that "money mingles family" deploring the phenomenon of the non-noble new rich demanding and getting more power, while at Mytilene, in the northeast Aegean, Alcaeus writes that "money is the man, and no poor man is noble or good." Thucydides, writing a century later, points to growing wealth in Greece when he notes that tyrannies arose when Greece became more prosperous. Although the history of the Alcmaeonid family shows that aristocrats could tap new potentials for money-making, it seems to be the case that this new wealth was not always in the hands of traditional aristocrats. Athens may have been the earliest and most extreme in shifting to a wealth standard, but eventually, many cities shared her experience.

Boeotia's Pindar, writing in the early fifth century, expresses the nature of the noble ideal clearly, and the scope of his poetry illustrates its prevalence and pervasiveness. The great majority of his surviving poems are praises of victors in games and contests, choral hymns describing their abilities and accomplishments. They celebrate aristocratic virtues like skill and honor, and were written for patrons all over the Greek world. Pindar was especially popular with the Syracusan tyrant Hieron and other Sicilian patrons. The world of contests, patrons and poetic praise was by no means unique to Pindar. Bacchylides, of Iulis on the island of Ceos, and his uncle Simonides among their work provided victory odes for patrons, although we do not have anything like the body of extant work we have for Pindar. Again, a wide range of patrons shows the inter-city quality both of the contests and of the practice of patronage and honor.

In the fifth century, aristocrats were still firmly entrenched in power in most cities, even if they had no longer the technical constitutional supremacy which they had held in earlier centuries. At Athens, where we can see developments best, all through the Persian Wars and well past the middle of the fifth century the leaders were all aristocrats, and most, if not all, members of the early eupatrid families. Even after Pericles, when finally non-noble *nouveaux-riches* like Cleon came to the fore, the aristocrats stayed in the game in the careers of Nicias, Alcibiades and the notorious Critias. The fourth century, however, moved more and more non-nobles to the fore. Although aristocrats of talent like Timotheus could still play major roles, the political and military scenes were dominated by people of non-noble, and often quite obscure or humble origins, men like Demosthenes and his rival Aeschines, or the general Iphicrates or the financier Callistratus. Outside Athens, the fourth-century move to democracy in many cities suggests some reduction in the political power of aristocracies, although again, the paucity of detailed information in most places leaves uncertainty. At Thebes, for example, Epaminondas was an aristocrat, although his father was not wealthy, and Pelopidas was of good family, but he was a member of the democratic faction in opposition to the oligarchs and Spartan control. At Sparta, the fourth century saw a shift away from the traditionally austere habits of the small elite group of Sparta citizens, as the Spartan community, plunged into the world of international diplomacy and finance by the relationship with the Persians in the Peloponnesian War, adapted to a monetary economy, the use of gold and silver, and the emergence of a wealthy class. The tyranny of Syracuse, which emulated the aristocratic values of the Aegean Greeks at the time of Pindar, gave way to democracy in the fifth century, but reverted to tyranny in the fourth. The democratic constitutions installed there and elsewhere in Sicily by the Corinthian general Timoleon were short-lived, as tyrants emerged again in some cities and at Syracuse an oligarchy held power, and later, the adventurer Agathocles rode to power on a wave of anti-aristocratic sentiment.

As a general phenomenon, then, the influence of aristocracies on civic policies declined in the Greek world in the century and a half after the Persian Wars, although at a different pace and to a different extent in the various cities. Correspondingly, the highly elitist values characteristic of aristocracies seem to have deteriorated, supplanted by a much greater respect for wealth and its comforts. Certainly this is our explanation of the decline in the Athenian citizen army, and the reliance on mercenary forces in many cities. The comedies of Menander, which we now have better represented by the papyrus texts from Egypt, show in dramatic form what might be called middle-class values. The purveying of education in formal schools rather than in the households of the rich may also be part of this shift as it is traceable at Athens. The biographies of the famous philosophers at Athens are instructive. Only Plato was an aristocrat, and he took up philosophizing as a rejection of what he considered a failed tradition. His teacher, Socrates, was at best of craftsman origin. Aristotle, Plato's pre-eminent student, was the son of a Macedonian court physician. Plato's contemporary, Isocrates, although of a prosperous family, was no aristocrat. The philosopher Diogenes, who impressed Alexander the Great, came from Sinope, at the remote end of the Black Sea, and lived in revolting poverty, "like a dog," which gave rise to the name of his cynic, "doglike" in Greek, philosophy. The fundamental concept of the man who began all this, Socrates, was a rejection of the aristocratic value system in favor of a pursuit of personal self-worth. In place of the philosophic "goods" of his time, wealth, fame, honor, good looks, physical prowess—the aristocratic goods—Socrates would substitute only one good, the cultivation of one's soul, or spirit, or personality, to be as good as it can be—a goal for a slave as much as a king. The ethical philosophy of the fourth century for the most part accepted this principle, adapting in various ways life-ideals which abandoned the reliance on the earlier aristocratic values.

Another important shift in civic attitudes is the value placed on individual membership in the community as citizenship. The perceptibly less jealous regard for citizenship is undoubtedly related to the changes in other values. For instance, the aristocratic value is, in the first instance and above all, a matter of family values. In most cities, the noble families were those particular families which had exercised power and authority or held prestige in early times, the origin of their status so obscured by the passage of time that it is explained almost entirely by hypothesis, suggesting, for example, that the noble families were those who had been advisers to the kings when kings ruled the cities, or that they had been a particular warrior caste, or the original landowning group. In any case, the preservation of aristocratic status interacted with the general appreciation of citizenship. If many in the city could not be nobles, they could have the privilege nonetheless of being Athenians, or Spartans, or Thebans, to enjoy some benefits to the exclusion of other people. In the prevailing attitude toward the relationship of members with the community, the common Greek attitude that membership provided benefits and some authority blended with defining membership on the basis of family only, to reinforce mutually the continuation of aristocratic privilege and the strong sense of exclusion represented by citizenship.

In the early stages of the development of the Greek cities, these attitudes supported the extreme particularization of the peninsula, and the characteristic indivualization of colonization. In only two areas were these factors insufficient to avoid the development of small and politically isolated units. In Laconia and the southern Peloponnesus, Sparta created a unification by force, while in Athens the union occurred for reasons that remain obscure. Apart from some groupings which are at least as much religious as political, like the so-called Archaic Amphictyony or the union of Ionian cities, there are no significant voluntary aggregations of cities in the sixth and fifth century, and even at the beginning of the fourth, Thebes' leadership of the Boeotian cities required force at times. Only the so-called "less developed" area of western Greece, or assemblages of what are villages more than cities, such as Phocis, show anything like federations or government in common.

Citizenship was everywhere a closely guarded privilege. Sparta's refusal to add citizens in spite of her need of soldiers is a good example of the attitude. Again Athens is exceptional, with the incorporation of new citizens by Pisistratus, the solidification of their status by Cleisthenes, and further expansions of citizenship until a stop was put to it in the fifth century. There are a few other instances, such as the importations of citizens to Syracuse by Gelon, but for the most part, citizens did not want to share their status and were willing to fulfil civic duties, including that of military service.

That began to change in a formal way at the end of the fifth century, again Athens leading the way so far as our evidence shows. In the crisis of the year 405/4, Athens granted the citizens of Samos what she called *isopoliteia*—equation of citizenship. This was not a unification of citizenship whereby all Samians were automatically citizens of Athens, but rather a right of potential citizenship. All Samians could become Athenians if they took up residence and formally became Athenians. The practice of conferring *isopoliteia* became more common in the fourth century and was often reciprocal, and the instances for which we have inscriptions may be only a small percentage of actual cases.

The extension of potential citizenship *en masse* is not the only phenomenon suggesting a decline in the value put on membership in a specific group. The creation of cities out of villages or completely anew in Greece itself became a feature of Theban policy. The acceptance of the reconstitution of Mantinea is easy to understand, and the populating of Messene by the Messenians offers no problems of loyalty, but Epaminondas' creation of Megalopolis required the abandonment, in part or full, of 40 villages. Athens' union of Attica did not call for the new citizens to abandon their homes, but the military exigencies calling for the fortification of the new cities in the fourth century required that people move to take up a new place of residence with citizenship. When we consider how local Greek loyalties were, with attachment not only to agricultural land but to the gods and spirits of their places, the implications of the creation of Megalopolis, and probably Messene as well, are striking.

A further aspect to the change in the depth of feeling connected with citizenship is the shift to mercenary warfare. Not only can we suppose that the preference of citizens to pay others to fight for them is indicative of underlying attitudes, the existence of the bands of professional soldiers also shows disregard of civic attachments. The emergence of large numbers of mercenaries can be explained in part by the civic disruptions of the late fifth century and early fourth, which exiled many people and impoverished others. While it may be understandable that those soldiers would take service with the Persian king's brother in an adventure to take over the throne, it is significant that they were also willing to sell their services to Sparta, regardless of their original cities. Athens could find enough paid troops for most of the fourth century, Phocis used them almost exclusively, and Persian kings wanted more of them than they could get. The mercenaries, free Greeks though they might be, lived without civic connections, and two leading Athenian commanders illustrate their versatility. In the early part of the fourth century Chabrias was a successful general for Athens and also for kings in Cyprus and Egypt. He was elected general at Athens a number of times, faced trial for and was acquitted of treason, and then later served an Egyptian king against the Persian king. A successor to Chabrias, a general named Chares, commanded in the Athenian war against the allies but quit to join a rebellious Persian satrap. He returned to Athens, fought against Philip of Macedon, was on the hit list promulgated by Alexander the Great but escaped, and shortly before he died was on the Persian side, commanding against Alexander. These were not disloyal men; they were men with new, non-civic, even non-Greek loyalties, and their followers' attitudes would be no different. The decline in civic devotion in that group must have carried on with their offspring.

The half-millenium between the time of the oral epics and Hesiod down to the life of Alexander the Great saw a number of major changes in Greek values. The very development of the Greek city as a political entity belongs to this period, and with the evolution of the city came shifts in the power and respect given to aristocratic elements and even in the worth laid on citizenship and membership in the community. Nevertheless, certain attitudes and values remained constant. It seems common and consistent for all communities that members expected to participate in the direction of the community and to share in the benefits of belonging to it. This seems to persist even when the membership was not protected with such exclusivity.

Beyond these social and political values we can see other, more fundamental ideas. At Athens, at least, we can follow the claim for a more open, more cultured environment. It is clear that the ideal of a more relaxed attitude toward war, along with a general devotion to civic affairs, was part of the self-image Athenian leaders might promote. A love of beauty and of philosophy, a willingness to debate and discuss, an equality before the laws and an openness to public life even for the poor and obscure were part of the picture. Put into the mouth of that most aristocratic of aristocrats, Pericles, at a time when Athenians put their affairs in the hands of none but aristocrats, these sentiments show ideals which contrave the facts of practice. Even more deep-seated an attitude, and one that is general for all Greeks, so far as we know, is the dislike of change. The new was unreliable, untested, even revolutionary. There was no pursuit of growth or improvement, and political institutions and economic activity were designed to preserve as much as possible the human environment unchanged. Greeks aimed at a stability in society, government and economics that accounts in great measure for the slowness of change over the 500 years before Alexander. Despite the shifts in some values and the modifications of attitudes, basic institutions, once developed, remained essentially the same. The structure of the Greek city, its officials, assemblies and its expectations of its citizens, carried on as they had been into the time of Philip and Alexander and even after. The fundamental relationship of society and its members remained the same, and it would take the subsequent experience of their major alteration in the location of power to modify it.

6 The Oppressive Society

In admiring the emphasis on participation in most Greek communities, or the openness, cultural liveliness and nascent egalitarianism at Athens, we should not forget that Greek societies depended fundamentally on the oppression of large numbers of resident non-members. There were virtually no Greek communities without large numbers of slaves, and none at all without women and children. It is clear from the start that Greeks operated with the presumption of slavery, and as their political, social and economic systems developed, the need for slaves increased and was met. In addition to using slaves, the system was predicated on a significant amount of work done by women and children, who worked without having any share in the policy-making or decisions. Although the large majority of male citizens had a very small portion of the overall wealth of most cities, political realities dictated at least a minimum concern for their interests in most places, and as democratic tendencies grew, there was more and more potential for the poorer males to pursue power and a greater share in social benefits. Women could only act through males, and were completely subject to them, and there is some indication in literature of a male recognition and even fear of female resentment.

Except for the Spartans and their helots, there was little fear of slaves, and from earliest time, Greeks looked to slaves to share their work or do it as substitutes. Hesiod's advice about priorities for a man setting out to farm puts a house first, a slave-woman second, and an ox third. Only when he is approaching thirty should a man marry, and even then, he should choose a young virgin who is teachable. Hesiod has been thought particularly anti-female by some modern writers, but his attitude is revealing and is probably indicative of the general situation. The slave is an essential part of a household; a wife should be deferred, and when acquired is best seen as part of the work force.

We have little Greek comment on slavery before the fourth century, and the significance of slaves to the society must be deduced from literature and inscriptions which deal with slaves. The situation of Sparta, with her helots, is both clearer than that of most cities, and unusual. The helots were not imported slaves. Some were conquered Laconians and others were residents of the Messenian territories which Sparta had taken in the seventh and sixth centuries, and in historical times they far outnumbered the Spartans who controlled them. They were state-owned, and had a specific status; unlike slaves, they were not salable, but were assigned to specific lots of land, which they worked for the benefit of Spartan owners. They were supported by payment of a fixed amount from the produce of the land. The Spartans were on the alert against them constantly, and as a matter of precaution declared war against them annually to justify any actions against them, and assigned their youth to duties as secret police to keep informed of their activities.

In addition to helots, the Spartans had the same kinds of slaves as had other cities. Our knowledge of slavery in any detail, there and elsewhere, begins with the fifth century, when we have historians and other writers to provide us with information. From literary references and from inscriptions, particularly manumissions of the fourth century and after, the technical and legal position of slaves is clear. Put simply, slaves were property, and did not legally have property. In practical terms, slaves might have families and possess goods and money, but the law was always clear on the technicalities. The manumissions which are recorded at Delphi and elsewhere illustrate the legal situation well. Slaves were manumitted as sales to the god; the owner sells the named slave to Apollo, and thereafter the slave is free. Some manumissions contain a provision that the (former) slave remain with the former master for a specific time or even until the master's death, and there are some inscriptions which record a later payment by the former slave to the master. What is happening in these texts is best understood as a sequence in which the payment to the master is the slave's own payment, but, since the slave is property and cannot legally own money or enter into such a transaction, the action, to have legal force, is made as a purchase by the god, with the resulting freedom for the slave. Later, when the now-freed person makes a payment to the former owner, that payment can be recorded in the payor's name, for it is now made by a free person.

The slaves came from all parts of the world with which Greeks had contact. Many came from territories controlled by the Persians, particularly areas close to the Aegean, like Caria, Phrygia and other parts of Anatolia. Some certainly came as children, sold by their parents to provide for the rest of the family, a practice deplored but not refused by Greeks. Others passed to slave markets as Persian booty in distant wars. Outside the Persian domains, Scythia, Thrace, and even the west provided large numbers. The prices, so far as we can see from late fifth-century Athens, could vary widely. A high-priced slave, valued for some skill, talent or potential, might bring as much as the equivalent of a year's wages of a skilled Athenian craftsman. Other could be bought for less than half that, and many prices fell between the two amounts. Although some modern scholars argue that slaves were inexpensive, published prices, compared to income levels, suggest that purchased slaves were not cheap. A high-priced slave might be comparable to the investment in a good farm tractor today, and very few farmers buy many of those in a lifetime.

Tractors, however, do not reproduce, and slaves could be counted on to try. While raising a home-born slave represented some investment, it was not paid all at once, slave children could be useful and help or completely earn their keep after a few years, and the parents, allowing for a little flexiblity in practice, would probably contribute something as well. There is a good deal of evidence for slaves "born in the household," and estates usually grew to some extent by this natural increase. There is no evidence for slave-farming, however, and life expectancy being poor under the best of circumstances, an owner could not expect a great capital appreciation from a slave couple given a few minutes of time-off.

The markets would therefore have flourished just to keep up with the natural attrition of the high death rate of antiquity. The indications for the fifth century, however, suggest a very large number of slaves on the market. The fifth-century supply would have been well started with the remnants of the Persian army and fleet. The Athenian actions against Persian territories produced a good deal more. Thucydides reports some slave-making explicitly. After Cimon's capture of Eion in the mid 470's, the Athenians enslaved the population, and then the island of Scyros was captured and the people were sold off into slavery. In Greece, when the Athenians captured Chaeronea in Boeotia in the mid 440's, they garrisoned the town and made slaves of the inhabitants. The destruction or capture of 200 Persian ships at the Battle of the Eurymedon River, which followed not long after, must have resulted in slavery for a large number of prisoners, and the continuing conflicts of the ensuing decades undoubtedly produced more. The great war between Athens and Sparta led to many enslavements of whole populations, and the Athenian army lost in the Sicilian expedition produced at least 7,000 slaves, according to Thucydides. Melos, with its males killed and women and children enslaved, is just one example from the Aegean. With so many slaves becoming available, it is reasonable to wonder how the market maintained the late fifth-century price as high as it did.

The answer can only be a great expansion in the use of slaves. Athens alone probably accounted for a great part of the demand herself. It has been estimated that there were over 115,000 slaves in Attica at the outbreak of war in 431, and in Athens and the Piraeus 70,000. The city used a number of slaves for civic and police services, and devoted many to mining the silver at Laurium. The discovery of the new and richer vein at the beginning of the century provided increased employment there, and the miserable conditions of the mining slaves meant a heavy demand for replacements. At the same time, the increase in commercial prosperity at Athens, brought about by the use and expenditure of the money from the league, meant an increasing need for slaves in the trades. Certainly the trades provisioning and outfitting the soldiers and the navy expanded and needed more workers, and the public construction activity of the Periclean era on the acropolis not only called for workers, slave as well as free, but left inscribed the accounts for their payment. Beyond these clear indications of increased employment of slaves for public purposes, we can reasonably suppose that the increase in commercial activity led to a general rise in prosperity for the owners of the enterprises, and thus a greater affluence to acquire slaves for private and household purposes.

The Persian financial support of the Spartans for war against Athens supported the same rise in military expenditure among the Peloponnesians that the league money underwrote for Athens. It is ironic to imagine that some of the 7,000 Athenians sold off by the Syracusans ended up building war equipment for their enemies, but it is likely that this was the case. Many also remained in the west, however, and there, as in peninsular Greece, both war and cottage industry provided employment. Although Syracuse went through a troubled time in the fourth century under tyranny, she always remained a great city, and thus always a major user of slaves. The fourth-century market continued to supply them, both there and in the east, although the wars in Greece may not have been a major source.

The issue of slavery in Greece has always touched a sensitive nerve for modern historians. During the early nineteenth century when they idealized the Hellenic world, these writers tended to deny the significance of slavery to Greek life, presenting the slave as a kind of trusty family retainer, like Odysseus' Eumaeus in the Odyssey, or the loyal mammy of the American South. Marxist historians naturally have devoted a great deal of attention to the question of ancient slavery as an aspect of exploitation of labor. Slavery should not, however, be seen as an isolated aspect of Greek society, either as a unique aberration of an otherwise liberal and libertarian structure, or as the fundamental resource on which the economy rested. It is best seen as a particular ancient response to particular ancient conditions, and must be considered along with the other aspects of the provision of cheap labor.

In the first place, it is worth noting the characteristics of Greek use of slaves. Rarely were there large gangs of industrial or agricultural slaves. The large numbers in mines, thousands at Athens, or in stone quarries as at Syracuse, were specific cases in which large numbers could be employed at one time. Their use in such numbers was encouraged by the nature of the enterprise and its profitability. Xenophon, addressing the problems of public finance at Athens in the fourth century, proposed that the city could earn what it needed by going into the slave-renting business, whereby it would build an inventory of slaves in a number comfortable enough to provide for the needs of the mines and an income for the city. In other service, there is a report that Nicias had 1,000 slaves, but there is no indication that large numbers were common. Certainly Greeks did not have the great tracts of agricultural estates for which the Romans and the Caribbean and American planters used so many slaves.

The application of slavery to profitable enterprise in Greece was characteristically small scale. On the basis of the late fifth-century prices, investment was high. To furnish a workshop with 20 capable slaves would call for an investment of about 6,000 drachmas, a sum which, converting it to wage equivalents in the modern world, would be the lifetime earnings of a skilled electrician or plumber. It is not a small sum, and although such a shop might make the owner rich, there were few who could afford to start so big and few who reached that size gradually. Lysias' father, a late fifth-century manufacturer of shields whose workshop is one of the largest known, had 60 slaves. In the next century, the workshop left to Demosthenes had a fairly large number.

Most profitable slave-owning activity was on a much smaller scale, because almost all commercial and agricultural activity in Greece was on a small scale. A workman—shoemaker, shield maker, stonemason, whatever—might buy a cheap boy and teach him the skill needed to make him useful. The boy would work alongside the master, be fed by him and sleep in a corner. As both grew older the master might buy one or two more, and perhaps even invest in a skilled workman, while the boy, now a man, might be living outside the house, with a woman and children of his own for the master to use, working in the shop, acting as his master's sales agent and keeping some of the profits of his sales himself. If the master lived to retire and had no children, he might sell or close the workshop, keeping some of the slaves to rent out to others, or he might turn it over to his favorite slave, whom he planned to manumit in his will.

All kinds of arrangements were possible, and the treatment of slaves on an individual basis could range from kindliness to the most extreme and perverted forms of physical and sexual abuse, but in most instances slaves were handled with an eye to profitability. Even when land became more commonly available for sale and investment in the fourth century, it was a relatively difficult investment to make, and slave-owning on a small scale was easier. To buy land, certainly the preferred investment for the prosperous and rich, required assembling significant capital, waiting for something suitable to come available, and then supervising its use closely enough to achieve a return. One or two slaves cost much less and brought immediate return.

Without the availability of these slaves the system could not have produced as much as it did. Greek attitudes did not seek growth in productivity, and with relative stability in population and life expectancy, there was not much potential for increased production by an increase in citizenry. Greater production had to be achieved in the same way any ancient society achieved increase in wealth—by taking it from someone else. Slaves taken from elsewhere provided the wherewithal to increase production. In an economic sense, slaves were like machines: they allowed their owners to do more than they could accomplish with their own two hands. This worked for individuals and cities alike. Individuals with more slaves had the potential for acquiring greater wealth by using the slaves to do it. Large numbers of slaves in a city were one factor which made it possible for the city to dominate others. The fundamental utility of slaves is one reason Greek thinkers rarely questioned the morality or value of the institution. Aristotle's only caveat related to the enslavement of free Greeks and the question of the appropriateness of people for the status.

The relation of slavery to the structure of society should not be evaluated in isolation from that of women and children, and here we turn also to the problem of production in agriculture. The Athenian use of slaves in urban production still represents a much smaller fraction of labor enterprise than the work devoted to farming. Even Athens, which was the most urbanized of Greek cities, surely left at least 80% of its population on the land. The density of slaves spread around the territory of Attica and owned by the 80% of Athenian citizens in the rural areas is much lower than the concentration in the urban center, showing that proportionately, there was much less use of slaves for agricultural production.

The reason for this relates to the nature of land and farm holding in Greece, and in the methods of agriculture applied. In general, farm plots were small—enough to provide food for the peasant owner and perhaps a little surplus to be sold. When land was accumulated by investors, it came piece by piece, and a rich landowner might have little properties all over the territory of his city. There is no indication that even the land held by the old families who had been wealthy in land for centuries came any other way. Land taken over by the wealthy in foreclosures before Solon, for example, would lie here and there depending on the placement of the mortgage investments. Small owners, like Mediterranean peasants today, would have plots here and there, and the great majority of owners would have very little to work. In modern times, for example, the average holding in Greece is an acre and a half per family. That the ancient pattern was similar is borne out by some recent surface surveys which help to delineate the landscape and farming.

The nature of the soil and climate also affect the working of the land. Greece is very mountainous, with only about 25% of the land usable for crops, and perhaps an additional 40% able to support pasturing animals like goats. Even though the cities were located in regions that were suitable for agriculture, the total available terrain for this was small. The soils in most places are, and were, poor—although relatively light and easy to work—and the heat and dryness of summer is a serious constraint on productivity. Winter rains, and snow in some places, provided moisture, but rivers were shallow, short, and often only seasonal, and not much good for irrigation.

The cumulative effect of all these factors makes for an agriculture very different from that of Western Europe or North America. There, farmers must deal with heavy soils, which turn with difficulty, calling for deep plows and teams of horses or oxen,—or tractors. Winters in many regions are harsh, with deep accumulations of snow, and springtime is rainy, so that the land is wet and difficult to work. In mediaeval times these problems impelled people to organize, and they farmed and bought animal teams or the new wheeled plows cooperatively.

Even Italy has a very different topography and climate from that of Greece. Although there are mountains, they do not cover nearly so much of the peninsula, and there are miles and miles of rolling hills and plains suitable for crops, with more precipitation and deeper soils, but still suitable to the light steel plows used in Roman times. As Roman society developed, the wealthy acquired larger estates outside of the territory immediately around Rome, initially in Italy and then in Spain, North Africa and the Mediterranean-like areas of southern France. Here large gangs of slaves could be used profitably, and were used, and the image of the great gangs of Roman agricultural slaves has distorted our view of the Greek experience.

The Greek farm was a different place. There was not much territory to cultivate in the first place, and the light soil could be worked with a wooden plow, often merely breaking the soil as a cultivator rather than turning it as a plow. Even a woman could pull it, hence the slave-girl before the ox, which was probably as useful for its manure as for its muscle. The poor soils did not produce a large return on seed, and unless the farm was devoted largely to a commercial crop like olives or wine, there was little revenue from it. However, if a farmer had good land, with a reasonable depth of topsoil that held moisture, and his holding was more than minimum size, he could probably count on a profit from his work, and would need slave help to work it. Hesiod's advice about working the land with a slave would serve such farmers for centuries: use oak for plow shares and two different kinds of plow, in case one breaks; use a forty-year old man behind two oxen, and give him a specified amount of food; have slaves plow in the right season, and use one to follow along after seeding to cover the seed from the birds, while in midsummer, have the slaves build barns. But this is for the prosperous. Many a farmer was happy to feed himself and his family regularly and have a little surplus for manufactured goods or luxuries. In such circumstances slaves could be more of a burden than a help, especially in numbers. They had to be fed, so that the farm had to produce enough to make feeding them profitable. Since they had to be purchased with hard-gained cash in the first place, a farmer would be reluctant to acquire more than he could be sure to place usefully on the land.

Wives, on the other hand, presented quite a different case. In the first place, they came free, and sometimes even brought in a little money as a dowry. They were as subject to their husband's will as slaves, had no legal rights, and could be expected to work hard for the common survival of the couple, and later the children. They probably did not require the same care as slaves, either, because they could be replaced free. Once children came along and grew a little, the women could spend much of their time in the field, for the little ones could look after the chickens, goats and plots of peas and beans. In the chilly winters all could make or mend clothes and fix implements, while the husband could ignore Hesiod's further advice and not pass by the blacksmith's shop, but sociably join the crowd in the warm room.

It would be difficult to overrate the harshness of life for most women, or exaggerate the contribution they made to the economy as unpaid labor. The activity of women in Greek society was, of course, not very different from that of most women in most societies until modern times, but historians have been distracted from its realities by literary portraits of women with independence and power. Clytemnestra, Agamemnon's queen who killed him in revenge for his sacrifice of their daughter, was the dominating figure during his absence at war. Medea, the barbarian witch who killed her children, overcame her maternal love to project her vengeance on her enemies. Antigone stood against her king to fulfil her religious duties to her dead brother, and willingly died for her act. All these and more present images of powerful and dominating women, and more than one modern reader has suggested that they reflect personalities the playwrights and audiences would recognize in their own families and acquaintances. In a similar vein, the female characters of Aristophanes' comedies take on personalities and interests which are hard to imagine for women isolated at home as most better-class fifth-century Athenian women supposedly lived their lives. The Lysistrata who incites her sisters to withhold sex in order to drive their men to agree to end the war with Sparta is a political leader, espousing a cause that the playwright himself believed in.

This is drama and imagination, however, and the other side of these representations of women is an unconscious recognition of the oppression of women, an unvoiced sense of the rage which must lie below the surface of placid obedience, and a fear of the effects of that rage if it ever came to the surface. We can read Xenophon's homily on household management, with its praise of the obedient wife who follows all her husband's instructions, and dismiss the subservience of the wife as typical of all but modern society. We can even pass by Hesiod's denunciation of some wives, or Semonides' misogyny, or Aristophanes' comic bawds and bitches. However, the women of tragedy are stunners, and Euripides' wild females in particular seem most understandable in terms of an intuition of the female as enemy, a sense which lurks just below the surface of thought.

The women of tragedy belong to Athens, and in the fifth century at that, when women's status and freedom seem to have been at their lowest levels in the Greek world. We can look at priestesses and goddesses to find examples of female prestige, and we can find at Sparta that the women not only own and manipulate property in their own names, as was common for Dorian cities, but also have a great deal more freedom than anywhere else in Greece. None of this touches the facts of women's activity as a major source of controlled labor. The Spartan women, after all, belonged to an elite society that subsisted on a huge mass of forced laborers, and Spartan families needed the women's work no more than the men's. Where work was needed, women did it, and they did it at the behest of men and under men's control, and they, unlike the men, had no say in the distribution of its benefits.

Like the value of slaves, women's value and their oppression is adaptive to the Greek economy as it existed in the fifth and fourth centuries, if not before. We know of the legal and social restrictions imposed on women in urban settings, or at least in Athens in those centuries. Among the middle and upper classes, women were discouraged from leaving the house, and were expected to send slaves to do the errands women must do. Women of lower classes, the much larger proportion, were undoubtedly more visible, and busier. Pericles remarked in his funeral oration that the best women were those talked about least, for good or for bad, an attitude that underscores the social pressure for women to be screened from the world. Women were presumed to be sexually adventurous by nature, and that male opinion was the justification for protecting them from corruption. Anthropological studies of a number of societies, more recent as well as ancient, argue for the focus on isolation of women as part of the male's concern that the children born are really his. "I know they are my children," a woman can always say, and males in some societies go to great lengths to be able to say the same thing. There may be some truth in this observation by anthropologists, but the concern for the purity of the line does not call for the legal disabilities or the heavy burden of work imposed on wives.

If slaves were machines to free the owners' hands for other work, wives served the same purpose. Except for the very rich, people used homemade products for most of their needs. Pottery was made by professionals, and had to be bought or traded, but baskets, most household furnishings, harnesses, clothing, blankets, even wagons, carts and plows were fashioned in the household. A great deal of this could be done and was done by wives. If city women did not have plows to help make and repair, there was still clothing to be dealt with. A tradesman's wife would have not only herself, her husband and children to look out for, but the slaves as well. Cooking the porridges and bean dishes served daily to the workmen was probably not so arduous a task, but keeping the garden, if there was one, and the chickens or other animals if there was room in a city compound, would keep her busy. There may have been slave-girls to help, but that took supervision. The work was often done in a state of pregnancy, or while nursing the newborn, and many a wife not only looked after those she had borne but those produced by the last wife, dead of childbirth or infection.

The wives were probably not the most stimulating companions, and men freely resorted to ordinary or fancy prostitutes, depending on what they could afford. A large number of female slaves were available for paid sex, and some free women maintained themselves in that way. Men with the taste for boys could resort to slaves or, in a society which tolerated homosexuality, that relationship between free citizens was accepted and respectable, although this may be particular to Athens, which provides the evidence in the matter. In the city in particular, the wives working at home left the men time to entertain themselves in various ways.

The case of Xanthippe, the wife of Socrates, and the hostile attitudes expressed toward her are, in fact, very revealing. She is portrayed as bad-tempered, a nag and complainer. But she obviously supported Socrates and his children, because the old philosopher did not seem to work at anything. His father had been prosperous, so far as we can tell, but Socrates lived in poverty, and it was Xanthippe who seems to have done all the work. This reminds us of the situation in the third world today, when fully two-thirds of the women are the sole support of families. In some cases, women did all the work, while men attended to other things.

What people saw when they watched women can be sketched by the pictures on hundreds of Athenian vases. Although some views show women relaxing or involved in games, or even reading, as in a rendition of the poetess Sappho, most of them are engaged in household tasks like spinning, weaving, cooking and the like. Men, when they are portrayed at work, carry on the tasks of shoemaking, blacksmithing and shiploading, but on most vases live the life of the athlete or warrior. There is a modern notion of ancient Greece as a place of leisured life made possible by a workforce of slaves. That is in part true, but the leisured life belonged to only a few at the top of the economic and social heap, and their wives shared with the slaves the responsibility for making it possible.

Without the wives, a lot of work would not have got done, and with the intensity of craft activity increasing as the Athenian empire grew, the free female workers played a bigger and bigger part in the economy. A large number of male citizens were engaged in military activities in the last half of the fifth century; the 7,000 captured and enslaved at Syracuse are a reminder of the number. While Pericles and his fleet sailed along the Black Sea coast, or a fleet besieged Samos, Naxos, or Thasos, someone carried on the tasks of household or business management. Trusty slaves may have done some of the commercial work, but wives often would have supervised that, and in many cases when the male hands were away the female hands substituted. We read nothing of Rosie the Riveter in fifth-century Athens, but she must have worked harder than ever as the men pursued Pericles' ideal of glory. Male awareness of their dependence on wives left behind, and an unconscious fear of their activities and attitudes, may lie behind some of the dialogue in Aeschylus' *Oresteia,* as Clytemnestra greets Agamemnon on his return from the Trojan war.

Fear of women was not far below the surface. Aristophanes' play *Lysistrata* is a funny presentation of a women's revolt against war, but it certainly touches on a male sense of how women might behave in concert if they were ever free enough to collude. Athenian men would have accepted the modern naval caution about sailors: "One will work, two will talk, and three make a mutiny." The bitter remarks of Medea, Phaedra, Alcestis and so many of Euripides' female characters show that at least one male was aware of a deep-seated anger and hostility on the part of women. When the men respond in drama they often betray an insensitivity to what the women are telling them, or react with patronizing disdain or even the hostility which is found in many ancient writers about women. Hesiod's myth of Pandora as the cause of all trouble in the world absolves men of responsibility totally, unlike the *Genesis* narrative which gives Adam some share. Hesiod's view, like that of so many writers, emerges from a male sense that society lives out an undeclared war between men and women, but as in most of the Greek male reports of that war, there is no indication that it is a war that men are forever winning. It is to Euripides that we look for some insight into the realities of the case.

In the Greek city, the male citizens had all the power. Although the lower classes were usually dominated and exploited by the rich, they in turn used slaves and women to make whatever advantages they could scratch out of the portion of the collective wealth left to them. Society as a whole was able to use this army, larger in numbers by far than the dominating group, to generate the resources and equipment the society needed. Even the communities without the great body of slaves which helped expansion and aggression had their women and children to generate some wealth and use little of it, so that in democracies men could at least consider devoting themselves to the time-consuming activities of the council, the assembly and the law courts.

Because fundamental assumptions created no anticipation of economic growth, political and social structures developed to meet the need for increased production. In modern societies a great effort is devoted to increasing the productivity of capital, machinery and individual workers, with the view of providing goods at costs which are economically supportable. Greek societies tended to satisfy the need for increased production by adding workers, and price stability, always a goal, was achieved by pushing production onto unpaid or poorly-paid workers. Slave acquisition was practiced by all, and the social attitudes toward women and children were inextricably tied to their labor utility and the need for their production. It is commonly agreed that the status of women in Greece was at its lowest in fifth-century Athens, and it is significant that this came when Athens had its greatest need for production. The structure of society and attitudes toward women hardened when demands on them were greatest, when male citizens active in politics and war were taken more and more from productive labor. There is little doubt that Athens could not have sustained so extensive or such frequent war from the 470's onward if the prices of military equipment had risen with the sharply increased demand. Even when the war with Sparta after 431 placed large numbers within the walls, possibly available for production, the drain of feeding them when agricultural production was cut would probably have more than balanced any cuts in labor costs from a possible increase in labor supply. That period also saw a much greater use of male citizens for war, and a public expense of the two-obol payment to the needy during the last decades of the century. The social restrictions of women increased as their work became more vital, and probably heavier.

Athens is the clearest example of the dependence of Greek cities on the slave and female labor supply. The greater a city's power and activity in the world, the higher the standard of culture, the more of its resources devoted to literary and political activity, the greater the need for the oppressed elements in societies. In all probability, democracy itself as practiced in the Greek city called for greater oppression, for the more the resources of the society were devoted to the lower element of the male citizenry, the more had to be produced by the unpaid. The more "liberal" and the more accomplished the city, the more the structure required extensive and intensive oppression. It has only been the modern development of the growth ethic that has allowed a net increase in material well-being among a large part of the population without the same extent of exploitation. Even today, many people see the persistence of an economic and social under-class as a major contribution to the prosperity of the majority.

7 One-Man Rule

Greek communities all emerged out of monarchic rule, it is generally agreed by modern and ancient writers. First ruled by kings, communities evolved into aristocracies or oligarchies, and some moved to a wider devolution of power as democracies. In this evolution, some had the experience of tyranny, a form of one-man rule different from kingship, defined in Greek terms as illegal power acquired and held by force, rather than by law or tradition. Tyrannies emerged in Greece in the seventh and sixth centuries as part of the stresses of social and political change, and they usually were part of political conflict.

At Corinth, for example, the ruling Bacchiad family was overthrown by one of their own number, Cypselus, in about 650, and the tyrant held power with the support of a wider group of the population than the earlier limited oligarchy. Under Cypselus and his successor, Corinth enjoyed great prosperity, expanding her trade westward in particular. Periander, Cypselus' son, who came to power around 625, founded the colony of Potidaea and involved Corinth in trade with Egypt, and his rule is associated with a great flowering of Corinthian industry, commerce and the arts. He outlived all his sons, and when he died about 585, the tyranny devolved to his nephew, but soon ended with the latter's murder.

Tyranny at Sicyon, near Corinth, had some different features. It began at about the same time, the mid seventh century, when Orthagoras gained control and elevated the non-Dorian elements in the city, which had been founded by Argos and was under some measure of Argive control until Orthagoras took control. The unrest on which Orthagoras capitalized, therefore, must have had ethnic as well as political and economic aspects. Under his successor Cleisthenes, who ruled from about 600 to 570, Sicyon took an active part in politics in west central Greece, and the anti-Dorian policies continued. Cleisthenes had close relations with Athens. His daughter married the Alcmaeonid Megacles, sometime ally of the Athenian tyrant Pisistratus, and she was the mother of the Athenian Cleisthenes, the political activist of the period immediately after the expulsion of the Pisistratids. The tyranny ended at the hands of the Spartans, and Sicyon came into their hands.

Tyranny flourished on the eastern shore of the Aegean, on the coast and on the islands. At Miletus, the tyrant Thrasybulus maintained good relations with Lydia even after the city came under the control of King Croesus, and the tyranny persisted under the Persians until Histiaeus and Aristagoras initiated the Ionian revolt and lost their position. On Samos, Polycrates seized the tyranny with his two brothers around 540, but soon took sole control. Polycrates built Samos into a naval power and played international politics with Egypt, Cyrene and Persia, in pursuit of his objective of maintaining Samian independence and leadership. Like tyrants in many other places, he was responsible for many public works in the city and encouraged the arts and literature. He was noted for his good fortune. Herodotus tells a story that a friend urged him to dispose of something he treasured in order to balance his good fortune, and so Polycrates threw a precious ring into the sea. When the ring came back in the belly of a fish, his friend would have nothing more to do with him, expecting him to attract some great misfortune. He did just that: lured to the mainland by a Persian governor, he was crucified, leaving the Samian tyranny to his steward and his steward's brother, Syloson. The city was turned into a democracy by the Persians after the Ionian revolt, and apart from short periods, remained so for the rest of the fifth century.

The tyrant we know best, of course, is Pisistratus of Athens, who ruled there in the mid sixth century. Like so many other tyrants, he took power as part of the unrest common in Greece in the period, and had the support of the poorer elements of the population, and ruled at the expense of the traditional aristocracy. The erratic history of his reign—on again, off again, gone again, Finnegan—clearly illustrates the political instability which opened the way to tyranny. The stories are dramatic. First, he made himself tyrant in about 560 using a bodyguard granted to him when he showed some self-inflicted wounds which he claimed came from his political enemies. Within five years, a coalition of "people from the plain and people from the shore," which included the aristocrats, expelled him. He was able to return by developing his alliance with Megacles and the Alcmaeonids, but when that collapsed because of his refusal to impregnate his Alcmaeonid wife, he was unable to hold on to power. After ten years of taking wealth from mines in the north, he hired mercenaries and returned to win control of Athens again by battle. He remained in power until his death in 528/7, maintaining himself with money and mercenaries, and building prosperity in Athens.

Everything we read about Pisistratus coheres with a picture of a power base different from and broader than the aristocracy. He established circuit judges for the rural areas of Attica, a procedure inimical to the authority of the family and clan leaders. He aided the small farmers and imposed only moderate taxation. He instituted a building and arts program which kept urban workers busy and brought craftsmen from Ionia, increasing the population of the city and providing new sources of support for him. He alienated only a limited number of the most powerful noble families, but they were forced to leave the city in some numbers. Ultimately, the Alcmaeonids were responsible for the expulsion of his son, Hippias, from the tyranny in 510, but that family was among the more commerce-minded of the aristocrats, and the leaders they later provided extended most of the Pisistratid policies.

Modern historians regard tyranny in Greece as a process which broke or weakened the power of the established aristocracies and moved cities toward more democratic constitutions. That seems to have been the case in Athens, at least. The earliest writers who deal with the tyranny of Pisistratus report a mild and beneficial rule, helpful to the poorer elements in the population. Pisistratus seems to have shared in the general tendency of tyrants to support commerce and the arts, and he, like many others, was outward looking, bringing in foreigners to settle, and developing close relations with other cities. He needed relatively little force in his control of Athens: the bodyguards which he used to obtain power in the first place do not reappear, and his final takeover of the city was achieved in a single battle. Pisistratus seems to have ruled with the support of at least one portion of the citizenry, again a pattern which applies to other tyrannies, as a process whereby members of the communities achieved their objectives by extra-constitutional means. The bad name for tyranny as it emerges in later Greek literature comes not from the tyrants of peninsular Greece, but from the later tyrants of Sicily, who represent a very different stage in political development.

Tyrannies began in the west at about the same time as they occurred in Greece, and in their early form followed the same pattern. The western cities are notable for their early formulation of law, as early as the early seventh century for Catana, where Charondas was active, and Epizephyrian Locri where Zaleucus served as lawgiver. Towards the end of the sixth century, tyrants established themselves in many of the Sicilian cities, developing powerful armies, political structures and economies. At Gela, in the final years of the sixth century the wealthy Cleander substituted himself as tyrant in place of the ruling oligarchy, and began a series of events which would remake the political map. Cleander's rule, lasting from about 505 to 498, was short and ended by assassination, but the power he established was enough to provide for the accession of his brother, Hippocrates, to power, with a base that allowed him to take over the Sicilian Greek cities of Zancle, Naxos, Callipolis and Leontini, and carried him to the subjugation of native Sicels and the conquest of powerful Syracuse as well.

By the time the Athenians had repulsed the Persians at Marathon in 490, Hippocrates had been killed on campaign against the Sicels, and his subordinate Gelon, who had been entrusted with the care of his sons, had replaced them in the tyranny. Gelon in turn began a series of manoeuvres which brought him to control of Syracuse by 485, leaving his brother in power as tyrant in Gela. Gelon enlarged and strengthened Syracuse greatly, incorporating into it the populations of Camarina and Megara Hyblaea and many of the citizens of Gela as well. Growing Syracusan power ultimately brought Gelon into conflict with Carthage, and in a battle which made Gelon's fame, he completely demolished a Carthaginian expedition to Sicily. When Gelon died in 478, he left Syracuse, in cooperation with Acragas, dominant over all the Greeks of Sicily. The alliance was more powerful than anything which had yet been put together in Aegean Greece. Tyranny had both lasted longer than those of Aegean Greece, and turned out to be a much more successful and powerful institution.

The fifth century was a time of instability for the western Greeks. After Gelon died in 478, his brother Hieron took the tyranny for a period of brilliant rule. As an ally of Cumae, near Naples in Italy, he defeated the Etruscans in a great battle which stopped them from presenting any threat to the Greek cities of Italy. In Syracuse itself, he was a patron of culture, according to our sources, if not a paragon of political virtue. Pindar praised his victories at games in Greece in several odes, and used these occasions to enumerate his accomplishments. Bacchylides, too, celebrated him, and the poet Simonides at his court served at one point to reconcile him to Theron of Acragas. Hieron provided hospitality to Epicharmus and Phormis, both comic writers of western origin, and was visited by Aeschylus.

After Hieron's death in 467/6, his brother Thrasybulus took the tyranny, but his rule was short lived, ended in the wave of revolution which was generally overthrowing tyrannies in the west. We hear of his repressive tactics immediately on taking power, executing or exiling wealthy citizens in order to take their property. The Syracusans rose against him within a year, and with the aid of forces from other Sicilian cities forced him to leave the city. The Syracusans established a democracy, but there was open war between factions of citizens and it was some time before civic order prevailed. The experiences of Acragas were similar. Thrasydaeus, the son of Theron, the tyrant there, took over when his father died in 472. Thrasydaeus had been ruling Himera, and the citizens there had been complaining about him while his father was still alive. When he moved to Acragas, he attacked Syracuse, was defeated with heavy losses and fled to Megara, where he was executed. An oligarchy then ruled Acragas, made peace with Syracuse, and seems to have granted Himera its independence.

Syracuse, under democracy and then the leadership of a general named Hermocrates, fought with success against Ducetius and the native Sicels in the mid fifth century, and repelled Athenian invasions, one in 427-424 and the second, in 415-413, with great loss to the Athenians. In 406 the Syracusans faced renewed Carthaginian interventions in Sicily. Democracy was in control in Syracuse again after the death of Hermocrates, but there was a good deal of dissatisfaction with the democrats after Acragas fell to the Carthaginians. A young lieutenant of Hermocrates, 23-year-old Dionysius, took advantage of the situation and managed his own election to a new board of generals, and next as supreme commander. He was then able to obtain a bodyguard, and with that, plus mercenaries who remained loyal to him, he was able to maintain control of Syracuse as tyrant, even when his military activities failed to prevent the Carthaginians from gaining control of the whole southern seaboard of Sicily. Dionysius, in fact, negotiated with the Carthaginians, and recognized their conquests in return for their acknowledgement of his position as ruler of Syracuse. He renewed war against Carthage with indifferent success, and after he died in 367 his son, Dionysius II, made peace with Carthage again.

Dionysius II, a man of very different nature from that of his father, seemingly was interested more in the manner of rule than he was in the expansion of power, and his mind turned more to philosophical speculation than to the practicalities of preserving power. Although one might admire this personality, the outcome of its decisions were not always good. His first actions set the tone: he remitted taxes and released prisoners, made peace in Italy and with Carthage, rebuilt two cities which Dionysius I had destroyed, and established bases in Apulia to protect the Adriatic from pirates. Although he was inexperienced, he had the advice of an uncle—brother of his step-mother—Dion, who persuaded him to invite Plato to his court in 366. The venture was not successful

Plato had visited Syracuse once before, in 389, when he became a close friend of Dion, and by the time of his invitation in 366 he was renowned for his writings and for his position as director of his philosophical school at Athens, known as the Academy. The invitation gave him an opportunity to attempt, through influence over the Syracusan tyrant, the implementation of his political philosophy. On his arrival, he went to work on a subject who seemed to be particularly malleable. It was an extraordinary time, as the philosopher from Athens discoursed with and advised the Syracusan tyrant whose reign rested mainly on raw force. Aside from Dion, however, the court of Dionysius did not welcome the new approach, and many felt not only that government by philosophy would not long serve a military tyranny, but also that Plato's influence over Dionysius served mainly to increase Dion's authority at court. When Dion wrote to the Carthaginians asking them not to negotiate with Syracuse when he was not present, his enemies showed the letter to Dionysius and, since there might be treasonable implications, Dion was exiled, but without dishonor and with full access to all his wealth. Although Plato remained for a while after Dion's departure, he focused primarily on philosophical matters with Dionysius, and on persuading him to recall Dion. In that regard Plato failed, and so he departed for Athens, and did not return to Syracuse for five years. When he did return in 361, he found Dionysius also interested in the philosophy of a rival, Aristippus, and somewhat suspicious of Plato's continued urging of the recall of Dion. Plato soon left again for Athens, his influence inadequate even to prevent Dionysius from confiscating Dion's property in Sicily after deciding never to recall him.

So much, one might say, for the impact of philosophers on the real world. But things got worse, as another philosopher mixed in, and tyranny in Syracuse degenerated to create such turmoil and repression that the name tyranny became synonymous with violence and brutality. One of Plato's associates was another philosopher, Speusippus, also a friend of Dion, and Speusippus accompanied Plato to Syracuse and back again. With Plato's full awareness, Speusippus urged Dion to use force to return to Syracuse, and Dion began his campaign in 357. Although Plato did not encourage the attack, neither did he warn Dionysius of it, so that Dion was able to land in Sicily and march on Syracuse while Dionysius was in Italy. He held the city for a while as liberator, but Dionysius returned with mercenaries and the city became a battleground between his forces and those of Dion's supporter, Heraclides, an exiled democratic leader. The slaughter in the course of the fighting was horrific, for the struggle was complicated by Dion's preference for oligarchic government and Heraclides' for democracy, so that these political rivalries also took their toll. It was not until 355 that Dion was firmly in control, and even then he felt impelled to murder Heraclides in order to quell democratic intrigues. In 354, Dion himself went the way of Heraclides, murdered at the behest of the so-called Platonic philosopher Calippus, who installed himself in Syracuse, beginning a decade of upheaval. In 352 Calippus was ousted and Dion's nephew (and half-brother of Dionysius II) seized the city, to be succeeded on his death by his brother Nysaeus, who was in turn expelled by Dionysius himself in 347. The tyrant now ruled with such ferocity that the wretched Syracusans appealed for relief from the tyrant of Leontini, Hicetas, in 344, and also asked for help from the mother city of Corinth. Corinth sent out a general, Timoleon, to help, and his success in getting control of Syracuse, and the good government he brought, gave him an enduring reputation for virtue, moderation and honor. But after his retirement in 337 the city was in turmoil again, only to be settled by Agathocles, who established himself in power by 317 and started calling himself king in 304.

In general, the nature of tyranny in the west was different from what it had been in Aegean Greece in the seventh and sixth centuries. For many cities it was the prevailing form of government, rather than a stage of development or an exceptional period of one-man rule interrupting prevailing democratic or oligarchic forms. The tyrants of Syracuse concentrated the resistance to Carthage, and when they could, they used the base of a powerful and populous city to increase the territory they controlled. Syracuse was probably the second greatest city of Greece under Dionysius I at the peak of his power. The tyrants there maintained courts that were centers of culture, attracting some of the greatest Greek poets and artists. Not only Hieron, among the early tyrants, but Dionysius I and II were noted for this. The first Dionysius tried to use the writing desk of Aeschylus and Euripides' writing materials to help him compose tragedies. Ancient reports tell us they were not very good, and that his victory at Athens with his *Ransom of Hector* was a political move. Plato's visits to the court of Dionysius II were part of the same pattern of the tyrants' involvement with culture.

The western tyrants were, however, essentially military adventurers who held on to power by force, and this expression of power and the degeneration of order at Syracuse under the later tyrants led to a general ancient attitude of disdain for the institution. Even though Herodotus and other early writers made it quite clear that at least some of the original tyrants of Aegean Greece were beneficial for their societies, that aspect of tyranny tended to be overlooked. Nevertheless, it is clear from what we know of Pisistratus and others that they were responsible for a great increase of commerce, and encouraged an expansion which was usually achieved by colonization, rather than the conquest of neighbors which attracted the western tyrants. Because they usually obtained power, and often held it with the support of significant elements of their populations, they were part of the expression of government in which the members of society expected to share in the benefits and control of the community. Even with that, however, the tyrants were always considered "irregular," in the sense that they did not hold their power by any entitlement or legitimacy, and as rulers they were not considered kings.

In the historical period, monarchy was extremely rare among the Greeks. Historical tradition claimed that Greek cities had been ruled by kings in very early times, but except for traces like the Spartan dual kingship or magistracies with references to royalty, it had died out in Greek cities. In the northern parts of Greece, however, dynasties continued on, and one of them, the Macedonian, ultimately developed to become the pattern of kingship and royalism for the rest of antiquity.

Some Greeks challenged the Macedonian claim to Hellenic status, but there is no doubt that the language which Macedonians spoke was a Greek dialect. The Macedonian dynasty came on to the stage of Greek politics at the time of the Persian War, with Alexander I, the first Macedonian king of whom we have much knowledge, who ruled from about 495 to 450. We have a story of his riding into the Greek camp with information for the Greek forces mustered against Persia, even though he himself had submitted. He advised the Greeks to abandon the forward line at Tempe, in Macedonia, and he provided intelligence to the Athenians before the Battle of Plataea in 479. As a result, he was admitted to participation as a Greek in the games at Olympia. He was also the first Macedonian king to pursue the acculturation of Macedonia along the lines of the southern Greek cities, inviting Pindar to his court and issuing a Greek-type coinage. The development of the Athenian-controlled Delian league limited his expansion to the east but he was able to annex territories in areas which did not obtrude on Athenian interest.

Alexander's successor, Perdiccas II, was deeply involved in Greek affairs. He managed to maintain control of a united Macedonia and expanded control of his coastal areas. The problems endemic in the Macedonian monarchy came to the fore when he promoted the revolt of Potidaea from the Athenians, for Athens responded by supporting the ambitions of his brother, Philip. Perdiccas came to terms with the Athenians, with the result that they could settle down to besiege Potidaea. His next problem came from his eastern frontier, as the Thracian king Sitalces invaded in 429. The Macedonian forces could not stand up to the large Thracian army, but Perdiccas escaped permanent damage as the Thracian king, with his army facing food shortages and the cold, withdrew on the advice of his chief commander, Seuthes. Perdiccas had used diplomacy on Seuthes, promising him money and his daughter in marriage, an agreement he kept. He was neither the first nor the last Macedonian king to protect or expand his domains by secret diplomacy or dynastic marriages.

During the Peloponnesian War, Perdiccas shifted alliances between Athens and Sparta. In 417 he was an ally of Sparta, switched to the

Athenian side two years later, and died just as Athens was experiencing her great disaster at Syracuse in 413. His successor, Archelaus, was another of the Macedonian kings to promote culture. He brought a number of poets, notably the Athenian tragedian Euripides, to his court, began celebrating Greek-type games in Macedonia, and moved his court to Pella, closer to the coast. He kept Athens friendly, avoided a revolt of one district by agreeing to a marriage alliance, developed trade and captured the city of Pydna. According to Thucydides, Archelaus built roads and fortresses, and improved the arms and equipment of cavalry and infantry. He was assassinated in 399, and for some time after that, Macedonia was pressed by tribes along the borders. Amyntas III, who ruled from 393 to 370, depended for his survival on alliances and help from outside Macedonia, as the more powerful cities of the south frequently dealt with Macedonia as a pawn in the general game of Greek politics.

Amyntas' death in 370 plunged Macedonia into a savage struggle over succession to the throne. First his eldest son, Alexander II, was murdered by an adventurer, Ptolemy of Aloros, who married Amyntas' widow and ruled as regent for the second brother, Perdiccas, from 367 to 365. Then Perdiccas turned around and took the throne himself by killing his stepfather. He lasted six years, preserving the kingdom by adroit shifts in alliances, but perished finally with 4,000 of his best troops in battle against the Illyrians, a people to the west whom he had attacked. Macedonia, now ruled by the infant son of Perdiccas, Amyntas IV, was in a parlous state. Philip, Amyntas' uncle, who served as regent for the child, had his work cut out for him if the kingdom was to survive. Enemies on all sides were ready to attack and dismember it, and Philip's half-brothers were also eyeing the throne, while a number of important cities in Macedonia had become independent of the monarchy during Perdiccas' reign.

Philip had spent some time at Thebes, as a hostage, between 367 and 364, and according to some ancient writers, had lived at the house of the great Theban general, Epaminondas, and had learned a great deal about war from him. Whatever that specific case might be, Philip's sojourn at Thebes at the height of her power could hardly have failed to teach him something. Upon his return to Macedonia he assumed duties assigned by his brother Perdiccas, who had become king by that time, and he was on the scene to take the regency when Perdiccas fell before the Illyrians. He was 22 years old at the time.

Athens was busy enforcing her will in the Aegean when Philip took power. A brief peace and alliance between the two, whereby Philip was to give Athens the city of Amphipolis, came to naught, but by the time the Athenians realized they had been tricked, Philip had met and defeated all comers along his borders and held Macedonia secure. At some time in these first years he began to term himself king, and so ruled as monarch rather than regent as he turned to the development of Macedonian power in Greece as a whole.

The kingship of Macedonia has been a much discussed institution, since it relates to the careers of two of the most powerful figures in the history of Greece, Philip himself and his son, Alexander, the Great. What we can say today about the Macedonian monarchy is both limited and a matter of generalities. The succession by the eldest son was not automatic, and the fact that Philip took the title of king even though his brother's son was alive shows that the kingship could move to another even while the earlier holder was still alive. Exactly how Philip became king we do not know, although one of the lesser ancient sources mentions an acclamation by the people. There are accounts of Alexander's accession which show that his succession was not a certainty, but that the army played some role. The loyalty the king could command was based in some measure on the support of the army and its leaders. Rather than merely ruling, the Macedonian kings had a relationship with the rest of the Macedonians that called for a claimant to be formally declared king, just as the people and the army had some role in the judgement of capital crimes. A Macedonian king had to make sure that his troops were rewarded, and his style of ruling left the impression that the soldiers, or the nobles or generals, were not completely subservient.

The interaction among king, senior officers and troops in the reigns of Philip and Alexander shows that the power of the kingship fluctuated with the abilities and achievements of those who held it. With the king subject to some limit and approval by others in the society—however vague and uncertain this group may be to us—the Macedonians exhibited a variation on the characteristic Greek attitudes toward political structure. Sovereignty wasvested in the collective of adult males who were citizens. Just as the fortunes of leaders in democratic Athens waxed and waned with the success of their policies, so the strength of Macedonian kings depended on their success. Before Philip, with the ups and downs of Macedonian fortunes in the fifth and fourth centuries, kings had been unable to accumulate prestige and power in quantities sufficient to overawe or overwhelm the body of soldiers. It took the sustained successes of the reigns of Philip and Alexander, stretching over 40 years, to make possible a significant shift of power in Macedonia.

This was the kingship Philip had to work with. For about 15 years, he pressed his eastern and southern neighbors in a relentless drive for expansion. His ambitions in the east brought him into conflict with the Athenians, who saw that area as vital to their interests. But a combination of military strength and clever diplomacy pushed his advance, and by 356 he had advanced past Amphipolis and had seized Potidaea. In August of that year he received, all on the same day, three pieces of good news. His horse had won at the Olympic Games that year, his general Parmenion had defeated the Illyrians in the west, and his wife Olympias had given birth to a son, Alexander. At the same time the Athenians were in disarray with the outbreak of a major revolt of their allies, and in the next year gave up their league, while Philip continued his drive east.

When the Thessalian cities called for Philip's help against Phocis in the Second Sacred War, he responded quickly. Although early success led to a defeat which forced him out of Thessaly, he had committed himself to intervention in the south. When he returned to Thessaly in 352, he destroyed the Phocian forces, establishing his dominance over Thessaly, and marched off to Thermopylae, heading south. He withdrew when allied opposition made forcing the pass risky, and he left central Greece for the moment, much stronger than he had been, having the Thessalian league under his control. He moved eastward in

Thrace, and on his western borders gained more territory, either under his direct rule or that of vassal kings. By 349 he was aiming on the complete takeover of the area known as Chalcidice, and Athenian aid against him was not adequate to slow his advance.

In 346, Philip finally brought the Second Sacred War to an end, and came to terms with Athens in a peace which he stalled signing for a few months, while he finished up with some acquisitions he had started to make. The hostility remained, however, shifting to the diplomatic arena, and by 342 Philip was protesting to Athens about some manoeuvres Demosthenes had undertaken. In 341 there were further acts of hostility on the part of Athenian forces in the northern Aegean, and Demosthenes delivered his *Third Philippic*, or speech against Philip, making it clear that he planned to commit Athens to open war with the Macedonians.

When war came in 340, after Demosthenes persuaded the Athenians and their allies in congress to pool resources, Philip struck at the cities controlling the Bosphorus, besieging Perinthus and then Byzantium. By 339, a new sacred war against the Locrians of Amphissa had broken out, and Philip accepted the invitation of the Amphictoynic Council to lead the League's forces. After quickly marching to Boeotia and wintering there, he won his final success over the opposing Greeks by defeating the allied Theban and Athenian army at Chaeronea. Supreme in Greece, he turned to plans for war against Persia.

In the midst of preparations, Philip decided on a new marriage. He had in mind a young Macedonian girl, the ward of his general Attalus. It was one of his many marriages, and did not cancel the union with Olympias, Alexander's mother, and it may have been an infatuation, as some ancient sources claim. In any case, it provided the possibility of an heir fully Macedonian, not half-Epirote, like Alexander. At the marriage feast, probably held in 337, a quarrel arose between Philip and his heir-apparent. He was celebrating with his nobles and, as well, the now 19-year-old Alexander, when Attalus, drunk, proposed that the Macedonians ask the gods to provide a legitimate—however meant—heir to the throne from Philip and Cleopatra. Alexander responded violently, throwing a cup at him, calling out, "What about me, shithead? Do I seem to you a bastard?" Philip rose angrily, drawing his sword, but fuddled with anger and wine, tripped and fell. Another remark from Alexander insulted the king: "This man, gentlemen, who is preparing to cross from Europe to Asia, even falls when crossing from couch to couch." The anger of both was great, and the falling out between father and son serious, for Alexander quickly took himself and his mother out of Macedonia, Olympias to her home in Epirus, Alexander going to Illyria.

The position was serious for Philip, for even if (as may well, in fact, have happened) Cleopatra produced a male heir, it was awkward for now to do without Alexander, and worse to have him hostile, in Illyria, if Philip was really to lead an army far from Macedonia. Thus he accepted advice and brought Alexander back, but the relationship of mutual trust and regard was impaired, because Alexander remained uncertain of his position. Philip was now in the full swing of his preparations against Persia, and had made an arrangement with the Persian king's governor of Caria to seal an alliance by joining his feeble-minded son Arrhidaeus to the governor's daughter. Alexander took it on himself to propose to the governor that he be the bridegroom, and the interference had the effect of confusing the issue enough that the marriage to Arrhidaeus did not come off. Philip was furious, and the relationship with his son worsened.

Philip was now, in 336, preparing for another marriage, this time of his daughter Cleopatra to King Alexander of Epirus, brother of Olympias. The marriage would give him a more secure relationship with the Epirote king than that of the tie with Olympias, and thus would protect Philip from trouble either from Epirus or from Olympias or Alexander. He put on a lavish show, with Greeks invited from all over. The guests enjoyed musical contests and spectacular banquets and watched Philip receiving gold crowns from cities and individuals alike. Philip even had his own statue carried along in procession with the images of the twelve major gods. Then suddenly, the bodyguard Pausanias rushed up and stabbed the king. Philip fell dead on the spot, and the amazing reign was over.

Senior generals quickly presented Alexander to the army, and the young man took over. After a purge of his enemies at court and a series of campaigns in Greece and to the north to ensure stability at home, Alexander and his Macedonian and Greek army left for their ten-year march which would bring the Persian empire and all its provinces, to the border of India, under Macedonian control. As Philip changed Greece, Alexander changed the world, and he left the east a heritage of monarchy based on the Macedonian tradition. In a way, the monarchy Alexander left was largely Philip's creation, for Alexander's campaigning did not give him much time for organizing and creating institutional structures. It was a monarchy dependent on a working relationship with the army, with authority flowing directly through the king's closest associates, or "friends." The friends would act as generals, emissaries, administrators. The monarchy also had a religious side, with the king in some way tied to the gods, either through distant descent as the family claimed, or in some more direct way. There may have been a cult of worship of Amyntas, Philip's father. Philip had a temple or "Philippeion," and there was the appearance of the king's effigy amontg the statues of the twelve gods. The oracle of Zeus-Ammon called Alexander "son of Zeus," either intentionally or as a mistake in Greek, and after his death, there was a cult devoted to Alexander-worship. While alive, Alexander had been very careful to worship his own and foreign divinities properly, and he followed the old Macedonian custom of maintaining a court in which cultural and artistic figures were active.

Macedonian kingship left a permanent impact on the world. Unlike the tyrannies,—*ad hoc* arrangements, temporary periods of one-man rule, or at worst, examples of depraved autocracy— the Macedonian idea of kingship and Macedonians' expectations of kings became the basis for the evolution of kingship over the next three hundred years, and then afterward, as Roman emperors established one-man rule. By the time the sons of Alexander's generals had taken over their fathers' monarchies, Greeks everywhere accepted the idea that leadership and power would be the prerogative of kings, and that government would be carried on by royal personages and their agents and appointees. Although individual cities might still administer their own affairs, and occasionally play some role in the larger world, the new world called for adjustments in people's attitudes. The single-city community, now insignificant in power compared to the kings, could survive as an entity if it adjusted to the new circumstances. That would work best for those who accommodated themselves to kingship, who accepted the kings as the embodiments of power and the expression of Greek political ideals. For many Greeks, it was easy to do this, as the kings promoted Greek culture and education in cities and towns all over the east, and most of the time used their power to achieve the political stability that was a fundamental Greek objective. An individual king might be good or bad, perform his duties well or badly, but the concept of kingship now included much more than mere political power. It had intellectual, moral, cultural and religious qualities as well, and not in the fashion of tyrants or in the age-old Homeric fashion of tribal leadership, but as an expression of the most advanced political and social ideas of Hellenism.

Monarchy, with all its responsibilities, became the expected form of government until the end of the 18th century of our era, and any republican challenges were laid down only for individual cities. Monarchs were endowed with divine blessing, and were seen as the embodiment of the state. The absolutisms of western Europe have confused our understanding of early Greek kingships, which were, for the most part, one pattern for the Greek practice of government and called for a two-way relationship between monarch and citizen-body.

8 Hellenism and Culture

Much of what is studied and remembered about Greek history would be ignored if the artistic and literary treasures of Hellenism did not exist. The story of the Athenian Empire and the war with Sparta would be, at best, interesting antiquarian information, no better known than the story of Assyria's great conquests, if Athens had not left us her tragedians, philosophers and sculptors along with her politicians and generals. We also put up with Athenian arrogance and ruthlessness because we have Athenian culture to enjoy. Cicero expressed a modern attitude when he wrote of his awe as he traversed the streets of Athens, and "sat where Plato sat." And there is more than Athens in the catalogue of our debts to Greece. From the time of the epic, Hellenism was developing art forms fundamental to western culture. To Hellenism we owe our concepts of the epic, of lyric poetry, drama, history, philosophy, our styles of sculpture, painting and architecture. More than just the forms, we also owe Greek writers many of the ideas which have persisted in western culture and ideology.

The cultural aspects of Hellenism did not exist in isolation from the rest of the social situation. As we can see in Greek history a particular approach to civic life, or a tension between narrow and broad visions of political control, and as we can trace the thrust to power, or attitudes toward foreigners, or dependence on oppression, we can connect those aspects of the Greek experience with much of what we know and admire in Greek culture. Cultural expressions are very much influenced by their environment, just as the environment is in turn influenced by the ideas of culture, so that there is a symbiotic relationship in which it is very difficult to isolate cause from effect. This was as true for the Greeks as it is for us. The *Iliad* and the *Odyssey* could not have emerged from fifth-century Athens any more than from nineteenth-century Europe, and Athenian tragedy needed its background in order to flourish. These cultural expressions are not slavish repetitions of dominant ideas, however, and they may in fact contain rejections of prevailing attitudes. Furthermore, in a civilization with as varied a history or as great a diversity of contemporary societies as Hellenism possessed, there will be in culture both forms and ideas which are contradictory or antagonistic, presenting an intellectual and ideological tension which is fruitful in itself. That tension, and a pursuit of its resolution, are characteristics of Hellenic culture which have come down in western civilization as important aspects of life and thought and art.

Some of these tensions emerge as early as we have Greek ideas. In the *Iliad*, for example, the great hero Achilles confronts a cosmos which he thought was ordered, with rules of conduct which he had been taught and which he had followed until they failed him. The great epic of war and battle, men and gods, is also an epic of a personal war, as one human being struggles to define for himself the right way to live life, and finds in the end that nothing works, that only the struggle itself makes human life noble. This philosophy is not explicitly stated, but it underlies the action. These are tacit assumptions common to the bards who carried the oral epic through time, and accepted by the audiences who listened to them. They make sense in an aristocratic society of warriors, physically strong and brave, whose short lives aim at a glory recognized and praised by others. It is the ideal recognized by Nietszche as that of the *übermensch*, the "over-man," superior to others, pursuing the complete fulfilment of his potential. It also belongs to a society which does not have an answer to the "meaning of life" or a concept of the cosmos which conceives of it as obeying a moral order.

There was, however, a contrary notion, that the universe was under control, and that the gods who act whimsically or in conflict in the *Iliad* were actually part of a system which made sense, and in which justice and virtue, or wickedness and crime received appropriate rewards. The Boeotian Hesiod, who wrote while the *Iliad* was still being sung orally, knew gods who punished injustice and who rewarded honest, hard labor. As his *Generations of the Gods* was influenced by Near Eastern mythology, so the ideas of justice in *Works and Days* may owe something to the east, but elsewhere, in Athens, Solon in the sixth century had the same confidence. Both Hesiod and Solon faced up to the problem that to appearances, wickedness went unpunished. To them, there was an explanation, for Zeus always avenged evil. Hesiod tells his wicked brother that at times Zeus punishes a whole city for the crimes of a single man, while Solon sees time as the answer: if a man escapes immediate punishment, it comes later, and if not, then to his sons. But it comes. There is in both these early writers a confidence that the gods deal with the world in conformity to human ideas of morality, a very different sense than that of the epic's Achilles.

With the same self-confidence that judged the order and morality of the universe in terms of human values, the Greeks proceeded to plumb the physical cosmos. In the sixth century, philosophers attempted to devise theoretical models of the manner in which the visible world functioned, but seeking the "real nature" of reality rather than descriptions of its surface manifestations. These models aimed at explanations for both change and constancy among the objects of the earth and the celestial phenomena of stars, planets, sun and moon. A number of theories emerged, but we know the ideas of the various philosophers only from fragmentary quotations and references by later authors. Some general patterns are clear, however. Heraclitus of Ionia, for example, argued that the fundamental nature of reality was fire, burning or expiring as regulated by an eternal principle, and that change was a real phenomenon as existence moved between related opposites. Others were not so satisfied to accept this kind of explanation of change, and the Eleatic school of Italy insisted on some unchanging principle, with one of its fifth-century members, Parmenides, describing reality as a unity, motionless, continuous and with no beginning or end, and unchanging. These concepts regarded change as an illusion, establishing for Greek thought a tradition which denied the apparent evidence of the senses, and substituted abstract reason as the human agency to achieve truth. Other fifth-century thinkers attempted models which allowed for both change and constancy. Leucippus and Democritus proposed a description of the cosmos as constructed of atoms, indivisible and invisible, infinite in number and type, which, as they fall through the void of empty space, link up to form the objects of the world, and then break apart to dissolve the phenomena which we know. The atoms remain forever, but the material things they make up are constantly forming, changing and disappearing. This atomic theory revived in later Greek thought, but it did not provide much basis for physical speculation in the fifth and fourth centuries.

Some modern analysts and historians of thought draw parallels between the earlier, Heraclitan approach, and oriental religion and mysticism, and, for that matter, some of the ideas of modern physics. The concept of the universe as a unified continuum, if in fact Heraclitan, would seem to have similarities to both Buddhist thought and modern physics. The proposition that phenomena occur in tension beween opposites, that hot and cold are merely descriptions of aspects of the same phenomenon which is a unity connecting two opposites, also appears in the cosmological descriptions of Buddhist writers. If there are parallels between the two cosmologies, it is very interesting that they both emerge in their respective areas at about the same time—the sixth century B.C. However, the Buddhist writings are complete, and clear in their statements, where the Heraclitan and early Greek ideas are in fragmentary quotes, often difficult to understand or uncertain in meaning. It many not, therefore, be a fair description of the evolution of Greek thought to say that the concept of unity and continuum gave way to Democritan ideas of diversity and separation which dominated western physics for two millenia after.

It is clear, however, that the Greek approach to the analysis of the cosmos was one which used reason and argumentation as the method of obtaining knowledge. Plato shared this view, even in proposing his theory of transcendent forms of which observable phenomena were merely imitations. Knowledge of the forms was achievable by reason, so that virtue, as Plato had Socrates say, was knowledge and therefore teachable. If the forms were transcendent, the process of learning was not. Greek ideas of the nature of reality established a definition of knowledge of the cosmos which required it to be teachable or repeatable. If the eastern mystic, having reached a perception of the nature of reality, will say "I can't teach you what I know, but I can teach you how to try to learn it yourself," the Greek, or western approach, insists that what is known can be taught, and that if it cannot be taught, learned, discussed, criticized and tested, it is not really known.

These are philosophical concepts, and they suited philosophy when it was refined as a discipline, practiced by Plato, Aristotle and the other professional philosophers of the fourth century and later. They may not have suited the approaches of the sixth and fifth century cosmologists, and they certainly did not apply to the Athenian dramatists, whose tragedies dealt with moral, religious and philosophical ideas before the schools examined them in an organized way. As tragedy developed in fifth-century Athens as part of the city-wide celebration of the festival of the god Dionysus, Athenians watched some of the most extraordinary works of popular entertainment the world has ever seen. Each year, at the festival of the Great Dionysia in spring, three dramatic poets competed with presentations of three tragedies and one satyric play each. Today we have only a few of the plays which were actually put on, undoubtedly close to a thousand in the course of the fifth century. Only three poets, Aeschylus, Sophocles, and Euripides, are represented by complete plays, and the total number is under forty. Most of what we have shows the focus of the tragedies on moral, ethical, religious and political issues. They might treat the just punishment of the king of Persia in Aeschylus' *Persians,* or divine endowment of human courts of justice in his trilogy, *Oresteia.* In *Antigone,* Sophocles presented the age-old human dilemma of a conflict between two good principles, the goal of order and discipline and law in human society as it contends with individual moral commitments. His *Oedipus Tyrannus* treats the outcome of an attempt to evade an oracle and the result of a ruler's self-confident pursuit of his goal, while other plays deal with mistrust or deceit, and in his last play, *Oedipus at*

Colonus, there is an optimism that in the long run, suffering may bring purification and reward. Euripides ranges widely over human moral and religious issues, and his plays were preferred by Socrates and most readers in later antiquity.

The extant tragedies are extraordinary in their force, still felt today, making the plays so formative of the ideas and the literature of western culture. They are also still vital, in that they frame issues which western culture has come to regard as fundamental: Why should human beings suffer? Is there a moral order in the universe, or are we the playthings of chance or hostile gods? Do people bring their troubles on themselves, or is human disaster sometimes inherent in the nature of things? The plays mark a high point in human literary effort and achievement in terms of their content and their influence on later times, but they are also exceptional in their role in society and the extent to which the citizens of Athens participated in their creation. The wealthier classes paid for their performance as a public expense on a par with the maintenance of military equipment, and the ordinary citizens attended the theater and judged among the plays presented. Thus the dramatic presentations at the festival of Dionysus are part of the complex relationship between society and citizen which characterized Greek life in general, and was extremely broadly based in Athens.

The deep discussions of the human condition were thus not addressed to an intellectual elite, as philosophy and some literature later was. The ideas of the tragedies had to be comprehensible to a wide audience, and an audience picking up on the spoken word, not able to look back and reread a difficult passage. This is undoubtedly the reason that some expressions of ideas tend to be blunt and sometimes repeated, or that simple moral maxims appear from time to time. However, any survey of Greek literature or discussion of Athenian tragedy will also show the subtlety and breadth of the concepts the tragedians treated, and which, presumably, they expected the audience to be able to follow. The audiences' abilities are also suggested by a play by the comic poet, Aristophanes. In his *Frogs* there is a contest between Aeschylus and Euripides, and the jokes and the references show that the comic poet expected his audience of ordinary citizens to have a high level of literary knowledge and familiarity with style of the playwrights he was burlesquing. It is clear that at the same time as the first professional philosophers, the sophists and Socrates, were educating the young of the wealthy aristocratic and commercial classes, ordinary citizens were receiving their philosophical and intellectual upbringing at the plays of the tragedians.

Historians of Greek literature have often observed that after the fifth century, tragedy and the drama became merely a form of entertainment, or at best an art form without deep probing of the human condition and human and religious values. Surely part of the reason for this is the emergence of philosophy as a discipline, and of schools within which it could be practiced. When these questions could be addressed in an organized and formal way, according to rules of reason and argumentation, with the expectation that Plato proposed, that reasoned argument could bring human beings closer to genuine knowledge, there was less inclination to pursue the tension and incompleteness which often was inherent in the dramatic treatment.

Socrates, claimed Aristotle, was the first person to pursue "deductive reasoning and definition by universals," and he relates this to the "beginning of scientific knowledge." Whether or not we accept Aristotle's specific and clear statement about Socrates, whose teaching remains a much-argued issue as he wrote and left us nothing in his own name, everything we know about Socrates suggests his interest in establishing some order in the human discussion of ethical issues. Certainly after him, teachers no longer wandered from house to house in the city, setting up shop at the behest of patrons. A number of Socrates' followers established formal doctrines, or wrote essays of a philosophical nature, or both. Socrates' most successful and influential student, Plato, created a place, the Academy, where the philosophically minded could come to learn. There Aristotle came at the age of 17, and developed his own philosophical principles. Some of those were opposed to Plato's basic notions, and some struck out into specific areas of knowledge, formal biology, physics, astronomy, logic, political science and the like. Aristotle too founded a school at Athens, having travelled from Athens to Asia Minor, to the court of Philip to tutor

Alexander, and then back to Athens after Philip's death. Aristotle's life spanned the period when city power gave way to the Macedonian monarchy, and his experience and role at the Macedonian court exemplifies the distance ethics and cosmology had traveled from the community stage of the Dionysiac festival to a closely argued and sometimes difficult to understand set of academic processes which could be supported by royal patronage.

A major reason for shifting the treatment of these issues from drama to technical philosophy is the emergence of a much wider use of writing in Athens in the latter part of the fifth century. In mid fifth-century Athens, drama dealt with the same issues as epic. In the religious context of the festival of Dionysus, audiences listened to plays which dealt with the natures and actions of the gods, human behavior, morality and ethics in private and public life, the interaction between the cosmos and the human domain. Narration was secondary, particularly in the works of Aeschylus and Sophocles, and reasoned argument was not only scanty but hardly necessary, the speeches and choruses instead aiming at producing emotional perception of the outcome of the actions of the characters. What happens when people do *that*? is a question that drama can ask, and the answers provide the nature of what drama can teach.

This kind of composition can present human problems, can demonstrate their effects and the actions they stimulate. It can present situations, and offer emotional and spiritual interpretations. It can probe deeply into religious and philosophical problems, and present them with stunning clarity and emotional force. It can even present solutions by way of examples and the simulation of action. What it cannot do, however, is present sequential argument, moving from starting point through a number of ideas and steps to reach a conclusion which is convincing because of the coherence of a series of statements. It conveys its truth through the directness of perception, rather than through the construction of its logic.

Logic belongs to the world of writing, rather than speech. It calls for a great deal more than just the hesitation of cogitation, reflection, revision, as Plato described Lysias developing a speech he was to deliver, writing "at his leisure, and over a long period of time." It calls for the reader to have leisure and time to read, reread, think and evaluate. And argumentative writing, itself, ultimately calls for some form of logic, some set of rules which a reader will accept as validating the steps of argument, and which can be used as the reader checks back over what has been read, rereading and rethinking to assert agreement or denial.

So writing both permits and calls for logical sequential developent in argumentation. It also permits lengthy, complex and variegated narrative. It can accept a bewildering array of people, places, events, can reach over a long period of time and can even allow for frequent forays back and forth in time. When the writing is presented on the pages of books, in the manner of modern texts, rather than in the rolls of early and middle antiquity, pages over which the reader can turn back and forth to be reminded of ideas and names, the complexity, subtlety and content can be almost limitless. Today, for example, historians can dump all sorts of obscurities into their texts, in the confidence that a reader who has got lost can be reoriented by using the index.

It is clear that the work of the extant prose writers of the fifth century does not show a deliberate rejection of earlier attitudes about humanity and the cosmos. There is neither that, nor a calculated endorsement of a new and different idea, or even an explicit endorsement of the value of writing itself. These were, after all, transitional figures, with attitudes reflective of the past and involved in activity leading to the future. Plato, for one, in the very act of writing, denigrated its value and its relation to truth, holding out written books as mere reminders of the valuable, discussable and refutable ideas and words of spoken discourse. These fifth-century figures were not the first, by any means, to compose in writing or in prose. What is new about their age and their work is the growing importance of writing as the mode of communication, so that by the time of Plato's death in the mid fourth century, the written work was the norm. And what is important about all these writers is their acceptance of the basic assumption of the validity of human reason and knowledge. Herodotus asserted a cyclical nature for human history, citing evidence by which one can deduce its truth, and his account of the vast panorama of Persian and Greek history and the Persian Wars is a validation of the possibility that humans can know their limits. The Lydian history of the dynasty of Croesus is so precise a prelude in microcosm of the great story to come that we must see his using the potential of writing to focus the attention of readers on his main points.

Thucydides, with his seemingly modern choice of a narrower focus to probe in depth, has a similar faith in the value of history. Who can read his pages without an awareness of his aim of moral education? To know the events of this "greatest disturbance of the Greeks" is to learn a great deal about right and wrong in statecraft and human behavior. In Plato's case, learning is what all the discourse is about—probing the potential of human reason to recognize true reality and abandon the deceptions of the world of seeming and becoming to which the senses respond. Even Xenophon, seen by many to have been of a lesser intellectual ability than the others, wrote with the same confidence in the capability of politicians and philosophers to make decisions on the basis of knowledge.

Yet, with all this, the heart of traditional Hellenism was still part of the world-view of these figures. The human being operates in a cosmos over which humanity has very little control. The king of Herodotus' cycle is as powerless to affect the broad sweep of events as is any figure of epic or tragedy. Thucydides' narrative takes place entirely on the human level and the author passes by all the questions of cosmic and human interaction, and for the most part, the same is true of Xenophon. Plato's work is concerned with knowing reality, not altering or affecting it. The difference between Achilles and Oedipus on the one hand and the historian or philosopher of Herodotus and Plato is knowledge, but it is *only* knowledge. Achilles at the end of the *Iliad*, like Ajax, Philoctetes, Prometheus, is unbowed but uncomprehending. Plato and Herodotus would lead us to comprehension and perhaps acquiescence, but they would not assert the modern confidence in the possibility of human control of the environment.

Knowledge itself would someday be praised as power, and the human confidence in the power of knowledge traces itself back to that point in Hellenism when some Greeks developed a confidence in the very possibility of knowledge, so that in the next generation, Aristotle could make his assertion that the human being by nature desires to know. From the fourth century on, many Greek writers based their whole approach to understanding on the tacit assumption that accurate, or true knowledge was not only abstractly possible but in some instances at least had actually been achieved. By the end of the fourth century we could have Epicurus assert the complete divorce between humanity and the cosmos: "If the gods exist, they don't care." Zeno, his contemporary and rival, as we understand the two schools of thought, began a tradition which in essence equated the divine force with that of reason.

This is a long way from the cry of one of Euripides' characters, "If you are a god you must be crazy," but the Euripidean vision of the cosmos as a moral shambles, at least from the human point of view, persisted in Hellenism for a long time. This is the view of life which the epic accepts, which fits the events of the plays of Sophocles and Euripides, which Aeschylus explores in some plays and rejects in the *Oresteia*, that remarkable account of transition from divine to human justice, from cosmic conflict tormenting humanity to the settlement of scores both divine and human. The view of humanity floundering in a cosmos neither understood nor manageable in any way never died out of Hellenism, but the manner in which it would be discussed changed radically. No longer an *Oresteia* on the stage, but dialectic and argument, recorded for reminding and discussion, as Plato would put it, carried the burden of human cosmological, ethical and moral investigation for Hellenism.

The atrophy of the tragic drama came quickly after the birth of written philosophy, and within a decade or two the stage was occupied by writers of comedy and of melodrama like Menander. The genre in which thought was carried on altered irreversibly. While enquiry into the human condition might in the future be carried on in a "literary mode," that was a long time in the future and would await an idealization of Hellenism many centuries away. Meanwhile, for the rest of antiquity, poetry and the drama would be devoted, for the most part, to entertainment and the expression of personal feelings—or at the most, impersonal ideas and ideals about society and human affairs, or metrical renditions of philosophical tracts.

It is the philosophical tracts that would carry on the exploration which characterized the religious drama of fifth-century Athens. The first creator of these, Plato, was himself suspicious of the very medium of writing which he was using, and tried to preserve the impact of orality and metaphor which he knew from his youth. He certainly did not move very far along the road of logic and controlled argument which writing allowed. This emerged in the work of his student Aristotle, whose extant philosophical tracts show a remarkable difference from Plato's in their confidence in writing and in their use of tools which writing makes possible. As history, once fixed as a genre by Herodotus and Thucydides, comprehended an assembly of information, opinion, values and experience of an extremely wide range of people, places and times, and could even spill over into poetry as in the *Aeneid*, philosophy could, now in an organized way, approach subjects like physics and metaphysics, astronomy, ethics, logic, rhetoric, politics and natural science. And all these are based not only on Aristotle's assumption of the essentially human nature of the taste for knowledge, but on a confidence in the ability of the human to achieve something significant in a quest for it. And it is a buildable, developable kind of knowledge, unlike that at the end of the *Antigone*, where the chorus tells us, "The basis of happiness is wisdom." What is the wisdom we learn from the misfortunes of Antigone, Haemon and Creon, in terms of knowledge we can use and expand for the future? Very different is the knowledge we gain from Aristotle, and his exposition of the route to human happiness in the *Nicomachean Ethics* and *Politics*.

Both Sophocles and Aristotle contributed to the medley which made up the music of Hellenism, and their very different harmonics continued to influence the manner in which the music was composed and heard. However, in Hellenism and in our culture, the confidence in human potential for knowing has run in a straight line from Plato to Popper. With all the differences in the style of philosophical investigation and the manner of its support, a central characteristic of Greek thought persisted. All was carried on in the confidence that the questions were soluble by human reason, and that the mysteries of the cosmos would ultimately yield to human investigation. Aristotle's fundamental assumption about the human being, that it was in the nature of humans to want to know, was coupled with a standing confidence that they could do so. This fundamental intellectual attitude was the philosophical version of the general Greek attitude toward the position of humanity in the cosmos: that it was the human that counted, and that institutions and processes should be designed and evaluated in terms of their benefit to living people—not for god or the gods, nor for ancestors or souls in transit to a future life. Tragedies were important and comprehensible to the citizens of an imperial city because they asked questions which those citizens had to decide: fundamental questions of law, order, morality and justice which Thucydides portrays them discussing in the pages of his history of the times. Later, the adaptation of ethics and morality to personal instead of civic needs still preserved the human orientation. Philosophers were less important to the populace as a whole, but valuable to the Athenian upper classes of the fourth century, as the members of those classes found less satisfaction in the leadership of a city now much less successful. Philosophy, in proposing the pursuit of personal virtue in place of traditional aristocratic values, became a helpful adjunct to those citizens less willing to give their all for the glory of their city, or follow the example of the fifth-century citizens Pericles had praised.

The development of the broader use of writing at Athens in the later fifth century, with its great impact on modes of thought and use of literature, was part of the more general social and political situation. Athens' imperial needs, for administration, financial record-keeping, and public communication, all called for the use of writing. It is no accident that the impact of writing on literature and thought came together with the expansion of power and administration and the advance to a greater democratization among the citizens of Athens. Just as the late fifth century is the time when public inscriptions first begin to appear in large numbers, and do so at Athens, so it is Athens where we can document a change from the orality of dramatic composition to the written texts of formal philosophy.

In tracing the relationship between cultural activity and society, it is important to note that what we call the arts were much more closely integrated into everyday activity than was the case even in Roman times. The Latin *Ars longa, vita brevis,* "Art is long, life is short," with its focus on art as cultural and particular, has no counterpart in Greek. In the parlance of Hellenism, what we call art is *techne*, not exactly "technique," in English, but also not a practice with some special cachet. The word for sculptor, for example, is *lithourgos*, which can be translated "stoneworker" and can refer to what we would call a mason as well as to a worker like the great Phidias, designer of the marble sculpture of the Parthenon on the acropolis of Athens. While the practitioners of *"techne,"* whether literary or in the plastic arts, might be praised and famous for their productions, they lived the lives of ordinary citizens and they did not make up a particular group as they do in modern society and have done for hundreds of years. Sophocles, for example, came from a wealthy family, was an active politician, an imperial administrator, a general and a diplomat, as well as a writer of plays. Aeschylus came from an old, noble family. Euripides is the first to attract descriptions as an iintellectual, a lover of books, a recluse, and even he served in a local priesthood and was a member of an embassy to Syracuse on one occasion. In the plastic arts, the creators of many of the most famous works are unnamed: there is no identification of the carvers of the many male and female figures of sixth-century Athens. Many of the potters and painters of the greatest examples of vase painting in the sixth and fifth centuries did not put their names on their work, and we do not know the names of those who executed some of the greatest sculptural work of the period.

The manner in which such activities as sculpture and literature were part of life was often religious. The connection between culture and divinity in the festival of Dionysus at Athens was by no means unique. At Athens itself, the art of Phidias and others was an expression of religious impulse, decorating the Parthenon, the temple of Athena, and creating the great gold and ivory statue of the goddess herself. Outside Athens, Olympia, in the Peloponnesus, and Delphi, in central Greece, were great scenes of artistic effort as well as religious centers, connecting art and service to divinities. At these sancuaries of Zeus and Apollo, architecture and sculpture brought the talents of the greatest artists from many Greek cities, and in cooperative service to divinity, the great quadrennial athletic games tied athletic competition to religion. At Olympia, the Olympic Games were first and foremost the honoring of Zeus, and at Delphi, Pythian Games were added to the musical contests in honor of Apollo. Just as the athletics—and the honor for triumphing—were not seen as separate, "professional" activities, but were integrated into the religious and social environment, so the dedication of temples, statues, vases and other precious goods was not an isolated practice of "art." Athletics and the plastic arts joined dramatic performances like those at Athens, the honorific and religious victory odes of Pindar, and many other cultural activities in the public and religious life of the Greek cities.

The practice of cultural and intellectual activity as a special category of activity began to be recognized toward the end of the fifth century, but even then tradition called for it to be part of, rather than apart from, the rest of life. Today we think of the artist or intellectual as separate from society, necessarily so to have the distance of vision from which to comment. The "ivory tower" is the home of academic activity. To Greeks, those activities were practiced like other trades, or carried on freely as part of the endowment of citizens. Comedy derided the sophists, professionals who developed rhetoric, ethics, political studies and the like, and taught them for pay. Literature was something of a special category, in the sense that writers were named and their works identified, and literature and its preservation were intimately connected with the spread of the practice of writing. Even before writing was general the most aristocratic of writers had their names attached to their efforts, and often, the names of early writers survive better than their works. We have the names of many lyric poets, philosophers, historians, dramatists, cosmologists of the sixth and fifth centuries, but the names of those for whom we have any real body of extant work can be numbered on a set of fingers. It was only in the sixth century that the Homeric epics were actually written down, according to the tradition which reports that Pisistratus of Athens had this done, and except for Homer and Hesiod, Greek literature before the fifth century is preserved only in quotations by later ancient authors or on papyrus texts found in Egypt over the last century.

It is interesting that literature is one of the very few areas in which women played a public role. Although they competed in athletic contests at Sparta, they did not do so elsewhere. In religious centers, they had some specific importance, as priestesses of female divinities and as the specially qualified priestess, or pythoness, of Apollo at Delphi, who received the oracle of the god and transmitted the unintelligible sounds to priests for translation and interpretation. In poetry, which was less directly connected to femaleness, a few women achieved great repute, although little of that work actually survives today. Sappho, who lived on the island of Lesbos in the northeast Aegean, at the end of the seventh and early part of the sixth centuries, was famous for her lyric poetry, and her love verses addressed to women established the sexual meaning of "lesbian" for all time. Although much of her work is now lost, it continued to be known in later centuries, and a great deal of what we have of her writing comes from papyrus fragments of the early centuries of the Roman period. A later woman poet, Telesilla of Argos, was esteemed for her poetry and also for arming Argive women against the Spartans. In Boeotia, Pindar had a successful rival in Corinna, who supposedly defeated him in verse competitions five times. Admittedly, none of these are Athenians nor date to the late fifth century, the nadir of women's freedom, when women of the better classes were expected to remain isolated from public activity as far as possible, but Athens does provide the example of Aspasia, Pericles' mistress, who maintained a cultural salon and promoted philosophical, literary and artistic activities in Athens. It is true that she was not a native Athenian, but a courtesan from Miletus, and that Pericles' political enemies attacked her. Nevertheless, she was of high intellectual ability, she was acquitted when charged with impiety, and her son by Pericles was legitimized when Pericles' sons by an earlier wife died. All these cases may be exceptions to the normal behavior and expectations of women, but it also may be that in cultural pursuits women had somewhat greater latitude than they had in other activities.

It is unfortunate that our picture of intellectual, cultural and artistic activity in Greece is so dominated by the Athenians. This is also the case in regard to another, extremely important aspect of Greek education and verbal and written activity, rhetoric. Because speechmaking is rather suspect in modern political and intellectual contexts, we tend to forget how essential it was, in terms of both content and style, in a Greek city. Athens provides us with many examples of speeches written for criminal, political and personal trials before law courts, and others written ostensibly for delivery but probably actually intended for circulation in writing. Fifth-century speeches in murder trials by Antiphon, for example, show an intricate tie between religion and political procedure in arguing the innocence of a defendent, and a wide range of speeches by Lysias show a master of language pleading public issues in speeches before law courts. Demosthenes' speeches in the fourth century show rhetoric in public assemblies, urging the adoption of Demosthenes' policies and denouncing Philip of Macedon. Although all these are Athenian, it is clear that in the fifth century, rhetoric was not, in the first instance, an Athenian specialty. When Gorgias came to Athens in 427 on an embassy from his native city of Leontini in Sicily, the Athenians were overwhelmed by his eloquence. He and others later taught rhetoric at Athens as part of the group of professional teachers known as sophists, and in the fourth century the art of speaking well was an important, if not the major, discipline taught in the new schools which emerged in Athens after the time of Socrates. The fifth-century sophists came from many different places: Protagoras, from Abdera in Thrace, Hippias, from Elis in the Peloponnesus, Gorgias, from Sicily. They taught not only rhetoric but ethics and political action, so that we can see philosophical and literary traditions existing outside Athens, even if we do not today have any of the written work that came from other places. The extent and depth of non-Athenian activity may be hinted at by the medical corpus of writings attributed to Hippocrates, a fifth-century physician who led a school on the island of Cos. Even if much of the Hippocratic corpus is not genuinely the writing of the fifth-century physician, it shows the existence of that kind of scientific writing then and in the succeeding century on the eastern side of the Aegean.

Although Athens dominates the cultural scene in Greece in the fifth and fourth centuries, there is enough left of the creations of other cities in the Greek world to show that the phenomena found at Athens were general. Lyric flourished in many places. Even at Sparta, in its early history, there were Tyrtaeus, who was almost surely a native, and Alcman, who may have come from Asia Minor. We know of lyric poets from cities all along the Anatolian coast, and that region also produced many of the first philosophers. In the west too, philosophy flourished long before the sophists began coming to Athens. Although Athens again was pre-eminent for vase painting in the late sixth and the fifth centuries, the rich cities of Greece earlier had their own vigorous traditions. Corinthian-style vases are found in many places in the Greek world, and even Laconia produced some fine vases at the beginning of the sixth century. The early Doric temples of Italy and the cities of Sicily show the vigor of the plastic arts in the west as well, and the court of Hieron of Syracuse was noted for the presence of many literary figures. Tragedy was performed outside Athens also, and a form of Doric lyric drama may even have influenced early forms at Athens.

Despite the presence of all this activity outside Athens, there is no doubt that once Athens built herself into the wealthiest and most powerful city of Greece, her prosperity also made her the outstanding cultural center in Greece in the fifth century. As Pisistratus brought Ionian artists to Athens in the mid sixth century, in the next, Athens could attract philosophers and sophists to make her into the first great eclectic city, a clearinghouse for Greek thought which gave Athenians the benefit of ideas from all over the Greek world. The wealth that flowed into Athens in the fifth century permitted the city and her citizens to devote great resources to artistic endeavors in both religious and civic service, and to create and support the growth of drama, which flourished at the Great Dionysia but also had performance at other Attic festivals to contribute to the sharpening of skills. The activities of the fifth-century sophists at Athens gave impetus to the schools of the fourth. Because all the arts flourished in a civic environment, the stronger the city the greater the cultural expression of her life. Before the dominance of Athens, the resources devoted to Greek culture were more generally distributed among many parts of the Greek world, but for the period of Athenian power, her resources could produce the greatest and most memorable expressions of Hellenism.

By the time of Alexander the Great in the latter part of the fourth century, the whole political and social picture had changed, and with it the cultural. Just as Athenian citizens seem to have been less willing to devote their persons to military service, the dwindling civic focus of life seems to have undercut the vitality of cultural life. Writing, with its shift toward the professionalization of culture and intellectual life, had remade the philosophical world and the art of writing history, but had not benefited other literary pursuits so well. With time, cities would be less and less the support for all these arts, and the patterns of cultural patronage in courts like that of Hieron of Syracuse and the kings of Macedon would prevail for much of the Greek world. It was fortunate that Alexander received from his father and forebears the tradition of supporting Hellenism, and transmitted that to his successors, for it was only they, for the most part, who could afford to be its patrons.

9 Forward from the Greeks

The stability the Greeks sought never came. As early as we know their history, we find them in turmoil, both within their individual cities and in the world at large. Civic disturbance, revolution and violent political unrest were frequent, and, when a city seemed to manage internal affairs well for a while, as did both Athens and Sparta, there was war with other Greek cities to disturb the enjoyment of civic quiet. The obstacles to stability were inherent in Greek society and attitudes. The fundamental orientation of the relationship between government and populace called for participation and sharing, at least to some extent, and in most cities, the civic conflict arose as a matter of disagreement over the allocations of resources to the different elements in society. Struggles for power were battles over control of shares, and without the concept of growth, the share of one group could only increase by taking from another within the city, or by taking from another city altogether.

The experience of the modern world has not been so different. The western democracies have been able to provide reasonable internal stability for the last two centuries by dramatically increasing their wealth. The idea of growth which underlies industrial society has helped to do this, but even here, a great deal of economic prosperity came from the politico-economic empires of the nineteenth century. The burst of genuine growth in the late 1940's and the 1950's encouraged western populations to an optimism that they could prosper and increase their material conditions without imperial domination, but then, convinced of the Club of Rome's "limits to growth," governments and people alike have turned inward to create "leaner and meaner" economies which threaten to produce permanent underclasses like those of the Greek world.

The problems of the Greek world were much greater than ours. The complete absence of any notion of genuine growth in an economy precluded the development of the industrial and technological infrastructure which is an assumed basis of modern life. There was simply no way in which an Athenian politician, for example, could meet demands of the poorer classes without finding new sources of income for the city. The struggles and shifts between oligarchy and democracy were not just disputes over political theory, they had at their heart the sense of the few and rich that the multitude, if they had power, would take their property. The opinion that the lower classes supported democracy for economic self-interest is implicit in the sardonic screed of the unknown Athenian aristocrat we call "The Old Oligarch," when he remarks, for example, that the multitude are mainly interested in holding the public offices which bring them pay and benefit their pockets.

It is true that the Athenian democracy of the fifth century brought more benefits to a greater part of the Athenian citizenry than governments in most other cities brought to their people. To do this, however, Athens used more slaves and controlled more other cities than other Greek cities did, and, it seems, imposed more restrictions on its women into the bargain. The parallels with Sparta are significant. Although Sparta has never been thought of as a democracy, the Spartan citizen "equals" enjoyed economic privileges and benefits which depended on the production of a huge under-class of Laconian and Messenian helots, and Sparta too had an overseas imperial adventure, though later and of shorter duration than the Athenian.

So long as the prevailing ethos called for some sharing of authority and benefits among all the citizens, and production growth could not be called upon to increase wealth, Greek societies were forced into exploitation. The huge numbers of women, slaves, helots, resident aliens, foreign cities and their populations contributing to the well-being of citizens were not even seen as oppressed or exploited. Their condition could be taken as a natural aspect of a world in which the only people who really counted in each society were the sovereign members of that society - the adult male citizens. Macedonian kings were concerned with satisfying the expectations of the warrior-troops who made up their armies, Spartan leaders aimed at the security of the Spartiate control of the helots, and democratic Athenian politicians framed policies calculated to benefit their citizens.

The attitude toward slavery was part of this limiting concern with the single city-society. Citizens of other Greek cities could be slaves, although there was some doubt about the propriety of this on the part of philosophers and social theorists. There was, however, no hesitation to use hordes of non-Greeks to fill the need for slaves, and slavery of barbarians could seem "natural" to Aristotle. This attitude towards barbarians was an extension of the sense of community which existed among the members of a Greek city population. The barbarians did not have any claim on participation in the Greek world. The common language, religion and culture giving Greeks some relationship across city lines did not extend to them. Greeks had only the interest of the curious about barbarians, and used them whenever Greek power made that possible. The attitude toward the barbarian world was an exaggeration and an extension of the attitude of one Greek society toward another, and Alexander the Great merely expressed it in an extreme as he swept eastward in the last third of the fourth century.

I do not write this to condemn the Greeks. With all their oppression and turmoil, Greeks managed to create societies with power bases and privileges and prosperity extended more widely than had been the case before - and, we should note, more widely than has been the case for almost two millenia after the triumph of Philip of Macedon. The great wrongs Greek citizens perpetrated on others were no worse than those inflicted by many other societies and peoples over the centuries, and those occurred without the ideal of participation and sharing. The Greek ideal could not progress to one of wider scope, impeded as it was by the failure to imagine a more prosperous world. It has remained, however, to inspire modern ideologies of participation, and combined with the conception of economic growth, has helped to make the sharing of power and wealth a reality for many, and a goal for others.

We should be aware of the extent to which we are advancing ideals rooted in Hellenism. The demands of developing nations for a larger share in the world's goods, taking some of the wealth of the industrialized world if necessary, evoke memories of economic attitudes of the Greeks, while broadening greatly their social ideal of participation. The condemnation of racism in the minds of many, and the assertion that women have a right to share power and economic benefits, represent a tacit expansion of the idea of "citizen" which first emerged in Greek societies. We should remember that the great burst of energy devoted to the liberation of women and minority groups in North America came in the 1960's, on the heels of the optimism of the 50's envisioning a future with more wealth to be shared. It was a time when Greek ideals could be expanded, because the Greek assumptions of limit and stability had been overturned. Today we face a crisis of confidence both in this social ideal and in the economic conception that has brought us so far. The Greek story will remind us that the penalties for falling back are great.

Bibliographical Note

In this book, I focus in particular on those aspects of Greek history which relate to questions of the control and direction of society, the population and their interrelation. This is not a study of democracy, although Athenian democracy in particular is an important aspect of the discussion. In recent years, there has been a great deal of discussion of Athenian democracy and the Athenian empire among scholars and thinkers, particularly in the English-speaking work and especially in the United States. I suspect this has to do with a discontent among and about Americans as the people address the weaknesses in twentieth-century democratic government. One of the most recent of these studies, Eli Sagan's *The Honey and the Hemlock: Democracy and Paranoia in Ancient Athens and Modern America*, Basic Books (1991), sees the development of democracy in both Athens and the U.S. as a "miracle" made possible as the societies felt less paranoid fear and hostility directed at opposition within and without, and Sagan is cautiously optimistic about the future of democracy in taking the view that there is nothing inherent in the situation which it makes it impossible for modern democracies to advance to a better stage of society with fewer paranoid defence mechanisms and the elimination some of the contemporary threats to human and planetary life.

One of the most rewarding books available to a person who wants to probe deeply into the society of Athenian democracy is Ellen M. Wood's *Peasant-Citizen and Slave: The Foundations of Athenian Democracy,*

London and New York (1988). While I came upon this work after I had formulated much of the material in my own book, I was deeply impressed by the cogency with which it argues many of the positions which I present without defense, and I find there valuable explanations of many important myths and prejudices about Athens, both ancient and modern.

Two books which look at the working of Athenian democracy and its institutions are *Democracy and Participation in Athens*, by R.K. Sinclair, Cambridge (1988), and *Mass and Elite in Democratic Athens*, by Josiah Ober, Princeton (1989). Both of these attempt to get at the issues of the manner in which the democracy functioned and the democracy's ability to govern effectively, and they go beyond accounts of structures to evalkuate the effects of institutions and practice. An account which focuses on structure and institutions is David Stockton's *The Classical Athenian Democracy*, Oxford (1990), while Mogen H. Hansen's *The Athenian Democracy in the Age of Demosthenes: Structure, Principles and Ideology*, Oxford (1991) offers a diachronic survey down to 403 B.C., introduces social considerations into the discussion of institutions, and carries the analysis of Athenian democracy down to Aristotle's time. A New book by Chester Starr, *The Birth of Athenian Democracy: The Assembly in the Fifth Century B.C.*, Oxford (1990), concentrates on the workings and impact of the assembly of citizens.

Many studies of Athenian democracy treat the empire as an integral part of the story, and most analysts of the empire condemn the Athenians for their brutality in maintaining it, if for no other reason. Something of an exception is Malcolm McGregor's *The Athenians and Their Empire*, Vancouver (1987), which takes the view, in the end, that the Athenians and their empire kept the Persians at bay and prevented the return of parts of the Aegean to Persian control, as happened in the next century.

Sparta, for which we have much less information and therefore receives much less attention, has a reasonably full treatment in one recent book, *Athens and Sparta: Constructing Greek Political and Social History from 478 B.C.*, by Anton Powell, London (1988). Powell balances the account of Athens and the empire with an analysis of Spartan actions in the fifth century, and an explanation of Spartan life and society. He also has a salutory chapter on the importance of religious prophecy, as well as almost 40 pages of text on "Citizen Women of Athens." Not as many books as might be thought have been devoted to the subject of women. Sarah B. Pomeroy's *Goddesses, Whores, Wives and Slaves*, New York (1975), was published almost two decades ago, and Eva Cantarella's *Pandora's Daughters*, Baltimore (1987) is now five years old. The study of slavery is not much better off. The general survey of Greek slavery, Yvon Garlan's *Slavery in Ancient Greece*, originally published in French in 1982, has had the benefit of translation and an update, Ithaca (1988). It is a synthesis of scholarship and opinion about Greek slavery and is extremely valuable, although readers today may not be so interested in Garlan's concern with discussion of Marxist analysis. Garlan's book shows that there is a good deal of data about Greek slavery, particularly in Athens, and points up a very useful contrast between the heavy use of chattel slaves at Athens and its much less extensive application elsewhere, as in Dorian societies. Garlan's book gets away from the unhelpful preoccupation with arguing for the use of slavery to provide the leisure which the ordinary Athenian used to operate the democracy.

A more general survey of social and economic life is Frank J. Frost's *Greek Society*, in a new fourth edition, Lexington (1992). An older, but much fuller and more analytical presentation is M.M. Austin and P. Vidal-Naquet, *Economic and Social History of Ancient Greece*, Berkeley, 1977. A new study of Greek agriculture by T.W Gallant, *Risk and Survival in Ancient Greece*, Palo Alto (1991), shows not only the nature of Greek agriculture but its role as the fundamental basis of Greek society. A very different approach to social history is G.E.M. de Ste. Croix' *The Class Struggle in the Ancient Greek World*, Ithaca (1981), which, while failing to convince critics of its thesis of class conflict at the basis of history, has probably helped focus attention on the issue of the broad extent of oppression in Greek society. Another important issue, that of the development of literacy, the use of writing, and their effect on society, has been raised in a number of books by E.A. Havelock, notably *The Literate Revolution in Greece and its Cultural*

Consequences, Princeton (1982).

While democracy and social history have received especial attention in the last decade or so, there have been many excellent histories of Greece of the more traditional sort published in recent years. Hermann Bengtson's comprehensive work has now appeared in English, under the title *History of Greece from the Beginning to the Byzantine Era*, Ottawa (1988), and provides an unusually full scholarly bibliography, brought up to date by the translator, E. Bloedow. The relevant volumes of the new edition of *The Cambridge Ancient History* contain extensive classified bibliographies of general and scholarly works. Simon Hornblower presents a clear account of the classical period, from the end of the Persian Wars to the death of Alexander the Great, in *The Greek World , 479-323 B.C.*, London (1983). Surveys of Greek literature provide information and bibliographies for the ancient sources, and *The Cambridge History of Classical Literature*, I, *Greek Literature*, Cambridge (1985) is an excellent introduction to the material, and texts, translations and critical studies of importance can be found in the bibliography to the translation of Jacqueline de Romilly's survey, *A Short History of Greek Literature*, Chicago (1985).

Chronological Table

B.C.

1000	End of palace-centered Mycenaean kingdoms
900	Period of infiltration of Dorian-dialect speakers
814	Traditional date of the founding of Carthage
800	Homeric epics being sung. Period of Hesiod
776	Traditional date for the establishment of the Olympic Games
	Colonizing in Sicily and South Italy
753	Traditional Date for the founding of Rome
	Development of heavy armor for infantry
700	Tyrannies in many cities (700-600)
675	"Lycurgan" reforms at Sparta
	Zaleucus lawgiver at Locri, South Italy
	Tyranny begun at Corinth by Cypselus (c.655-625)
650	Beginnings of colonization in Black Sea area
	Foundation of Cyrene in North Africa (c. 630)
625	Approximate date for Greek establishment at Naucratis, Egypt
	Periander tyrant at Corinth (c. 625-585)
	621- traditional date for first Athenian lawcode of Draco
600	Approximate date for founding of Massilia (Marseille)
	594 - traditional date for Athenian year designated as archon year of Solon
	585 - an eclipse of the sun which the philosopher Thales is said to have predicted
	End of tyranny at Corinth (c. 583)
575	Poetic, and possibly political, activity of Solon

	Reign of Croesus, king of Lydia (560-546)
550	Pisistratus establishes tyranny at Athens (546)
	Tyranny at Samos under Polycrates (c.540-522)
	Defeat of Croesus by Cyrus of Persia (546)
	Ionian Greeks subject to Persia (545)
	Homeric epics written down
	Activity of Theognis of Megara
	Western Greeks defeated by Carthaginians (540)
	Activity of Pythagoras in South Italy
	Beginning of tragic performances in Athens
	Death of Pisistratus (528)
525	Etruscans defeated at Cumae (524)
	Expulsion of tyranny from Athens (510)
	Reforms of Cleisthenes (508)
500	Activity of Hecataeus of Miletus (historian) and Heraclitus of Ephesus (philosopher)
	Beginning of Ionian revolt (499)
	Alexander I king of Macedonia (c. 495-450)
	Ionians back under Persian control (493)
	Persian attack on Greece; Battle of Marathon (490)
	Gelon tyrant of Syracuse
	Ostracisms at Athens
	Discovery of new vein of silver in Athens' Laurium mines
	Second Persian invasion of Greece; Battle of Salamis (480); Battle of Plataea (479)
	Establishment of Delian League (478)
	Pindar's first *Olympian* ode (476)
475	Syracuse defeats Etruscans at Cumae (474)
	Production of Aeschylus' *Persians* (472)
	Athenians begin compelling allies to remain in Delian League
	Birth of Socrates (c. 469)
	First victory of Sophocles (468)
	Thasos revolts from Delian League and forced back (465)
	Ostracism of Cimon from Athens (461)
	War between Athens and Sparta (461-451)
	Oresteia of Aeschylus (458)
	Death of Aeschylus (456)
	First production by Euripides (455)
	Delian League treasury transferred from Delos to Athens (454)
	5 year truce between Athens and Sparta; Pericles' law defining Athenian citizenship
450	Perdiccas II king of Macedonia (c. 450-413)
	Beginning of construction of Parthenon (447); sculpture of

Phidias
Revolt of Euboea, Pericles' campaigns of 446
30 years' peace between Athens and Sparta (445)
Activity of Herodotus the historian
Athenian founding of Thurii in South Italy (443)
Pericles dominant in Athens
Sophocles treasurer of league (443/2), then general (441/0)
Production of Sophocles' *Ajax* and *Antigone* (c. 441)
Activity of sophists in Athens
Euripides' *Alcestis* produced (438)
Athens excludes Megara from league ports (432)
Outbreak of war between Athens and Sparta (431)
Activity of Socrates (to 399)
Production of Sophocles' *Oedipus Tyrannus*
Activity of Hippocrates of Cos, physician
Plague at Athens
Death of Pericles (429)
Revolt and recapture of Mytilene (428-7)
Sophist Gorgias of Leontini on embassy to Athens (427);
Athenian expedition against Syracuse (427-424)
Leadership of Cleon at Athens

425
Acharnians (comedy) of Aristophanes produced (425)
Thucydides the historian exiled from Athens for failure as a general (424)
Production of Aristophanes' *Clouds* (423)
Peace between Athens and Sparta (421)
Athenians force Melos into league (416)
Sacrilege of the herms; Athenian expedition to Syracuse (415)
Destruction of Athenian force at Syracuse (413)
Archelaus king of Macedonia (c. 413-399)
Sparta renews hostilities against Athens
Oligarchic revolution, restoration of democracy at Athens (411)
Carthaginian attack on Sicily (409)
Alcibiades prominent at Athens
Deaths of Sophocles and Euripides (406); Battle of Arginusae
Leadership of Cleophon at Athens
Dionysius becomes tyrant at Syracuse (405)
Athens surrenders to Sparta (404); oligarchy (tyranny) of the Thirty at Athens; political activity of Theramenes and Critias
Postumous production of Sophocles' *Oedipos at Colonus* (401);
Xenophon and 10,000 Greek mercenaries join attack on Persian king by his brother

400
Execution of Socrates; Death of King Archelaus of Macedonia (399)
Activity of Socrates' students, Antisthenes the Cynic,

Aristippus, and Eucleides of Megara, to about mid-century
Activity of Plato (to 347) and Isocrates (to 338)
Plato's Academy founded (387)
Birth of Aristotle (384)
Sparta dominant in Greece
Thebes expels Spartan garrison (379)
Second Athenian League founded (378)

375
Thebes defeats Sparta in Battle of Leuctra (371); period of Theban supremacy begins
Death of King Amyntas III of Macedonia (370)
Aristotle in Athens to join Academy (367); Plato in Syracuse to educate Dionysius II, the tyrant there
Thebes wins Battle of Mantinea against Sparta (362); death of Epaminondas ends Theban supremacy
Second visit of Plato to Syracuse (361)
Activity of Dionysius the Cynic (to 323)
Philip II king of Macedonia (359)
War begins between Athens and Philip (357)
Birth of Alexander the Great (356); Dion, pupil of Plato, rules at Syracuse (to 354)
Sacred War, Philip in Central Greece (356-352); war between Athens and her allies (to 355)
Demosthenes active in Athens

350
Death of Plato (347); Speusippus head of Academy; Aristotle leaves Athens
Dionysius II back in control at Syracuse (347)
Peace of Philocrates between Athens and Philip (346)
Timoleon active in Sicily, ending the tyrannies (344-337)
Aristotle tutor to Alexander the Great (343)
War renewed between Athens and Philip (340)
Battle of Chaeronea (338),
Philip supreme in Greece; Philip assassinated (336);
Alexander king of Macedonia

Index

Academy, 163, 181
Achaea, 115
Achilles, 131-2, 177, 184
Acragas, 47, 161-2
Aegina, 78-9, 82-3, 94, 99
Aegospotami, 107
Aeschines, 134
Aeschylus, 31, 161, 179-80, 182, 185, 188
Aetna, 47
Agamemnon, 29
Agathocles, 135, 164
Agesilaus, 109
agriculture, 148-50
agroiki, 18
Alcaeus, 15, 133
Alcibiades, 104-6
Alcmaeonid family, 18, 21-2, 26, 82, 133-4, 158-9
Alcman, 192
Alexander I, of Macedonia, 80, 86, 168
— II, of Macedonia, 167
— III, the Great, 5-6, 13, 56, 119-20, 132, 135, 168-72, 182
— of Epirus, 171
Al–Mina, see Posideion
Amasis, 54-5
Amphipolis, 97, 101-2, 116
Amyntas, of Macedonia, 112
— III, of Macedonia, 167
— IV, of Macedonia, 167
Amyrtaeus, 89, 92

Antigone, 150
Antigone, 179, 186
Antiphon, 191
apella, 35
Apollo, 189–90
Arcadia, 115, 117
Arcadian League, 115
Archelaus, of Macedonia, 167
Archidamus, 100
Archilochus, 132
archon, 12
areopagus, 30, 132–3
Arginusae Islands, 106–7
Argos, 11, 13, 91, 93–5, 102–3, 105, 109, 158
Aristagoras, 51–2, 158
Aristides, 82, 88–9
Aristippus, 163
aristocracy, 18, 31–2, 37, 82, 131–6, 157, 159
Aristogiton, 21
Aristophanes, 152, 180
Aristotle, 14–5, 20–1, 28, 33, 62, 81, 124–5, 129, 135, 179, 181–2, 185–7
Artaphernes, 78–9
Artaxerxes I, of Persia, 89, 92, 109
— II, Memnon, of Persia, 112, 115–16
— III, Ochus, of Persia, 116–1
arts, 49, 188–9, 192–3
Aspasia, 190
Astyages, 66–7

Athenian Empire, 28, 87–108, 127
Athens 10–1, 13–14, 16–18, 23, 28–9, 31–4, 46–7, 52, 59, 68–71, 76–121, 123–4, 126–134, 136–7, 139, 144, 151, 162, 168, 187–9, 191–3
authority, 12–13

Babylon, 83
Bacchiad family, 13, 36, 157
Bacchylides, 134, 161
barbarians, 53, 60–2, 70, 72–3, 121, 197
bilingualism, 57
Black Sea, 43–4, 47–50, 60, 96–7
Boeotia, 94–5, 101, 117, 119
Boeotian League, 102, 109, 110–11, 113, 119
boulé, 36, 133
Branchidae, 56–7
Brasidas, 101–2
Bronze Age, see Mycenaean period
Byzantium, 96, 119, 170

Calippus, 164
Callistratus, 134
Cambyses, 66
Carthage, 45, 161–4
Carystos, 88
Catana, 46–7, 160
Chabrias, 138
Chaeronea, 119, 144, 170
Chalcidice, 101–2, 118, 170
Chalcis, 42–3
Chares, 138
Charon, 64
Charondas, 14, 46
children, 143, 146–8, 150
Chios, 51, 117
Cicero, 175
Cimon, 89–91
citizenship, 24, 26–7, 36, 73, 126, 136–7
Cleander, 160
Cleisthenes, of Athens, 24–7, 82, 137
– of Sicyon, 158
Cleombrotus, 113
Cleomenes, 25, 79,
Cleon, 32, 101–2, 127, 134
Cleophon, 127

cleruchs, 26, 116
Clytemnestra, 150
colonization, 41–6, 54, 60–1
Constitution of Athens, 18, 24–5
Corcyra, 43, 97–8
Corinna, 190
Corinth, 13, 15–6, 20, 26, 36, 41–3, 93, 96–9, 102, 109, 157, 164,
Corinthian War, 109
Cos, 117
Crete, 41, 43, 75–6, 94–5
Critias, 108, 134
Croesus, 1–2, 158
Croton, 4–6
Cumae, 43
cultural exchange, 45–9, 53, 58–9, 60–2, 68–72, 177
Cypselus, 157
Cyrene, 42, 44
Cyrus, 65–7, 109

Damasias, 17
Darius, 48, 50–2, 57, 67, 77–8, 82–3
Datis, 78–9
Delian League, see Athenian Empire
Delos, 20, 61, 88, 93
Delphi, 21, 95, 114, 119, 188–91
Delphic Oracle, 1, 79, 84–5, 118
– Amphyctyonic League, 117–19
Demaratus, 26, 71
demiourgoi, 18
democracy, 14, 17, 25–31, 33–4, 37, 82, 88, 104, 106, 129, 131, 134–5, 157, 162, 190, 195
Democritus, 178
demos, 28
Demosthenes, Athenian general, 101
– Athenian orator, 118–9, 127, 134, 146, 170, 191
diakrioi, 19, 23
dialects, 40–1, 166
Didyma, 56
diobelia, 32, 131
Diodorus Siculus, 87, 91
Diogenes, 135
Dion, 162–4
Dionysiac Festival, 179–80, 182, 188, 192
Dionysius I, of Syracuse, 110, 162, 165

— II, of Syracuse, 162–5
— of Miletus, 64
Dorians, 40, 42–3, 75, 151, 157
Ducetius, 47, 162

Egypt, 54–6, 62–3, 72, 83, 89, 92, 158
Eion, 144
Eleusis, 108
Elis, 91, 102, 115
Epaminondas, 110, 113–16, 137
Ephesus, 13
Ephialtes, 90
ephors, 35–6
Epicharmus, 161
Epicurus, 185
Epidamnus, 97
Epidaurus, 16
Epizephyrian Locri, 46
Eretria, 43, 78
Etruscans, 45–6
Euboea, 95, 116–17
Eumenides, 30
eupatrids, 18, 132–4
Euripides, 151, 155, 167, 179–80, 185, 188
Eurymedon River, 89, 144

Fifty Years Peace, 102

Gela, 160–1
Gelon, 45, 137, 160–1
gerousia, 35–6
Gorgias, 191
Gortyn, 95
growth, 124, 155, 195–6

Harmodius, 21
Hecataeus, 64
Hellanicus, 64
hellenotamiae, 88
helots, 35, 90–1, 120, 124, 141–2, 196
Heraclides, 160
Heraclitus, 177–8
Hermes statues, 104–5
Hermocrates, 162
Herodotus, 15, 20–1, 31, 51–3, 62–8, 81, 87, 158, 183–4, 186
Hesiod, 15, 50, 132, 141–2, 151, 154, 177
Hicetas, 164

Hieron, 45–7, 134, 161, 165, 192
Hipparchus, 20–1, 81
Hippias, 1, 3, 20–1, 159
— the sophist, 191
Hippocrates, medicus, 191–2
— tyrant of Gela, 160
Hippodamus, 46
Histiaeus, 51–2, 158
history writing, 186
Homer, 12, 61
hoplite, 23–4

Iliad, 12–13, 20, 23–4, 131–2, 176, 184
improvement, 124
Inarus, 89, 92
inscriptions, 128–9, 187–8
Ionian Revolt, 51–3
Iphicrates, 134
Isagoras, 25–6
Isocrates, 135
Italy, 15–16, 37, 43–6, 161

Karga Oasis, 56
kingship, 11–14, 36–8, 157, 165, 168–9, 172–3
King's Peace, 110

Laconians, 35, 77
Laurium, 127, 130, 144
law, 19, 30–1
Leonidas, 79, 85
Leontini, 103
Leotychidas, 82
Lesbos, 51
Leucippus, 178
Leuctra, 113
Libation Bearers, 29
Linear B texts, 12, 40, 75
literature, 189–90
Locris, 117, 119
logic, 182–3
Lycurgus, of Athens, 18–19, 26
— of Sparta, 7, 16
Lydia, 50
Lygdamis, 19–20
Lysander, 55, 106–8
Lysias, 70, 146, 182, 191

Lysistrata, 151
Lysistrata, 154

Macedonia, 13, 165–72
Mandane, 66
Mantinea, 102, 115–16, 137
Marathon, 79
Mardonius, 77–8, 83, 85–6
Massilia, 43–4
Medea, 150, 154
Media, 65–66
Megabazus, 92
Megabyzus, 92
Megacles, 18–20, 22, 82, 158–9
Megalopolis, 115, 133
Megara, 16, 41 3, 93, 97 8, 101 2, 133
Melos, 103, 120, 144
Menander, 135, 185
mercenaries, 109, 117, 129, 138, 164
Messene, 115, 137
Messenia, 35, 77, 117
Messenians, 90–1, 126
metics, 69–70
Miletus, 43, 51–2, 56–7, 158
Miltiades, 79–81
mining, 19, 146
monarchy, see kingship
Mycale, 86
Mycenae, 11–12
Mycenaean period, 39–40, 95–6
Mytilene, 13, 32, 100, 120

Naucratis, 44, 53–55, 60
Naxos, 16, 19–20, 78, 88–9
Neapolis, 43
Nicias, 104, 134, 146
"Nine Ways," 90
Nisaea, 101–2
Nysaeus, 164

Odysseus, 131
Odyssey, 12, 20, 131, 145, 176
Oedipus, 1–2, 184
Oedipus at Colonus, 179–80
Oedipus Tyrannus, 179
oikistes, 42
Olbia, 48

"Old Oligarch," 196
oligarchy, 15, 33, 38, 106, 108, 157
Olympia, OLympic Games, 61, 166, 188–9
oracles, 1–3, 20–1, 42, 55–6, 76, 172, 190; see also Delphic Oracle
– of Ammon, 55–6; see also Siwah
Oresteia, 29, 154, 179, 185
orientalizing style, 40–1, 50
Orthagoras, 157–8
ostracism, 25, 36, 81–2

Pallene, 19
Pandora, 154
Pantipacaeum, 48
paraloi, 19
Parmenides, 177
Parthenon, 188
participation, 23, 27, 32, 34, 37, 44–5, 61, 130–1, 136, 139, 195–6
Pasion 130
Pausanias, of Sparta, 108
pediakoi, 19
Pella, 167
Pelopidas, 113–15, 134
Peloponnesian War, 99–108
Perdiccas, of Macedonia, 98
– II, of Macedonia, 166
– III, of Macedonia, 167–8
Periander, 157
Pericles, 33–4, 46–7, 94–7, 99–100, 127, 129, 134
Perinthus, 119, 170
periokoi, 90
Persia, 24, 48–54, 52–3, 57, 63–7, 72, 92, 105, 109–10, 112, 115–17
Persian Wars, 28, 77–87, 166
Persians, 179
petalismos, 36
Pheidon, 15
Phidias, 188
Philip II, of Macedonia, 13, 117–19, 167–71, 181
Philolaus, 15
Philomelus, 117
philosophy, 135–6, 177–9, 180–7, 191–2
Phocis, 93, 95, 112, 114, 117–18, 123, 137, 169
Phoebidas, 110

Phormis, 161
Pindar, 31, 133–4, 161, 166, 190
Piraeus, 46, 108, 110
Pisistratids, 3, 21–2
Pisistratus, 18–20, 23, 26, 81, 137, 158–60, 165, 190
plague, 100
Plataea, 79–80, 85–6, 100, 102, 112
Plutarch, 7, 90–1
Polycrates, 20, 158
Posideion, 58–60
Potideia, 98, 116, 157, 169
pottery, 20, 40–1, 188
Propontis, 43, 96, 105
Protagoras, 46, 191
Psammetichus, 53, 55
Ptolemy of Aloros, 167
Pydna, 167
Pylos, 11, 75, 101
Pythagoras, 45

religion, 27, 54–5, 189–91
Rhegium, 42, 46, 103
rhetoric, 33, 191
Rhodes, 117

Sacred Band, 113, 119, 126
Sacred Wars, 114, 117–19, 169–70
Salamis, 85
Samos, 20, 51, 96, 107, 116, 137, 158
Sappho, 152, 190
Sardis, 52
Scyles, 48
Scythians, 44–5, 48–9, 67–8
Second Athenian League, 111, 116–17
Segesta, 103
Semonides, 151
Sestos, 86
Sicels, 47, 160, 162
Sicilian Expedition, 103–5
Sicily, 16, 43–7, 103–5, 160–1
Sicyon, 16, 157–8
Simonides, 161
Sitalces. 166
Siwah, 55, 172
slavery, 62, 70–1, 125, 130, 141–50, 152, 196–7
Smyrna, 41

Socrates, 31, 107, 135, 152, 179–81
Solon, 7, 15–17, 22–3, 30, 126–7, 132, 177
sophists, 31, 181, 191, 193
Sophocles, 31, 179, 182, 185–6, 188
Sparta, 13, 16, 21, 25–6, 34–6, 52, 55, 76–7, 79, 80, 82, 84, 86, 90–110, 123–6, 134, 136–7, 141, 151, 192
Spartiates, 35
Speusippus, 163–4
Sphacteria, 101
Sphodrias, 110
stability, 123–5, 139, 147, 155, 195
strategoi, 36
Sybaris, 43, 46
Syloson, 158
Syracuse, 36, 43, 45, 47, 101, 103, 134–5, 137, 145, 160–4, 192

Tanais, 48
Taras, 43, 46
Tegea, 115
Telesilla, 190
Thasos, 89–90
Thebes, 11, 77, 95, 100, 109–19, 123, 126, 134, 136
Themistocles, 82, 85, 89, 91
Theognis, 15, 133
Thera, 42
Theramenes, 107–8
Thermopylae, 85
Theron, 161
Thessaly, 91, 115, 169
Thirty, 108
Thirty Years Peace, 95, 97, 99
Thracians, 49, 90, 96, 166
Thrasybulus, 158, 161
Thrasydaeus, 161–2
Thucydides, 4, 15, 20–1, 31–2, 87, 91, 99–101, 103–4, 120, 124, 127, 129, 133, 186–7
Thurii, 46–7
Timoleon, 135, 164
Timotheus, 116, 134 Tiryns, 11
trade, 50, 53–4, 58–60, 69, 125, 127, 129, 160
tragedy, 29, 128, 151, 176, 179, 180–2, 187, 192

tyranny, 15–16, 18–19, 45, 47, 130, 134–5, 145, 157–65
Tyrtaeus, 192

warfare, 23–4, 27, 126, 131–2
women, 125, 141–2, 148, 150–6, 190–1, 196
writing, 182–4, 187

Xanthippe, 152
Xanthippus, 82, 89
Xanthus, 64
Xenophon, 116, 146, 151, 184
Xerxes, of Persia, 56, 83–5, 89

Zaleucus, 14, 46, 160
Zeno, of Citium, 185
Zeus, 177, 189
Zopyrus, 68–9